IMAGES
of America

PHELPS AND CONOVER

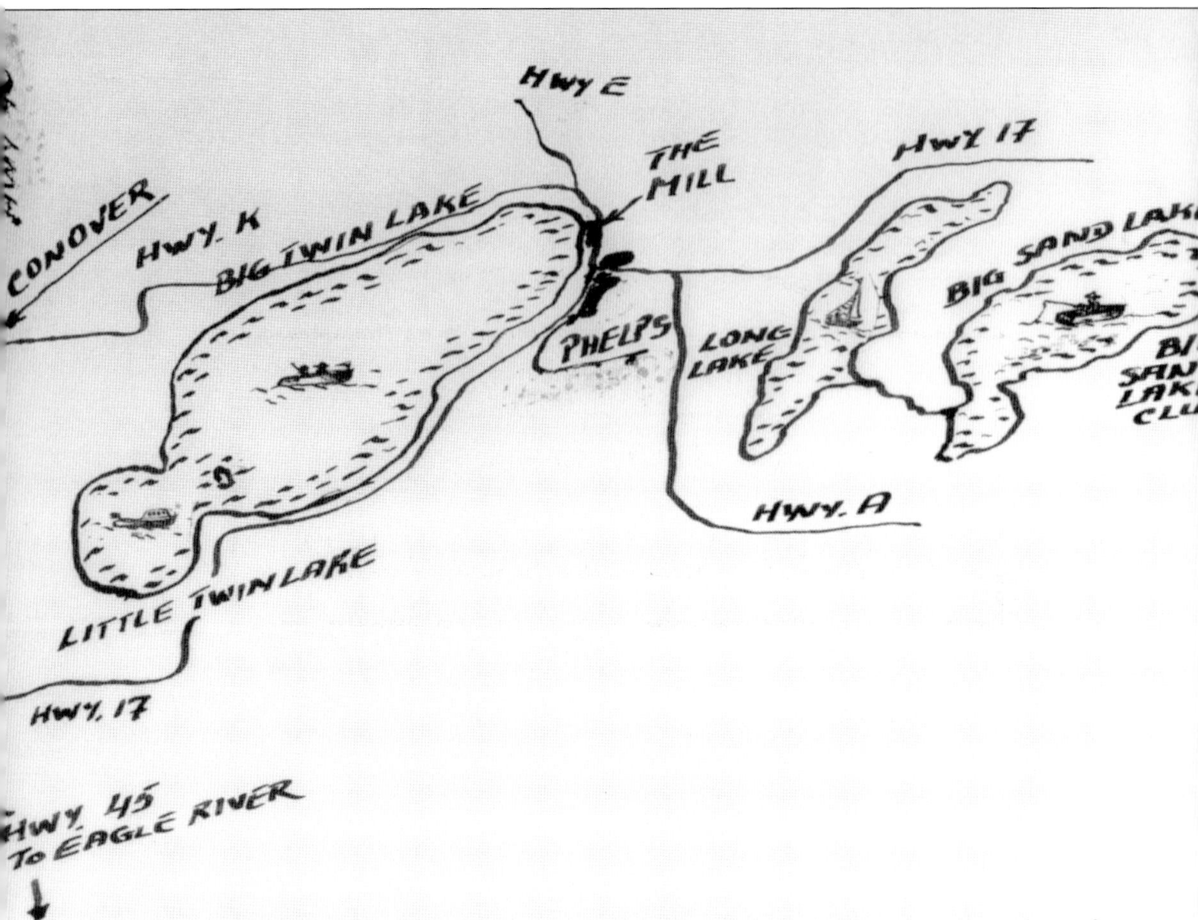

Although not intended to be a perfect depiction, this map shows the larger lakes around Phelps and Conover. This image was hand-drawn by the author, Gerd Klausmeyer. (Courtesy of Gerd Klausmeyer.)

On the Cover: For many resorts on the lake, the mode of transportation for guests was via boat. With the vast forests and limited roadways, this made for an easier route at times. (Courtesy of Gerd Klausmeyer.)

IMAGES
of America

PHELPS AND CONOVER

Gerd Klausmeyer

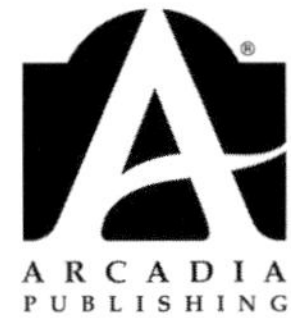

ISBN 978-1-4671-0637-5

Published by Arcadia Publishing
Charleston, South Carolina

Printed in the United States of America

Library of Congress Control Number: 2020949641

For all general information, please contact Arcadia Publishing:
Telephone 843-853-2070
Fax 843-853-0044
E-mail sales@arcadiapublishing.com
For customer service and orders:
Toll-Free 1-888-313-2665

Visit us on the Internet at www.arcadiapublishing.com

In memory of the late Jim Hedberg, whose contributions to this book reflected his immense interest in the history of Conover, his hometown

Contents

Acknowledgments

History has been handed down to us for millennia through artifacts, oral accounts, and written records—and for more than a century through the lens of the camera. Acquiring the images and selecting which ones to include was only part of the challenge in creating this book. Identifying the exact location and facts about the images proved to be more difficult. Fortunately, I was able to do some research and have some insightful conversations with people. The format of this book is intended to present only a glimpse of the past rather than a comprehensive history. I hope you enjoy this book, as it was truly a joy for me to create it.

I have been collecting postcards for over 25 years of my hometown in Illinois and of towns within Vilas County, especially Phelps, Wisconsin. Unless otherwise noted, all images appear courtesy of myself, Gerd Klausmeyer. However, there are others who contributed their historical treasures and are deserving of thanks as well.

Thank you to Pauleyn Ray Nystrom and the Phelps Historical Museum for providing access to some of their displayed items as well as other members' photographs. Thanks also to Jack Carlson of Phelps, who generously loaned his collection. Jack also fabricated a large three-dimensional model of Phelps (Hackley). The layout of the town is displayed at the Phelps Museum.

Many thanks to Donna Lapisto and Steve McMillan for sharing their collections. Additional thanks to Donald and Margaret Oberg, Ronald Buell, Russ Monty, Charles Requa, Dale Engberg and Bill Zahn, and Ed Champeney for sharing their historical knowledge.

Thank you to Anne Grogan and other Big Sand Lake Club members, including Rick Beyer, Alexandra Adams, Jan Largay, and Lois Milburn, for providing me the club's history. Thanks also go to Melinda Conrad for her help with some elements of review.

Another note of great gratitude goes to Jes Spooner for her time in assisting me through the technicalities and the adding and editing that was needed for publication. Her support helped me to finally bring this book to life.

Last but not least, I would like to thank Sheryn Olander for sharing Jim Hedberg's historical photographs and information pertaining to Conover, which he had compiled up until his passing.

INTRODUCTION

The northeast corner of Vilas County, Wisconsin, and the area just over the border into Michigan has a rich culture of Native Americans that predates European settlements by hundreds of years. The Ojibwa, or Chippewa, one of the largest groups of Native Americans who were formally located near Sault Ste. Marie and the Lake Superior region of Canada, dominated this region.

The hunter-gatherer lifestyle of the Ojibwa required they separate into smaller bands. In 1840, while platting the boundaries that formed the Wisconsin-Michigan border, surveyors and engineers encountered one such band on the north shore of Big Sand Lake. They called these Indians Ma-ta-wun-gaunk.

One of the first non-Natives to explore the region was probably Jean Nicolet in 1634. Claude-Jean Allouez, a Jesuit missionary, built a mission on Lake Superior.

The next major expedition to northern Wisconsin was that of Fr. Jacques Marquette and Louis Joliet in 1673. Natives, Jesuit priests, fur traders, merchants, and early settlers used the river and lakes as the highway of travel.

Since most of Northern Wisconsin was heavily wooded, these waterways provided shipping routes for supplies, transportation, clean water, game, and fish.

In March 1863, Abraham Lincoln signed an Act of Congress enabling the states of Michigan and Wisconsin to begin construction of a road between Fort Howard at Green Bay and Fort Wilkins near Copper Harbor. This road was called Military Road.

Military Road was built to connect the two forts during the Civil War for access to rapid reinforcements. This road followed the old Superior Trail, which was used by the Indians for hundreds of years. Early trappers and traders also used this route.

In later years, suppliers to the copper mines used this road. The construction of the road also made the timber resources of northern Wisconsin and Michigan available to the nation, enhancing the logging industry for these areas.

Nestled in this region of the Chequamegon-Nicolet Forest, with rolling hills and lakes created by the last receding ice sheet about 10,000 to 20,000 years ago, lie the towns of Phelps and Conover on opposite ends of the Twin Lakes.

In 1900, Hackley, Phelps, and Bonnell traveled by rail from Chicago to Conover. They proceeded to Lakota Resort, located on the southwest end of Big Twin Lake. From there, the three men secured a boat and toured the lake intending on locating a place for a community and a mill. They chose the northeast end of the lake, and they built a sawmill in 1903. The town of Hackley was established in 1905, taking its name from the Hackley-Phelps-Bonnell Company that owned the sawmill. In 1912, the name was changed to Phelps. This was supposedly because of the confusion between Hackley and Hatley, which was a lumber town in Central Wisconsin. Today, Phelps is often confused with Phillips.

Conover is named after Seth H. Conover, a prominent cheese buyer who came from Plymouth, Wisconsin. He enjoyed fishing and hunting. He came to the Northwoods on the logging trains to do just that. After stopping at the same place for several years, the railroad men began referring to it as "Conover's Place" and decided to build a station there. In 1891, Seth Conover was deeded acres of land on Big Twin Lake. From there, he founded the Twin Lakes Hunting Club. He then sold the resort to Harvey Goodall, and the name was changed to Lakota Resort, one of the most popular resorts in later years. Shortly thereafter, the sawmill and logging camps were established, and the town had its beginning. Conover was separated from the Town of Eagle River on January 3, 1907.

Surrounded by some of the greatest recreational and fishing lakes, including the lumber industry, the towns of Conover and Phelps continued to grow with the building of resorts, clubs, schools, churches, and storefronts.

In 1905, a railroad spur connected Conover with Phelps, mainly for lumber transportation. Later, a Chicago & North Western passenger train was introduced to bring tourists and club members from the city to the Northwoods. The tourism industry for this region exploded. People would take the long venture from the city, including powerful politicians and city businessmen, to partake in the resort life.

Over the years, Conover continued to grow, expanding the town limits. In 1914, more land was added to Conover, including the acquirement of Twin Lake property from Phelps in 1920.

In 1928, the Hackley-Phelps-Bonnell Company fell, and in 1929, C.M. Christiansen purchased the assets. It would later be named under the C.M. Christiansen Lumber Co. The lumber mill flourished as one of the largest mills until 1935, when the forests had started to become bare and regeneration was needed. Soon after, the rail operations ceased. Alternatively, transportation via automobiles had increased, and the routes to the Northwoods had improved.

Over the years, the population of Conover and Phelps dropped, attributed to the decline in the timber industry and the closing of the Phelps sawmill in 1957. The last train left Conover in 1960, and shortly thereafter, the station was torn down. Today, one can still see the old tracks overgrown with grass in the fields.

However, Phelps and Conover today remain an attraction for a chance to experience hunting, fishing, hiking, and the vast outdoor activities the area has to offer. People are drawn to visit year-round. Long gone are the opera house, sawmills, train stations, and railroads. The dense forest and multitude of rivers and lakes, however, still remain. The resorts, both old and new, offer an opportunity to get a taste of the relaxing and refreshing lifestyle of the Northwoods—a getaway that has been sought after for more than 100 years.

One

The Rise of Logging and the Mill

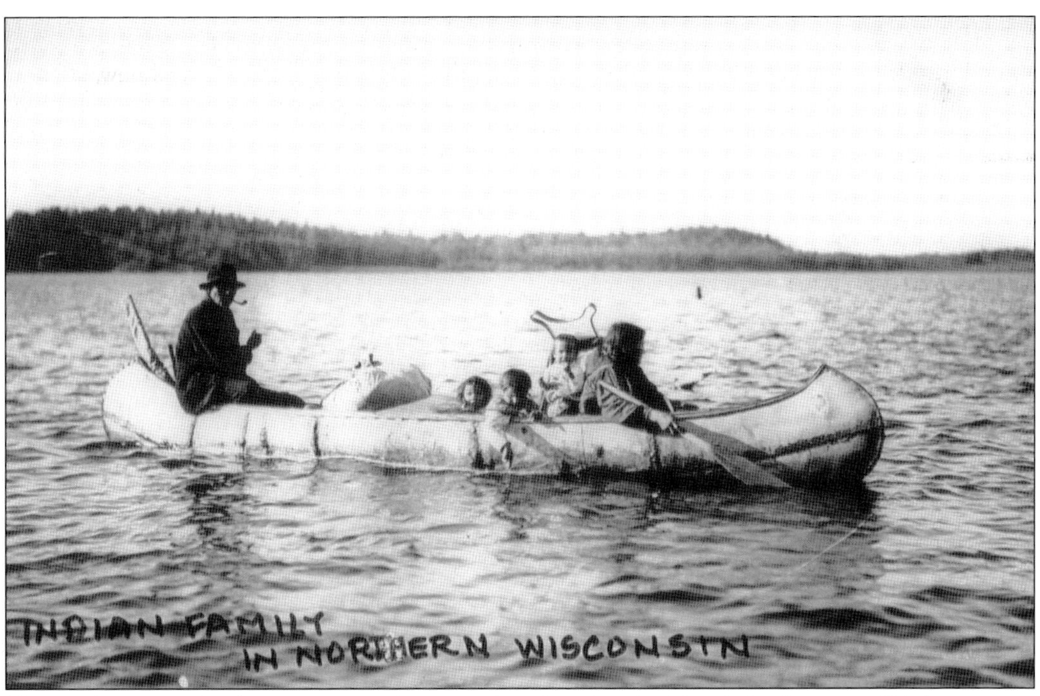

Native American Indians are seen here in their handcrafted birch-bark canoe. With so many lakes and rivers, it was the most efficient way to travel. Harvesting goods or visiting other families and friends would have been a common sight.

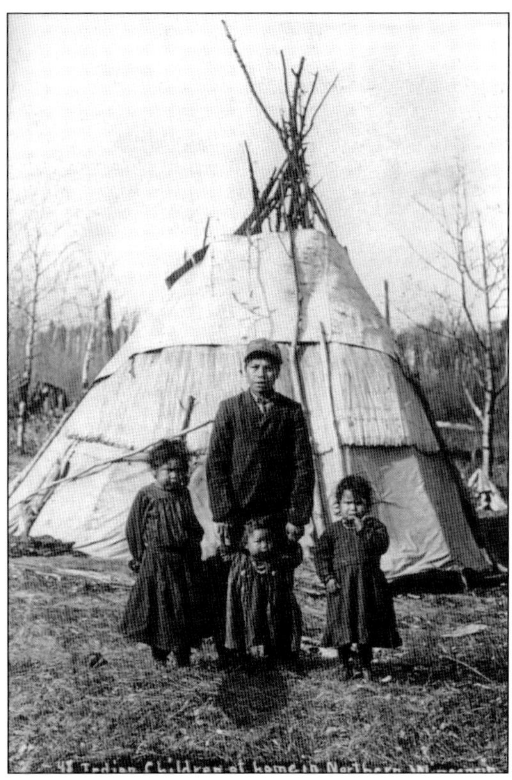

This 1908-postmarked photograph shows a family man with his children in front of his tepee. The shelter is constructed with poles in a cone-shaped configuration and then covered with blankets, canvas, birch bark, and animal hides.

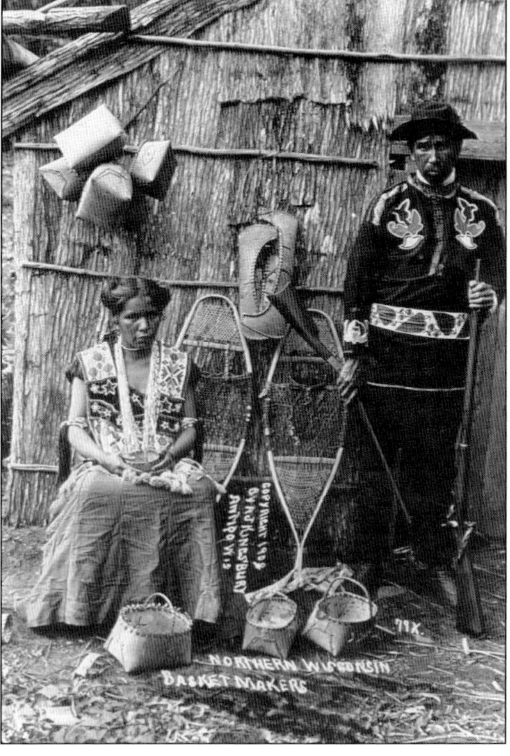

This photograph by Arthur J. Kingsbury of Antigo, Wisconsin, shows Chippewa Indians in 1908, probably husband and wife, in front of their wigwam showing weaved baskets and other handmade objects. Dressed in exquisite clothing, they proudly display their goods. The two rifles he is holding must have been his prized possession.

Ojibwa, or Chippewa, Indians lived in hunting camps in late fall and winter. Trapping and hunting occupied a lot of their time. Indians traveled by foot on snowshoes during the winter, transporting goods on dog sleds. A family is seen here in front of their lodge. Note the sleds piled on a snowbank.

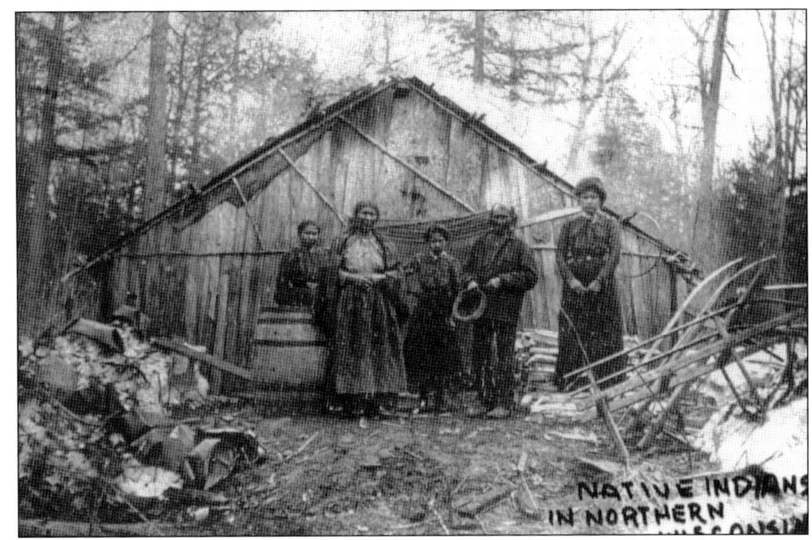

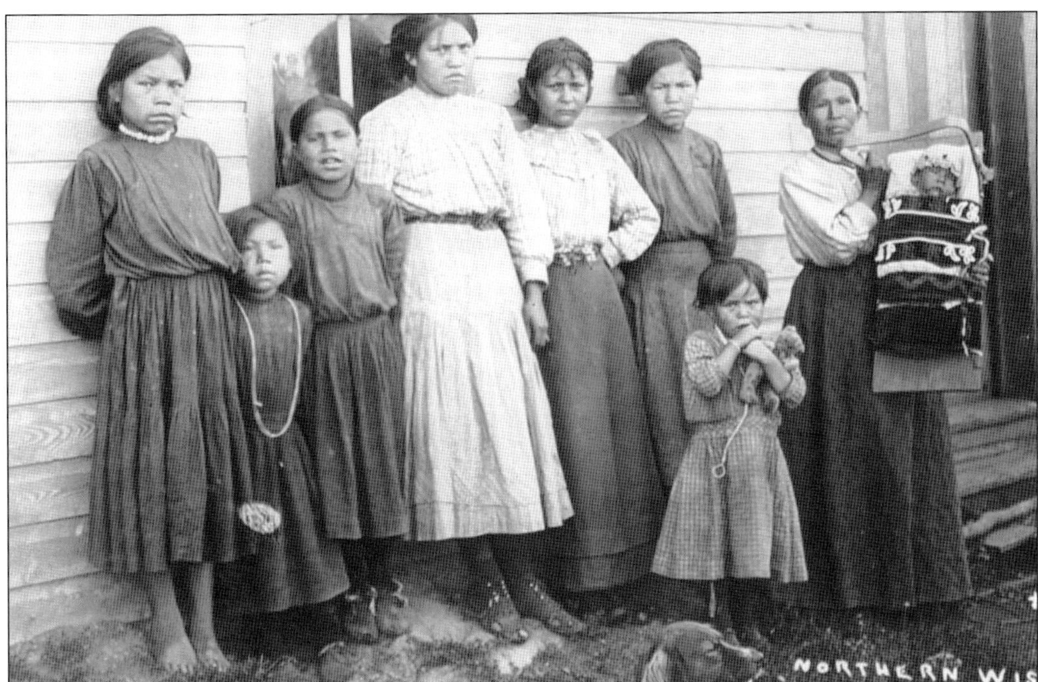

As Native Americans had continued contact with Europeans and white settlers, their ability to continue making clothing according to their traditional ways was destroyed. Resettled on reservations in the late 1800s, Native Americans lost the ability to hunt or gather the necessary materials for their clothing and were forced to buy clothing from whites. This photograph of a woman and children was taken in Antigo, Wisconsin.

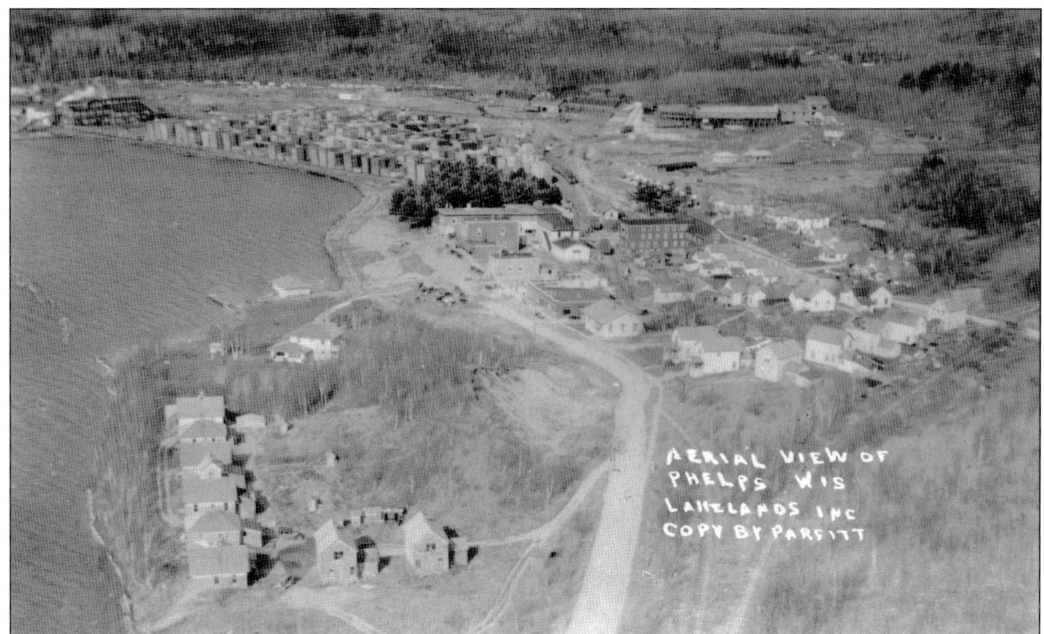

This is an aerial view of Phelps, Wisconsin, in 1927. The three men who founded the community of Phelps (previously named Hackley) were Charles Hackley, William Phelps, and John Bonnell. In about 1900, they secured a boat at the Lakota Resort on North Twin Lake and toured to the east end of the lake with the intention of locating a community and a sawmill. Thus, the town of Hackley was born in 1905 and renamed Phelps in 1912.

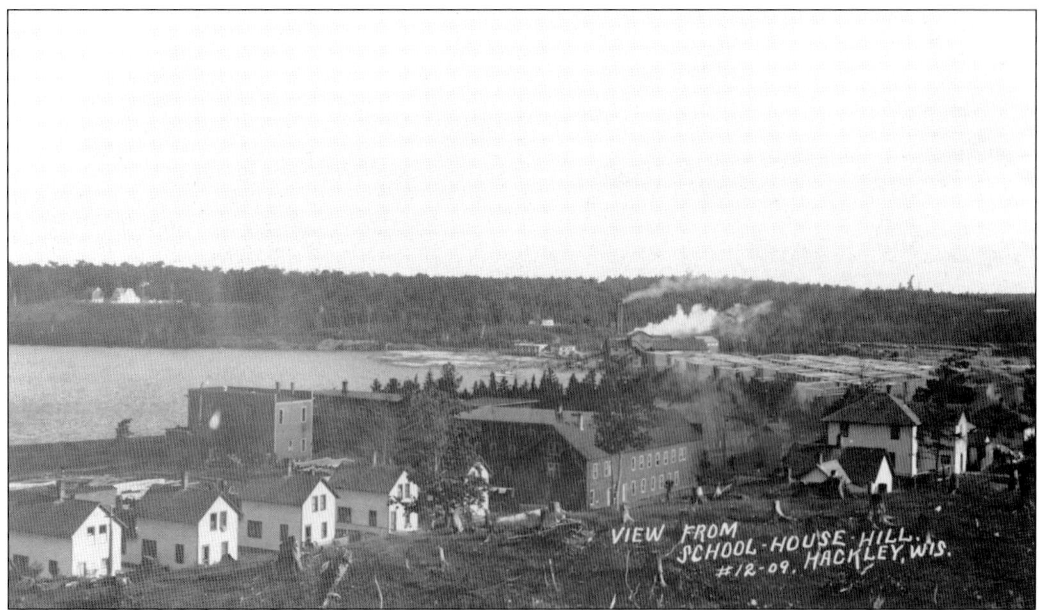

Company houses (front right), the opera house (back right), the general store, hotel, and the white hospital (far right) can be seen in this photograph from School House Hill in 1909. The mill in the background is in full operation. (Courtesy of Donna Lapisto.)

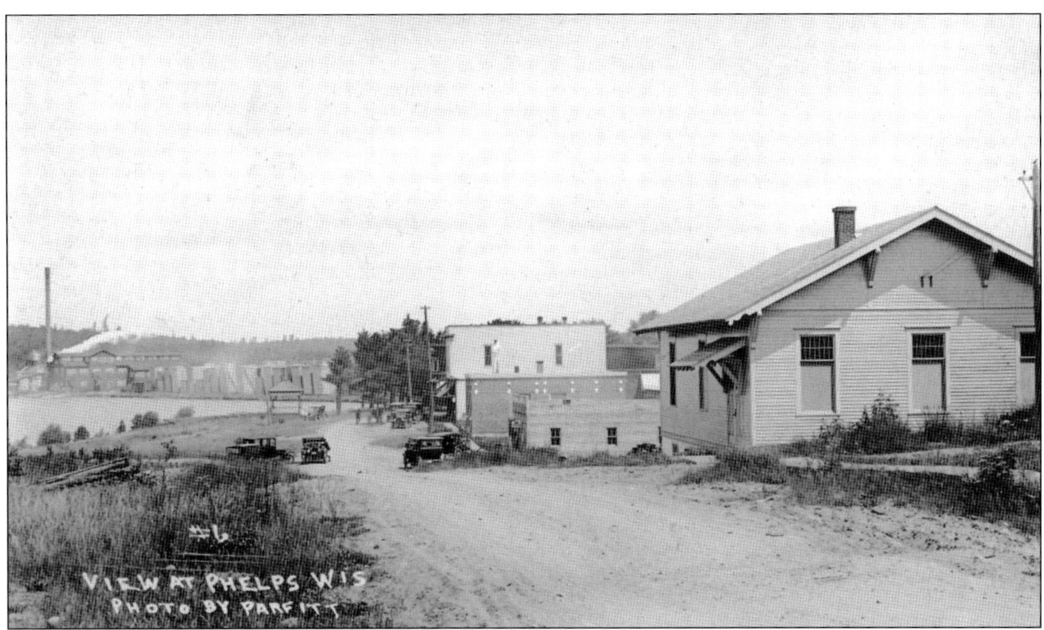

This photograph shows entering Phelps in the 1920s on a gravel Highway 70 (now 17). The building on the right is the Congregational church, built in 1921. The first church burned in 1919, and it was located on the lakeshore and across from the present church. The other buildings on the right side of the street, from foreground to background, were a car dealer and service station, the Northern Lakes Theater, and last, the opera house.

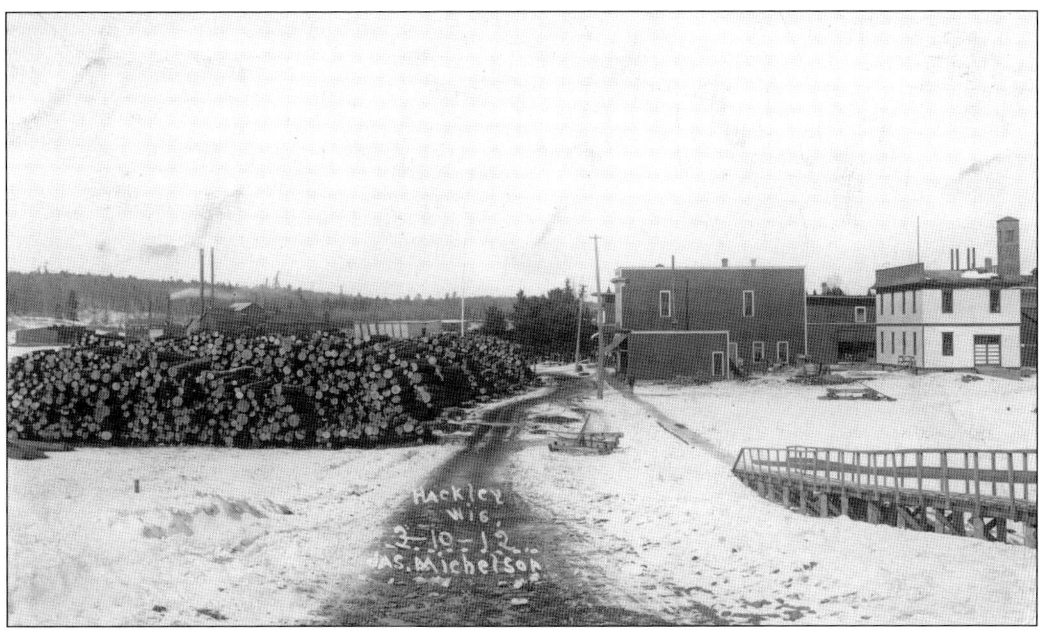

A similar view of Hackley in 1912 shows a dirt road leading into town with a boardwalk along the side. The white building on the right is the town hall. In the early days, lumber was also piled up on the south end of town. A railway spur (seen in another photograph) ran just to the left of the log pile along the lakeshore.

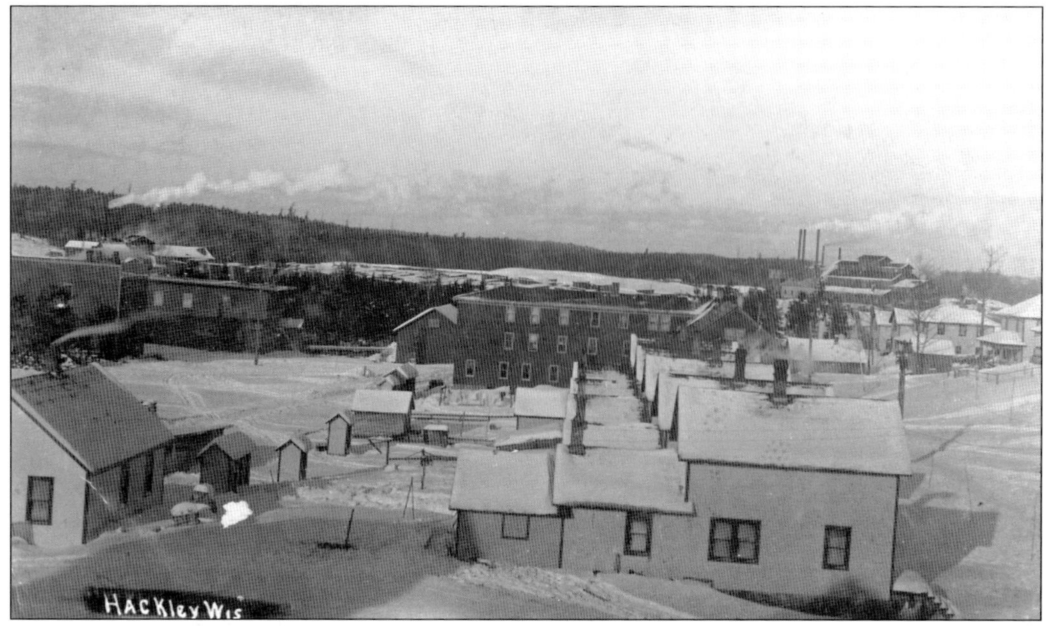

This photograph of Hackley, taken in the winter of 1910, shows company houses, the hotel, sawmill, and the chemical plant. Houses seen here were all identical, equally spaced, and perfectly aligned. Many of those original houses have been torn down or remodeled and modernized.

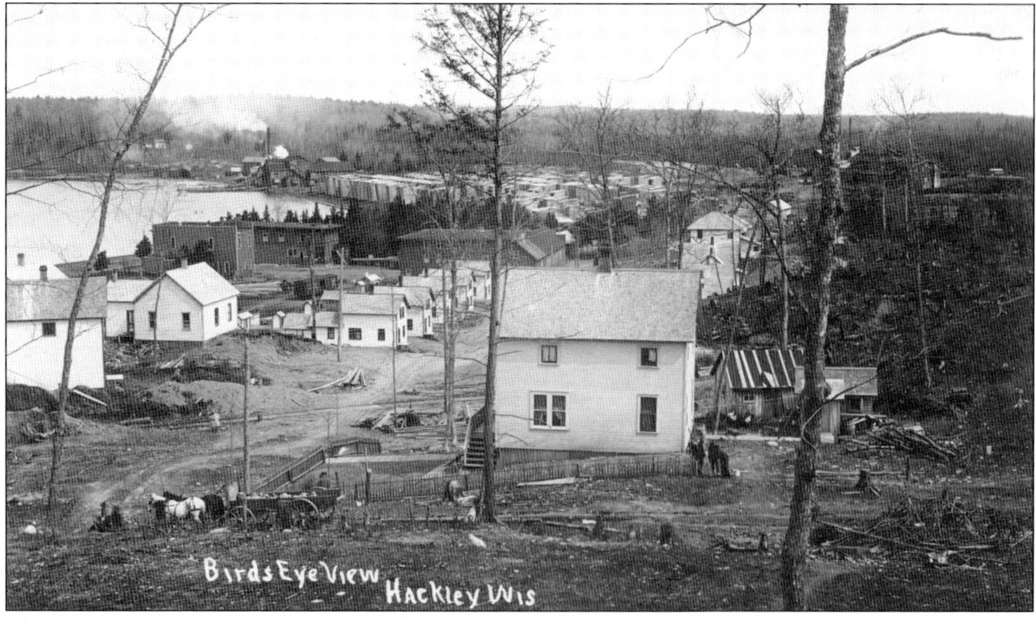

This 1907 view of Hackley looks north on Phelps Street, now Hill Road. Surrounding trees were cut down for firewood with stumps remaining, giving the landscape an eerie look. A horse-drawn wagon is seen going down the road, and a railroad spur crossing is between houses, probably leading to one of the lumber camps.

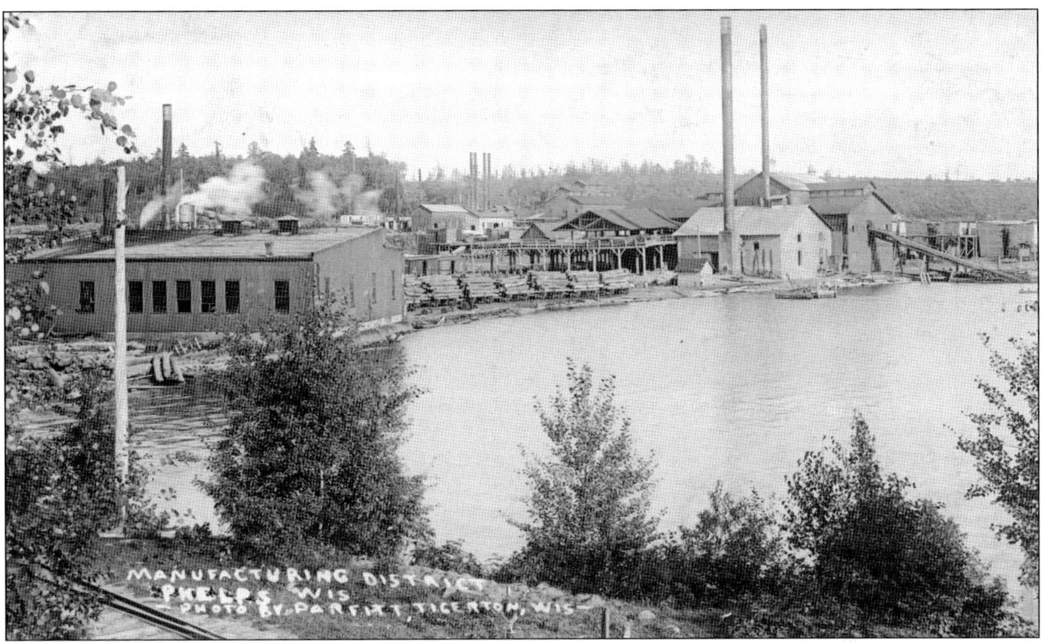

This postcard, dated 1913, shows the Hackley-Phelps-Bonnell Planing and Saw Mill, located on the east shore of Big Twin Lake. The sawmill burned in 1916 but was immediately rebuilt and resumed operation in 1917. The chemical plant can be seen in the distance with its four chimney stags. Note the railroad tracks leading to the mill.

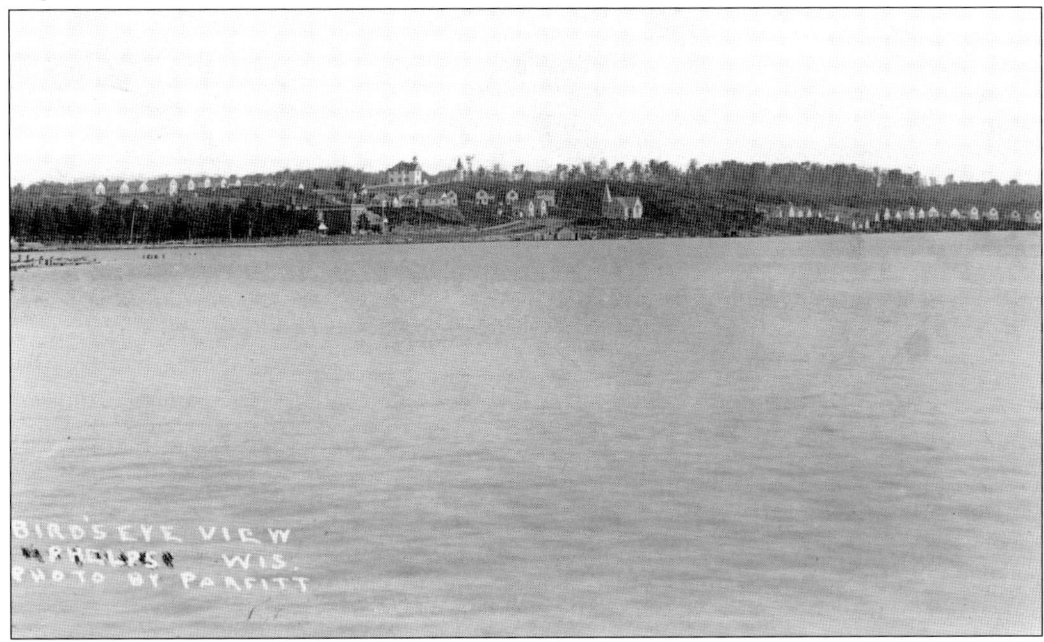

This early photograph across the lake shows the town of Phelps in about 1913. Company houses were on the hill, along the lake, and a few scattered throughout. The Congregational church was on the lake, with the Catholic church and schoolhouse on the hill. Also seen in this photograph is the opera house, the general store, boathouses with docks, and a log corral, which was part of the lumber company.

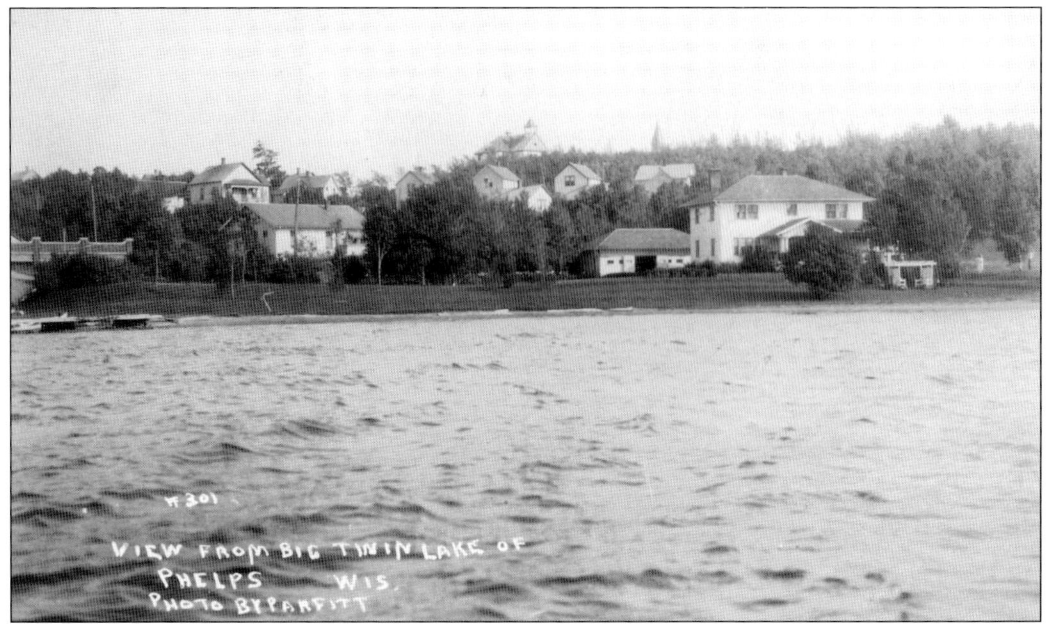

This view from the shore of Big Twin Lake shows part of Phelps in 1928. To the far right is the C.M. Christiansen home. The brick building at the far left is Yahr's garage, and to the right of that is the Congressional church. The school on top of the hill and the steeple of the Catholic church can be seen in the distance.

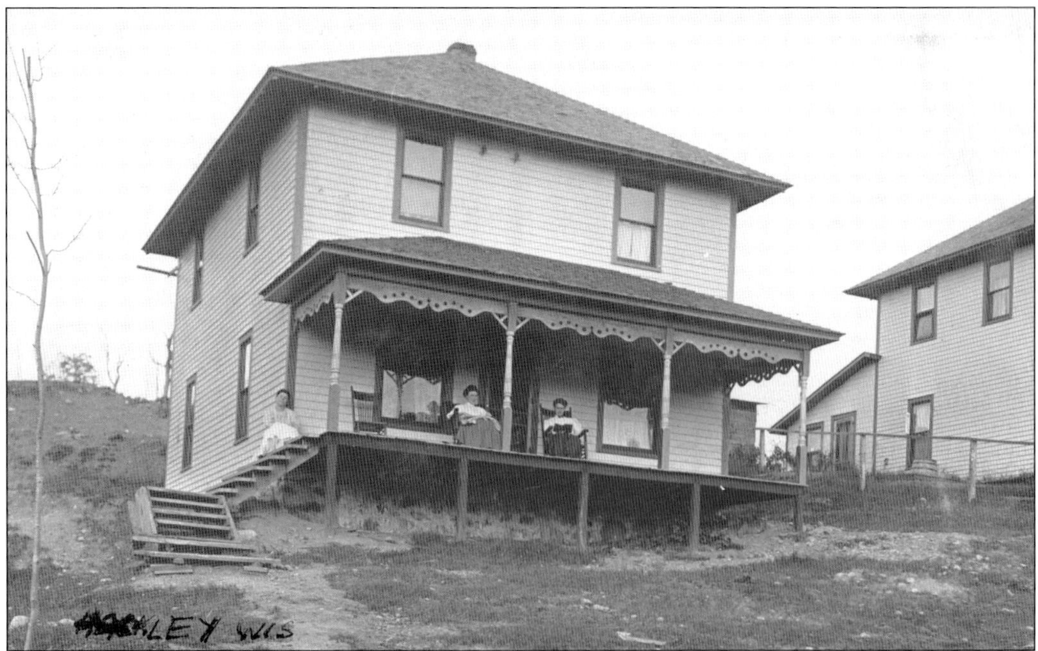

Located on the corner of Highway 17 and Hill Street is a house once occupied by supervisors working at the mill. This postcard, dated 1908, shows Rose Morgan and a Mrs. Connie sitting on the porch. The Jaaskas family lived here in 1930. Note the hospital building on the right.

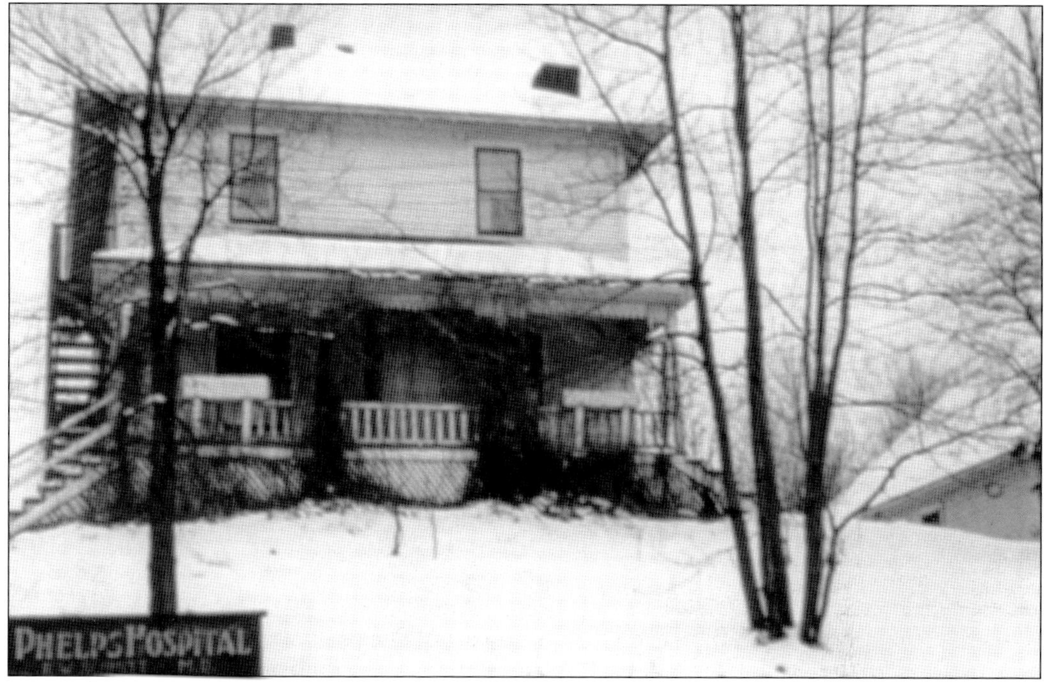

C.M. Christiansen lived in this house situated on the east side of Hill Street and the second house south of the corner of Hill Street and Highway 17. The Christiansens moved to their home on the lakefront in 1921. Dr. Norlander established a hospital in their vacated house in 1928. The house has since been torn down.

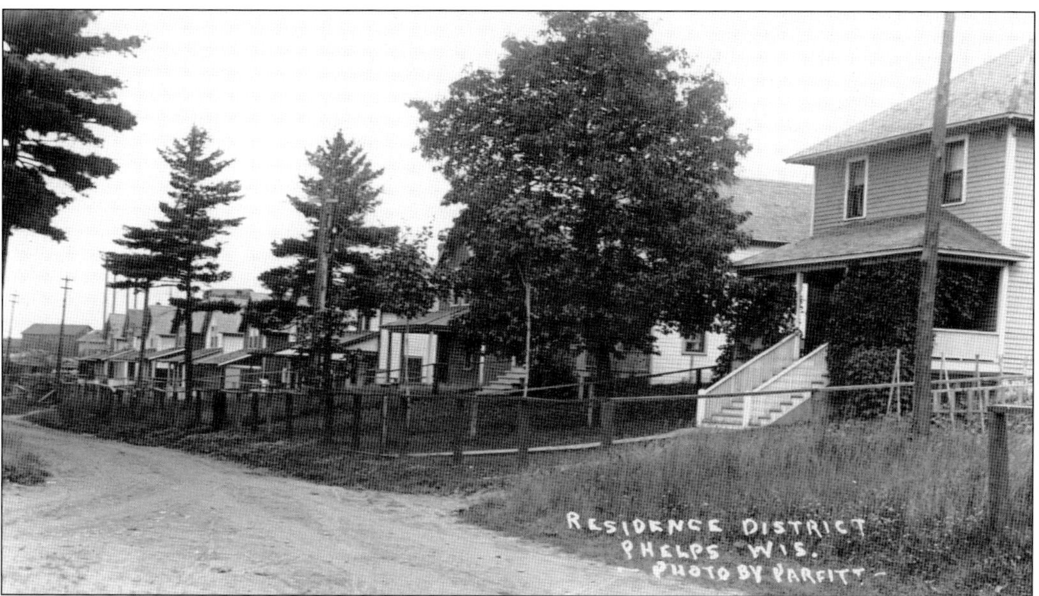

Foremen, like Otto Klabunde, who was employed at the mill, also occupied this house located on Highway 17 and County Road E. The Hackley Bonnell Lumber Company sold the house to Wentworth. In 1927, C.M. Christiansen granted the house to his wife, Leta. In later years, it was known as the Hackley House. The two-story house and the one opposite on the corner of Highway 17 and Hill Street are still standing as of this date.

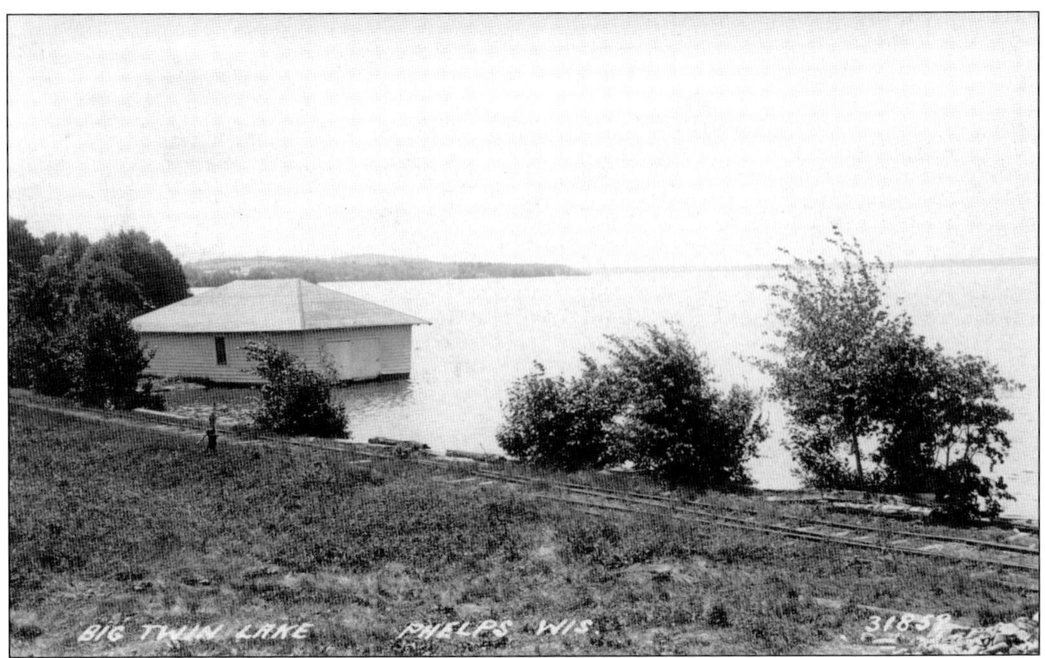

A boathouse next to the Christiansen house is shown on the southeast shore of Big Twin Lake in 1932. Some boathouses were built on posts driven into the lake bottom. Note the lumber company railroad tracks running along the lakeshore.

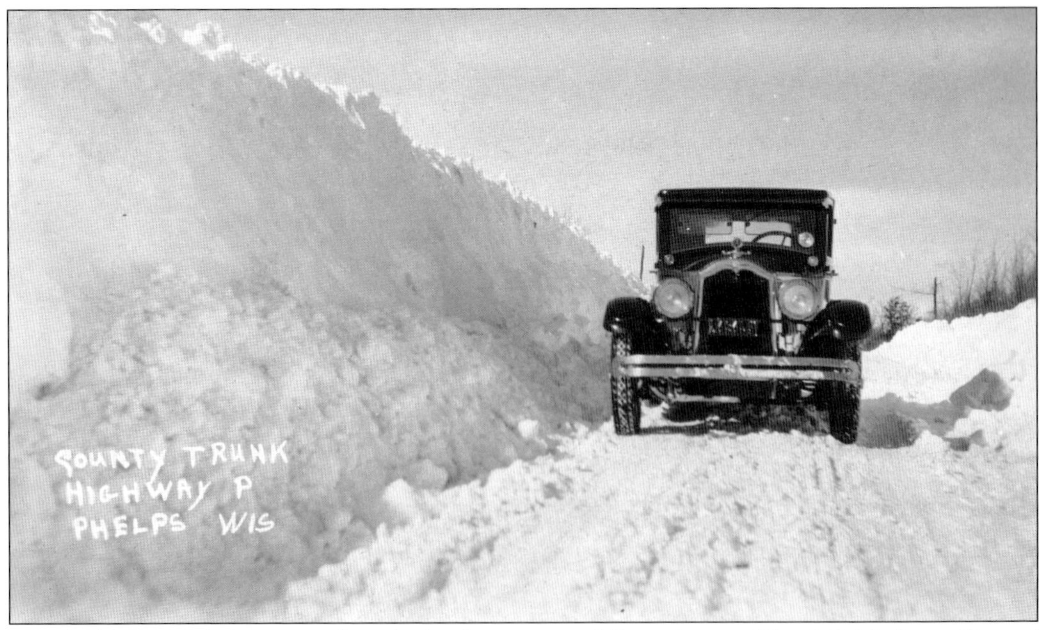

It looks like a single lane was plowed after heavy snowfall on County Trunk P, Highway 70, and now Highway 17 near Phelps, Wisconsin. The driver of this 1926 Buick Standard 6 took this photograph of his car, probably purchased at Yahr's GMC dealership in Phelps.

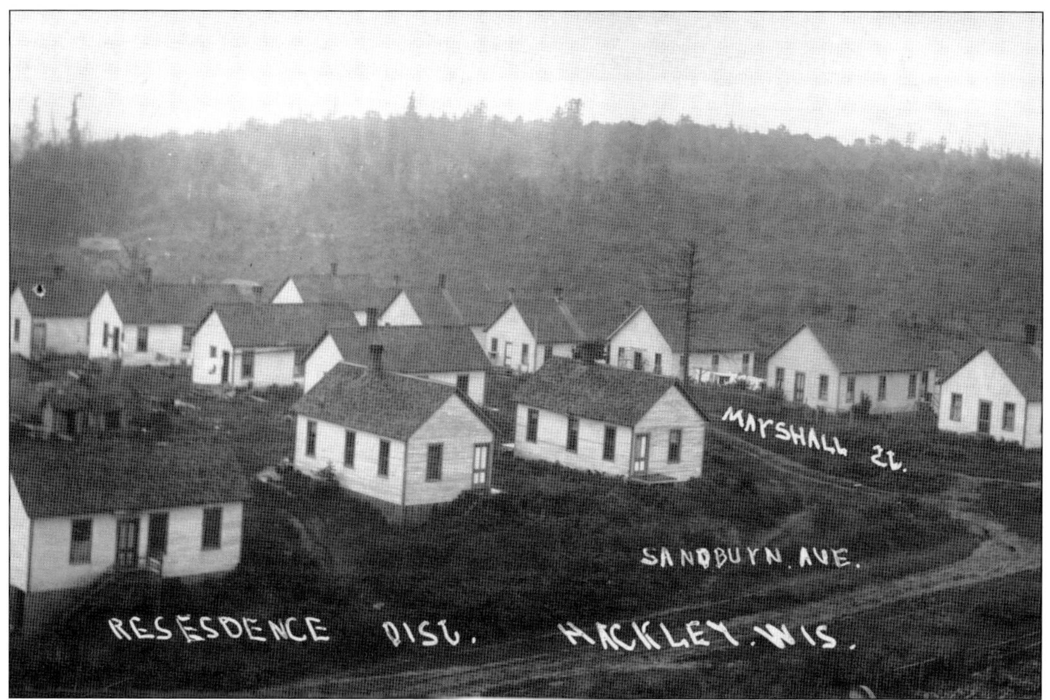

Company houses were built in groups. This 1912 postcard shows the houses on School House Hill. Millworkers paid $10 a month rent for them. Not only did the town change its name, so did some of the roads. Marshall Street became Old School Road. Sandburn Street became Phelps Road, which is now currently Hill Street.

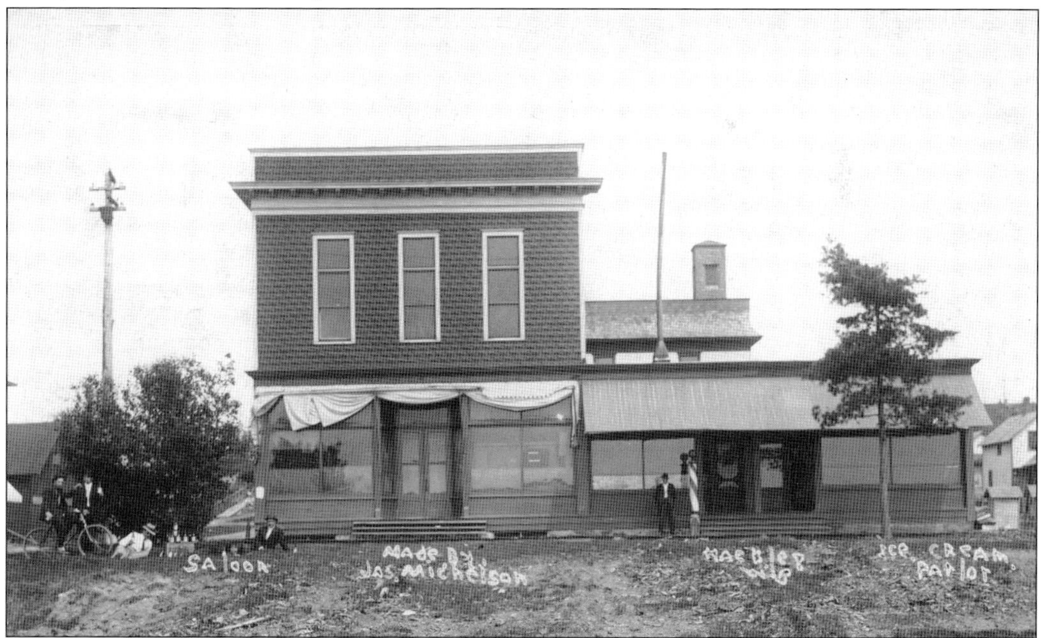

An early building to be erected was the opera house, shown here in 1912, which was located on Highway 17 just before it turns east and across from the company store. In later years, it became the Sportsman's Spot.

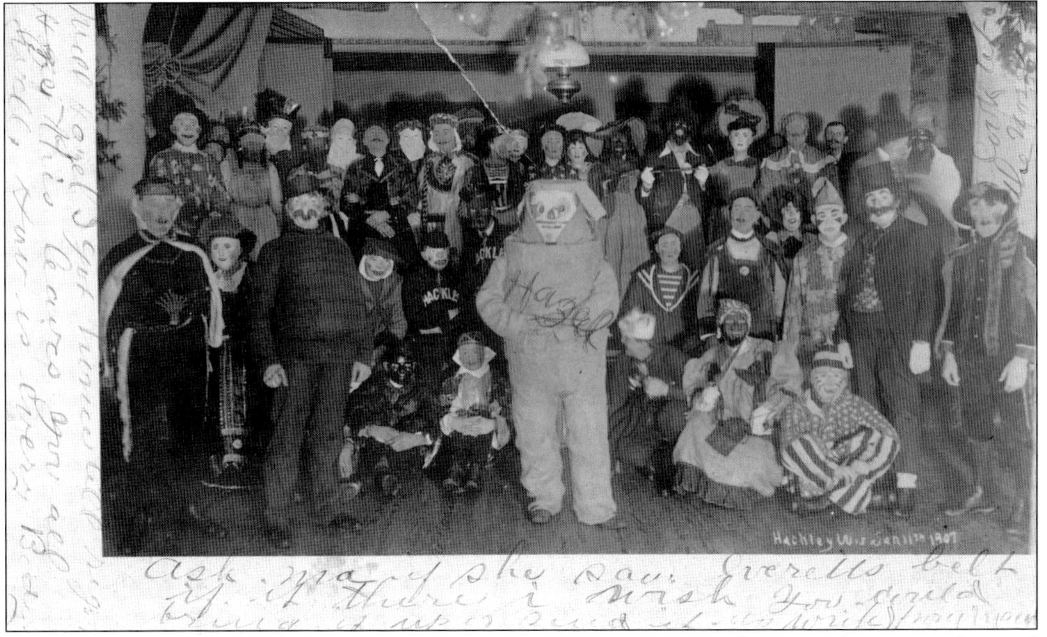

A cast of actors performs at the opera house on January 11, 1907. The opera house was located on the second floor of the building. Many home-talent shows were held here. Later, that area became a pool hall.

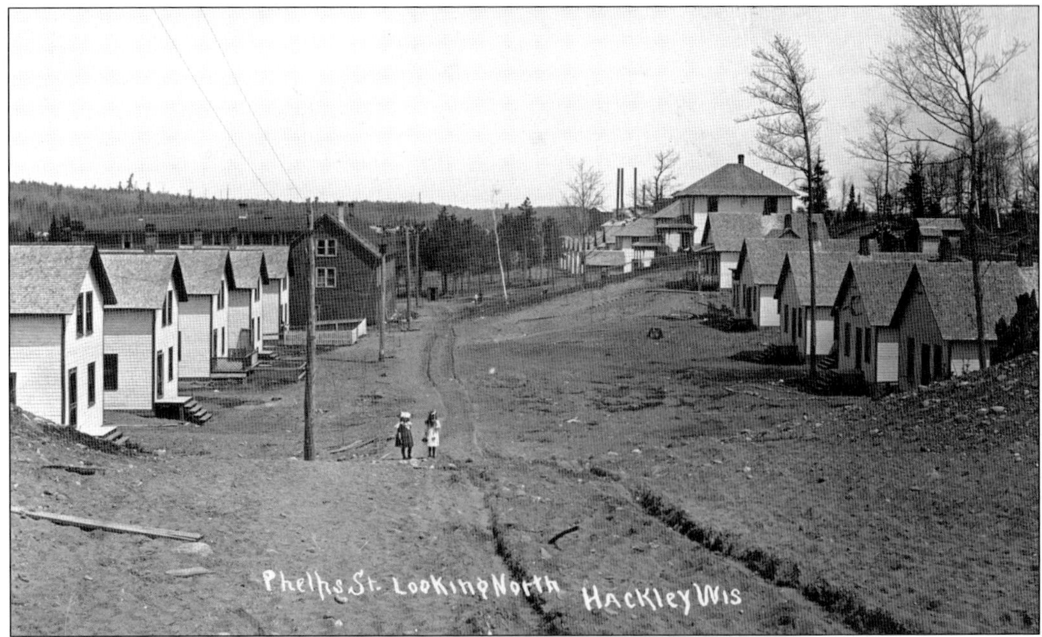

The dirt road Phelps Street, now Hill Street, followed the contour of the land. A wagon rut is clearly visible, and two girls are coming up the hill. On the left, past the company houses, is the hotel, and across the street are the hospital as well as the doctors' and supervisors' houses. In the distance are the chimneys of the chemical plant.

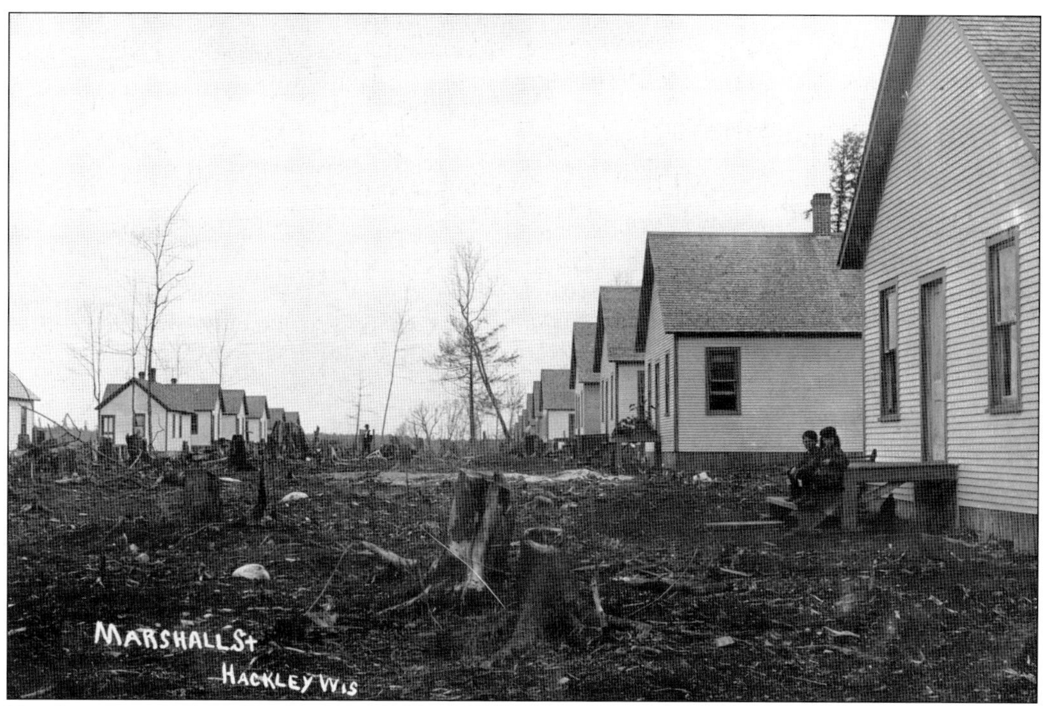

Two boys sit on the steps in front of one of the houses on Marshall Street in this view looking north from School House Hill. Only a few trees are remaining. Not much of a road here in 1907, with a lot of tree stumps still to be removed.

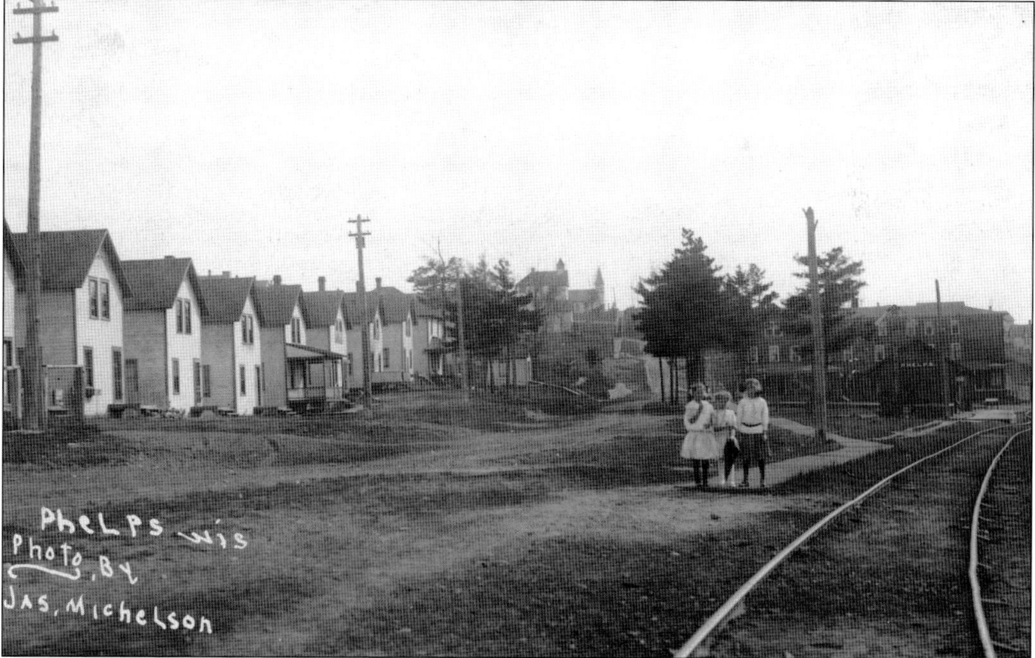

In this 1910 postcard, three girls pose along the railroad track, which runs south to the depot. The dirt road in front of the houses is now Highway K. On the hill in the distance are the school and church. The hotel can be seen behind the depot.

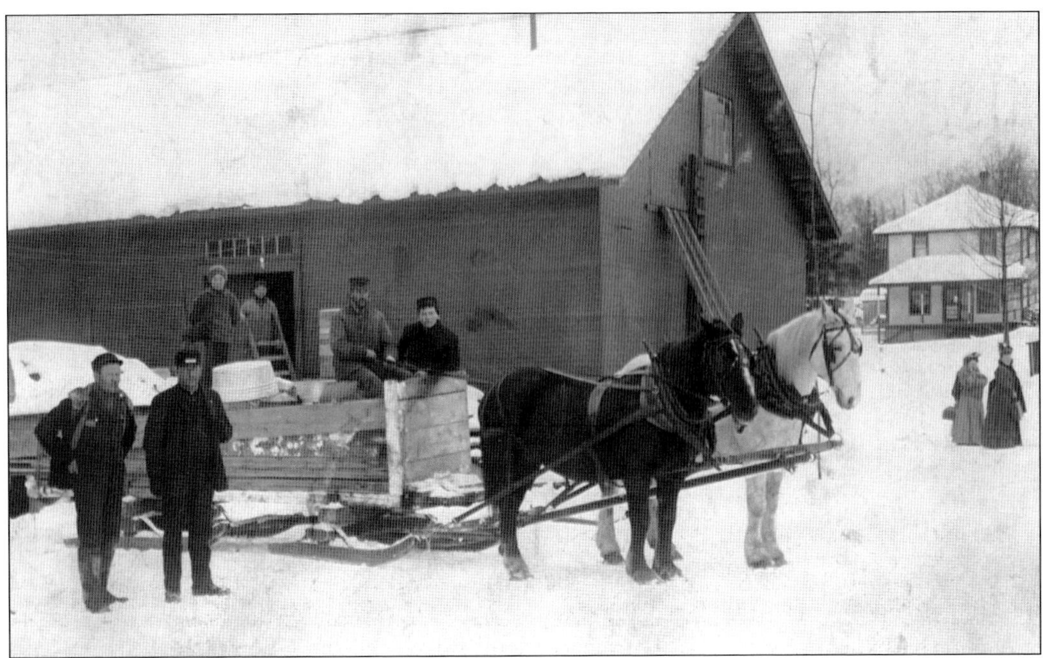

The railroad supply depot stored fodder such as grain, hay, and straw for animals. A sleigh pulled by a team of horses is being loaded for delivery. The ladies in the background, dressed in their finest, could be coming from the railroad station located behind the supply depot. (Courtesy of Donna Lapisto.)

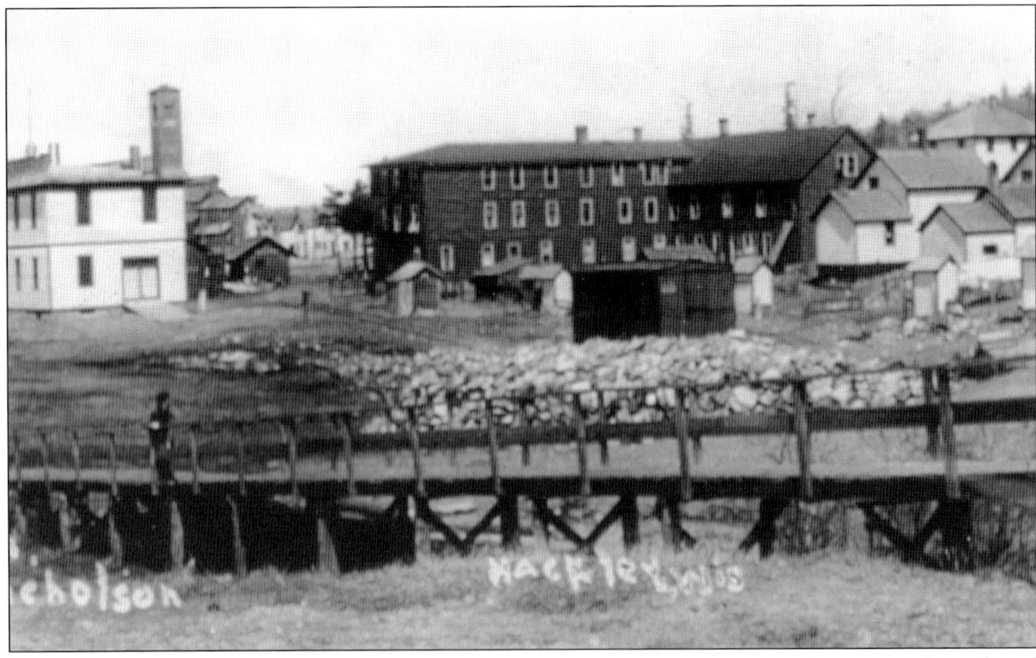

A boardwalk crossing a gully is seen here parallel to what later became Highway 17. The railroad spur runs between the town hall (left) and the hotel. The track ended at the boxcar where stone fill is being dumped. Eventually, the whole gully was filled, and the boardwalk was removed. (Courtesy of Phelps Historical Museum.)

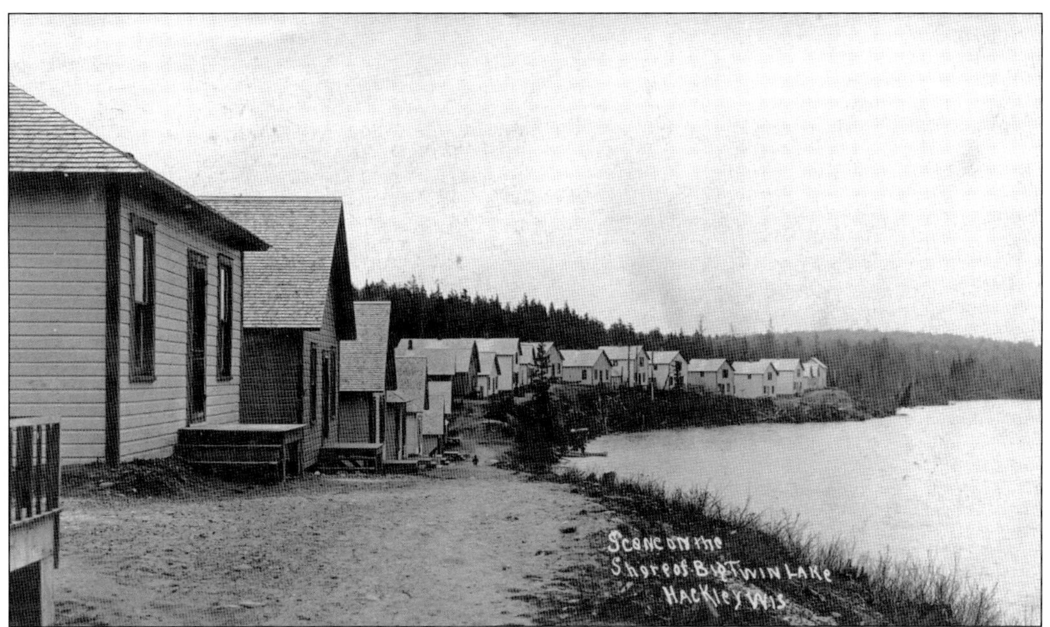

Stretching south along the lake is this row of company houses called "Hungry Hollow" in Hackley. This shoreline property on Big Twin Lake became a lot more valuable as time went on. Hungry Hollow originated in that people residing in the company houses were often transient workers that tended to be more on the poverty side, hence hungry.

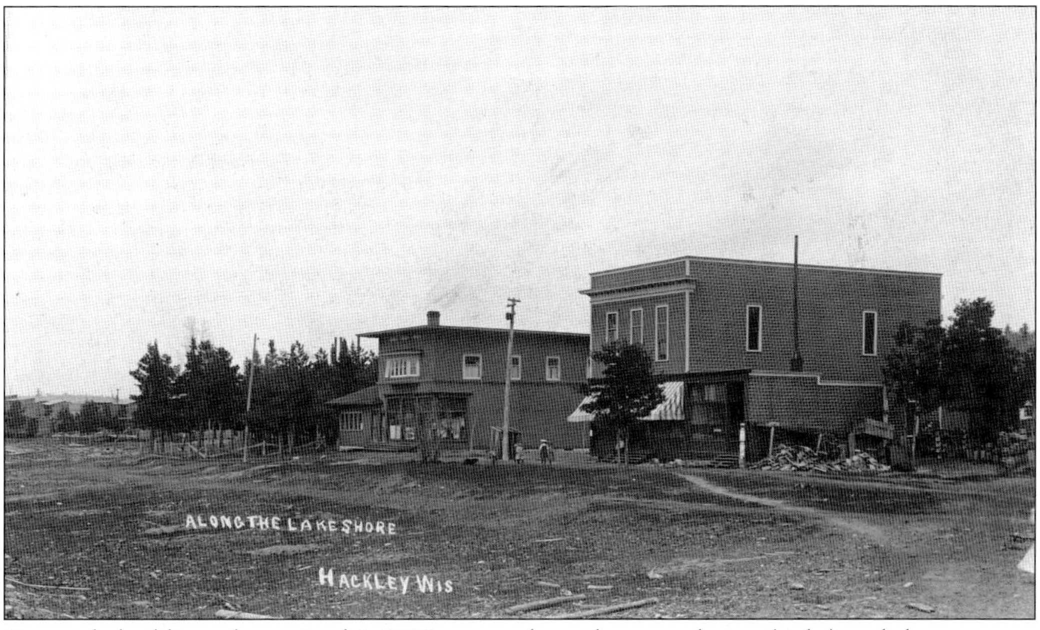

Two early buildings shown in this 1907 postcard are the opera house (right) and the company store. The opera house later became the Sportsman's Spot. The first floor had a saloon and barbershop. Operas were held on the second floor. The Hackley-Phelps-Bonnell Company Store and office building were erected in 1905. The store contained a butcher shop, icehouse, and post office. The company store carried all sorts of items. The building closed and was eventually torn down in 2015.

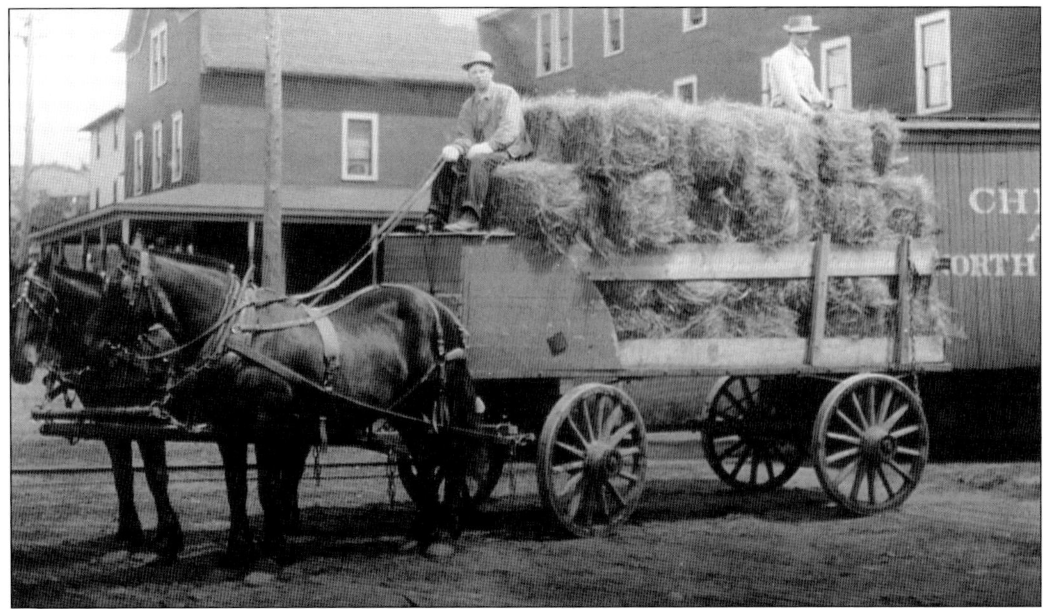

A load of hay is ready for delivery to one of several locations for livestock and other uses. The hay was probably unloaded from the Chicago & North Western boxcar seen behind the hay wagon and the hotel. (Courtesy of Jack Carlson.)

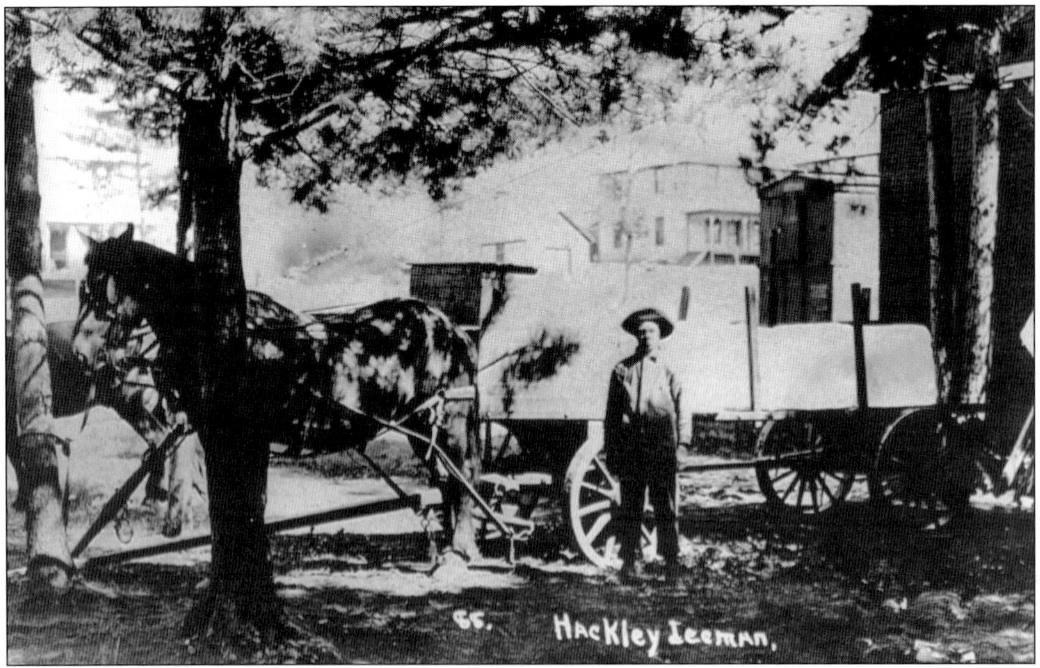

The Hackley Iceman is shown here. Prior to the invention of the refrigerator, blocks of ice were cut with ice saws on Big Twin and other lakes. They were then stored in a section of the railroad supply depot, as shown here. Covered with sawdust or straw, the ice would last through the summer months. On the far right is an ice block sliding down the ramp to be loaded. Most of the ice was delivered to businesses, especially the general store. They were placed in iceboxes to keep perishables, such as meat, from spoiling. (Courtesy of Donna Lapisto.)

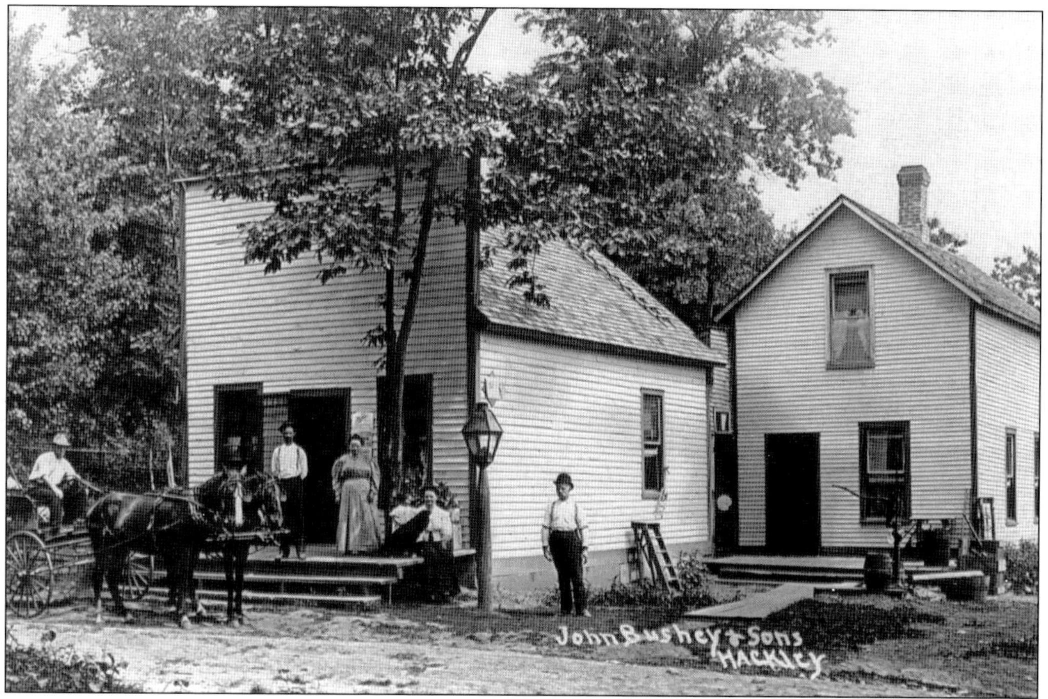

John Bushy operated a small store located almost at the corner of County K and County E when the town was still called Hackley. A Sunday afternoon treat was a 5¢ dish of ice cream or a chocolate sundae for 10¢ at Bushy's. (Courtesy of Donna Lapisto.)

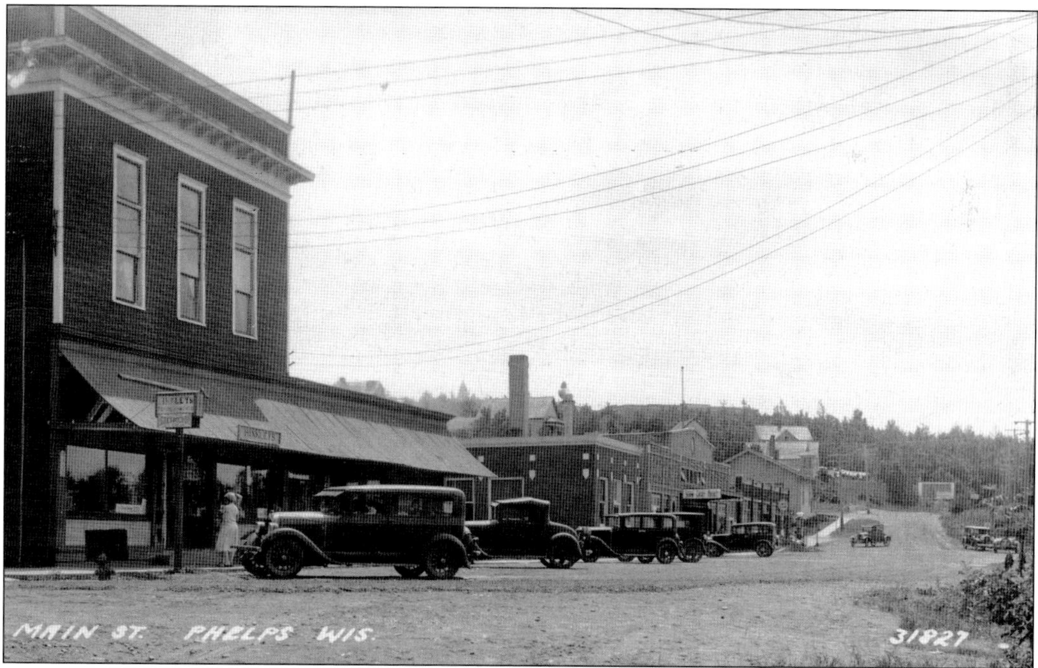

It looks like a busy day on Main Street in downtown Phelps in 1927. Located from left to right are the Sportsman's Spot, the bank, the theater, Yahr's Garage, and the Congregational church.

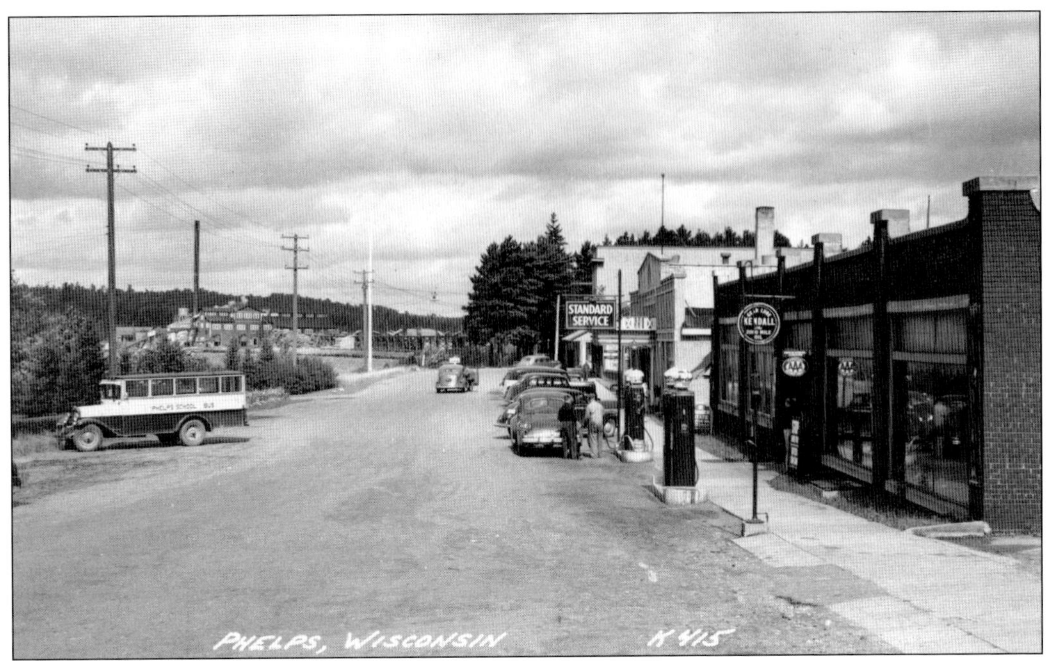

Pictured here is Main Street looking north in the late 1930s. In 1921, Art Yahr, a GMC dealer selling Chevrolets and Buicks, built a garage on Highway 17 in downtown Phelps. It was a full-service station with Standard Oil gas pumps. On the left is a school bus.

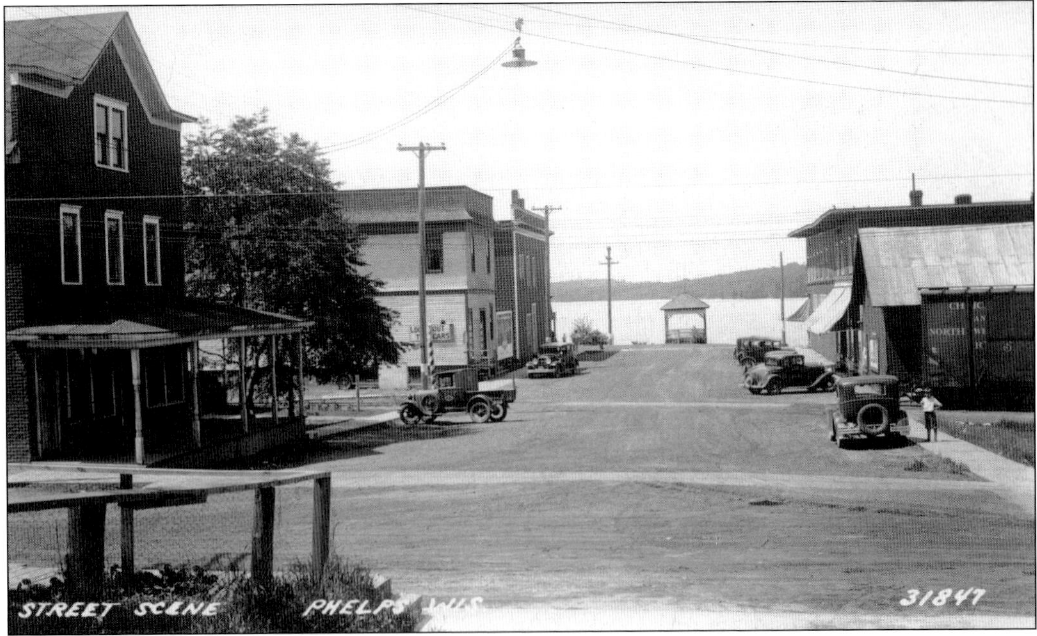

This scene is down the hill and looking west on Highway 17. Part of the hotel is visible on the left. Beyond that is the white town hall, and behind that is the two-story Sportsman's Bar on the corner. On the right are the supply depot (in the foreground) and the company store. This photo postcard was taken in the early 1930s, a year or two prior to the hotel burning down in 1934.

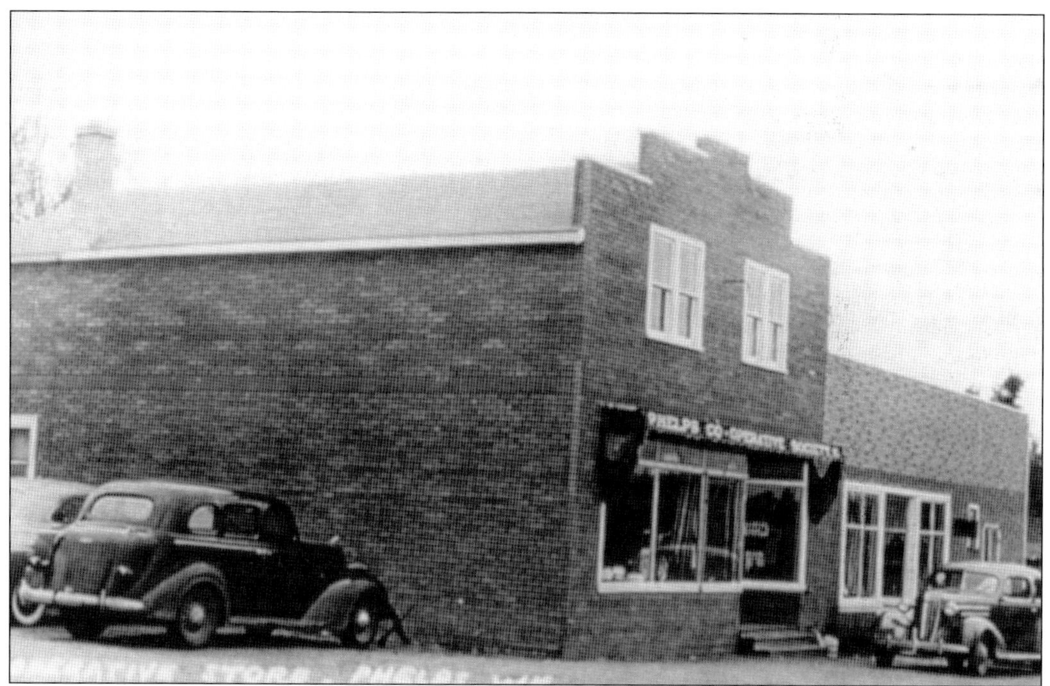

Finnish settlers formed a farmers' co-operative and built a store a half-mile east of town in 1916. The store was enlarged several times. In March 1976, the co-op closed. This photograph dates back to 1940. (Courtesy of the Phelps Historical Museum.)

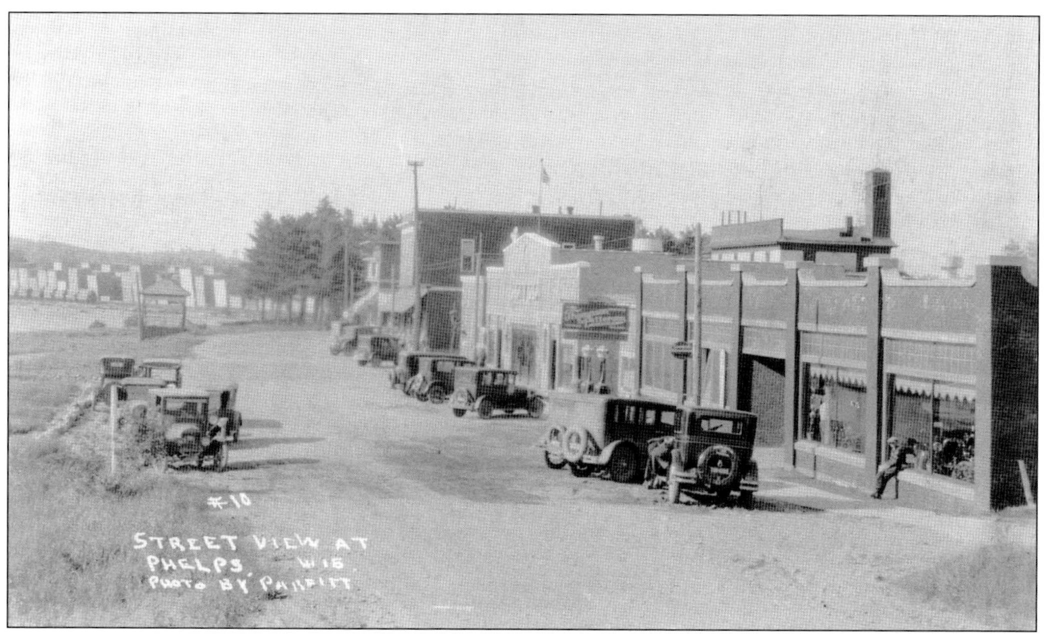

This is a street view of Phelps in 1922. A man is sitting in front of Yahr's Garage, probably awaiting his car repairs. Note the garage entrance in the middle of the building and no gas pumps as of yet. The bandstand can be seen in the background to the left.

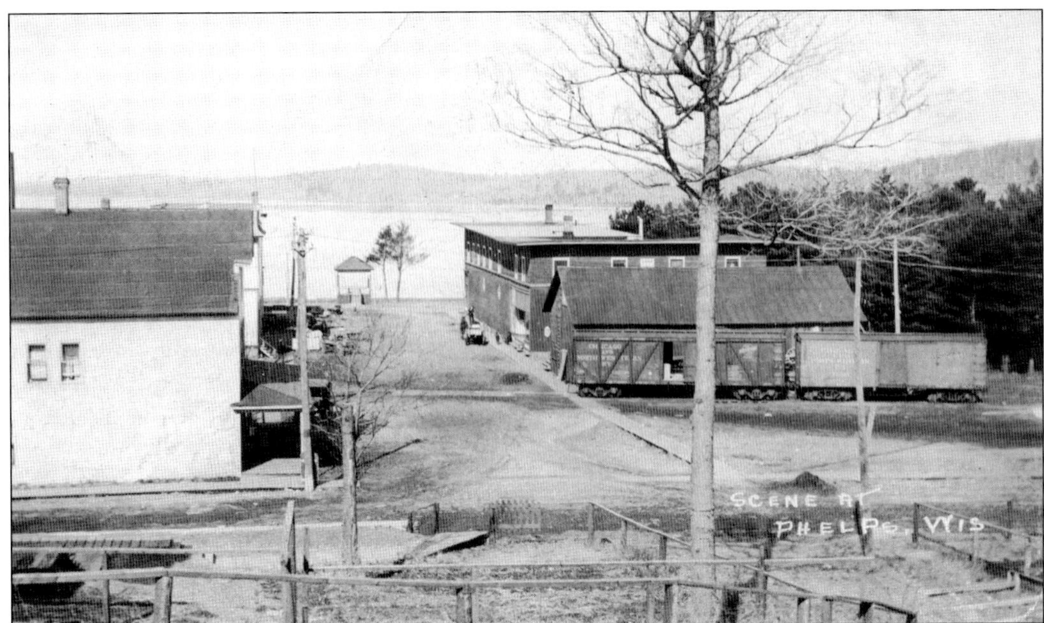

In this postcard dated 1927, the railroad tracks crossed Main Street (Highway 17) and ran between the hotel and the town hall. They continued to about Yahr's Garage. Boxcars were unloaded with supplies to be delivered to nearby businesses. The spur also served as a staging area for freight cars so as not to interfere or block the passenger train. Note the boxcar in front of the supply depot. The freight train delivered service items to all the stores around town, being the grocery store or even the mill. Today, the tracks have been removed, and the passenger train nor the freight train are operational.

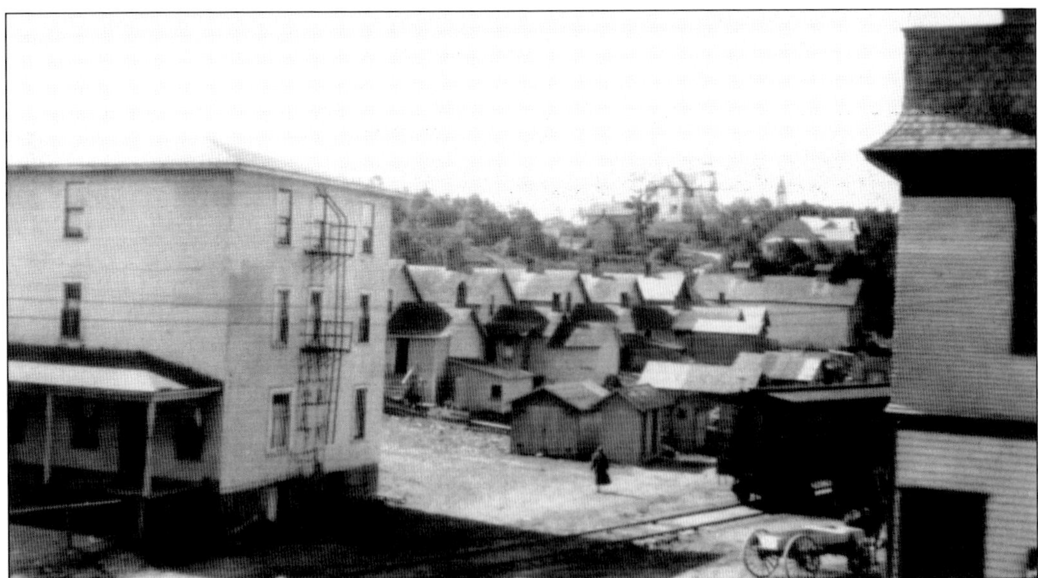
In this scene, company houses and sheds can be seen along Hill Street. In the background is the school on top of the hill. A boxcar is parked between the hotel and the town hall. (Courtesy of Phelps Historical Museum.)

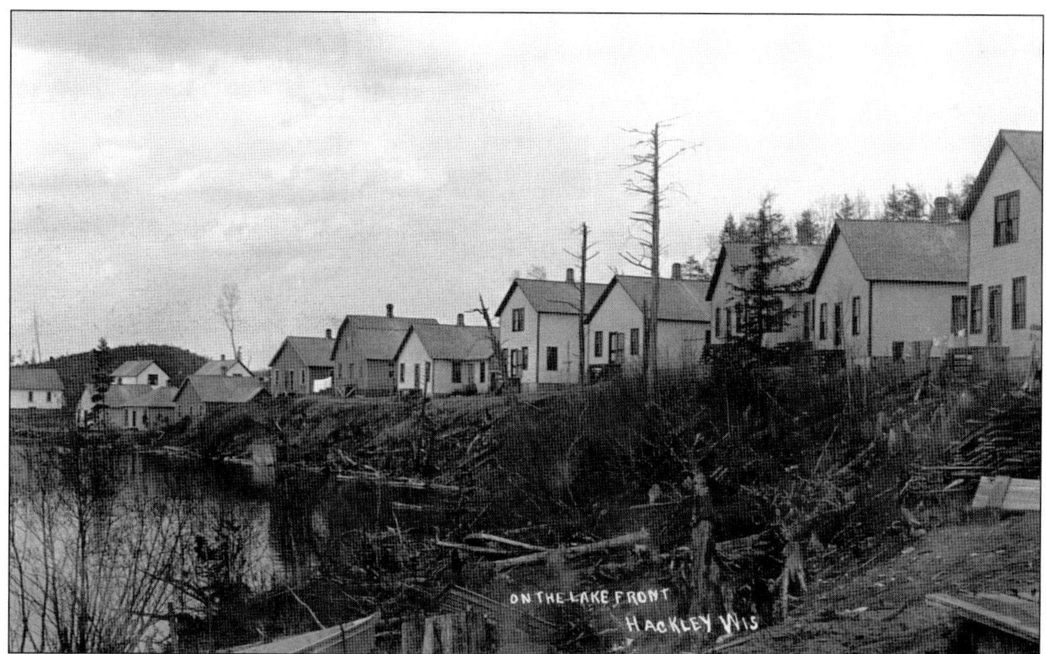

This is another view of company houses in 1909 when the town was named Hackley. The town was changed to Phelps in 1912 to avoid confusion with the town of Hatley. Company houses were owned by the lumber company and housed workers. Note the cutover along the steep shoreline along the lake.

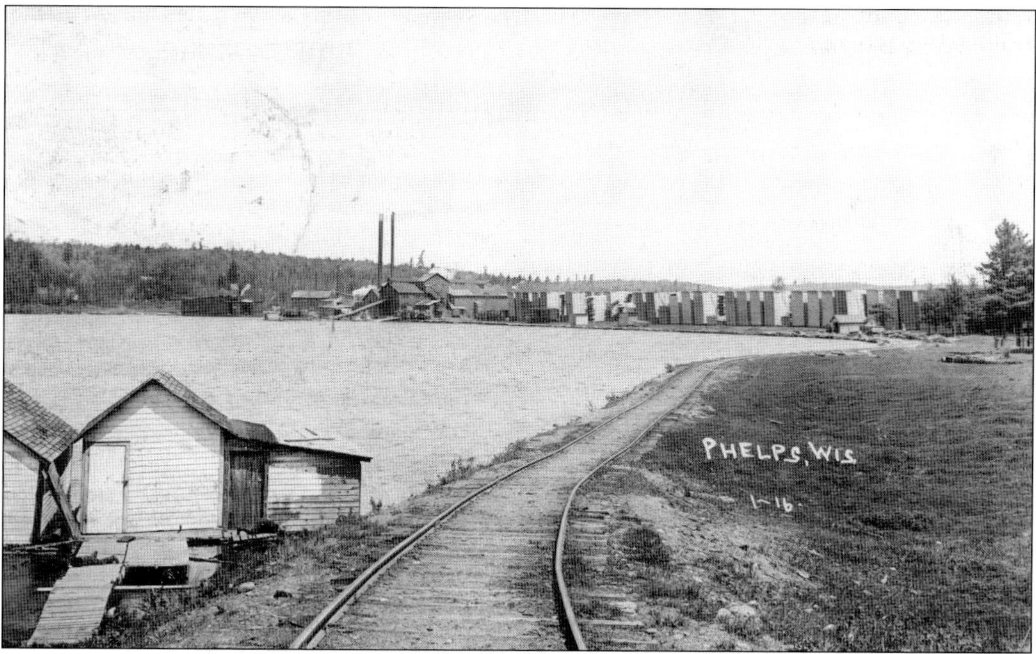

This track along the shore of Big Twin Lake ran from the mill (seen in the background) to about the Christiansen home. Access logs were piled along the right side of the track. This section of shoreline in this 1917 photograph has changed after the track was removed, and the lake reclaimed part of the land.

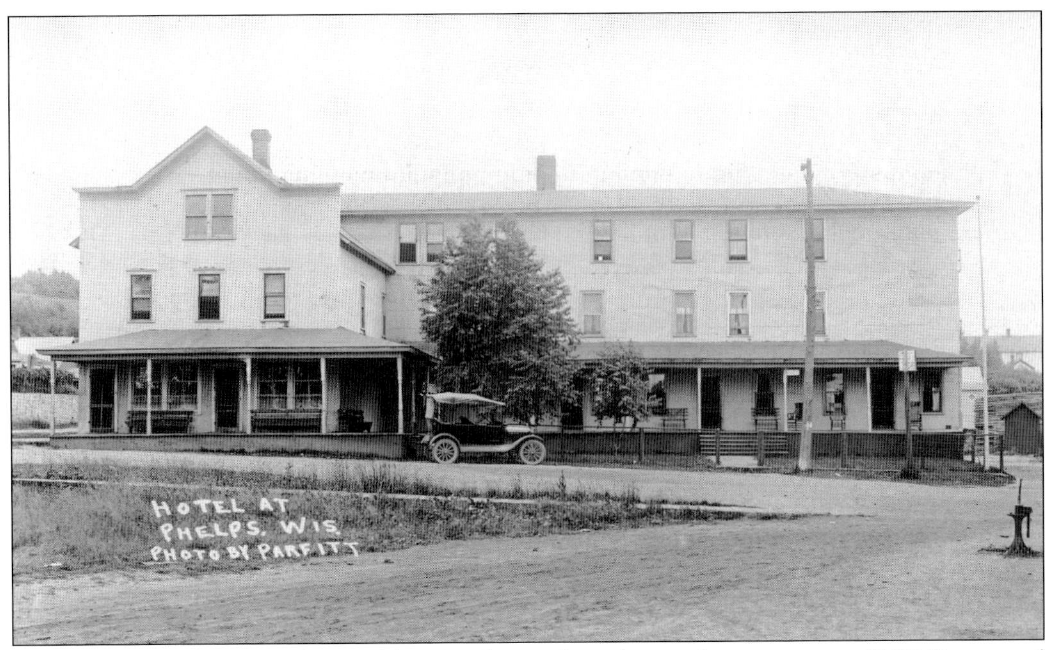

This hotel, referred to as the Hackley Hotel, stood on the southwest corner of Hill Street and Highway 17. It had the upper-class section where tourists, office workers, and teachers stayed. The lower-class section was allocated for transient mill workers. Note the Ford Model T in this c. 1923 photograph.

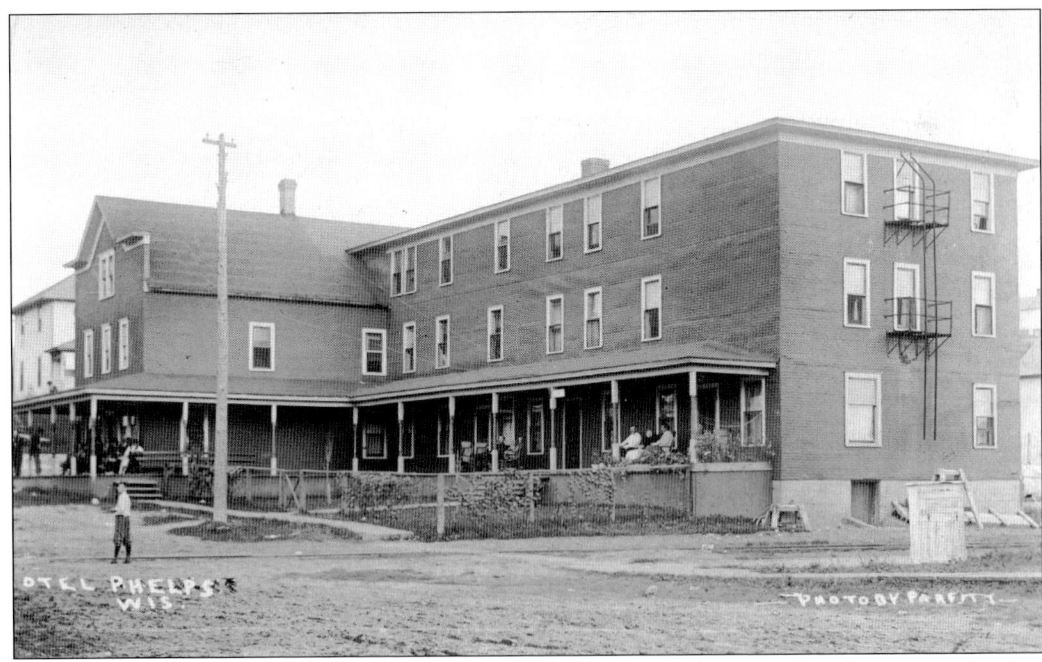

Sitting under the outside porch of the hotel, these folks seem to be relaxed and enjoying the day. The hotel also provided meals for patrons. Built in 1915, the hotel ultimately burned down in 1934 and was never rebuilt. That same year, John Briggs built the Briggs Standard Service Station on its location. His service station changed several hands over the years, ultimately closing in 2019.

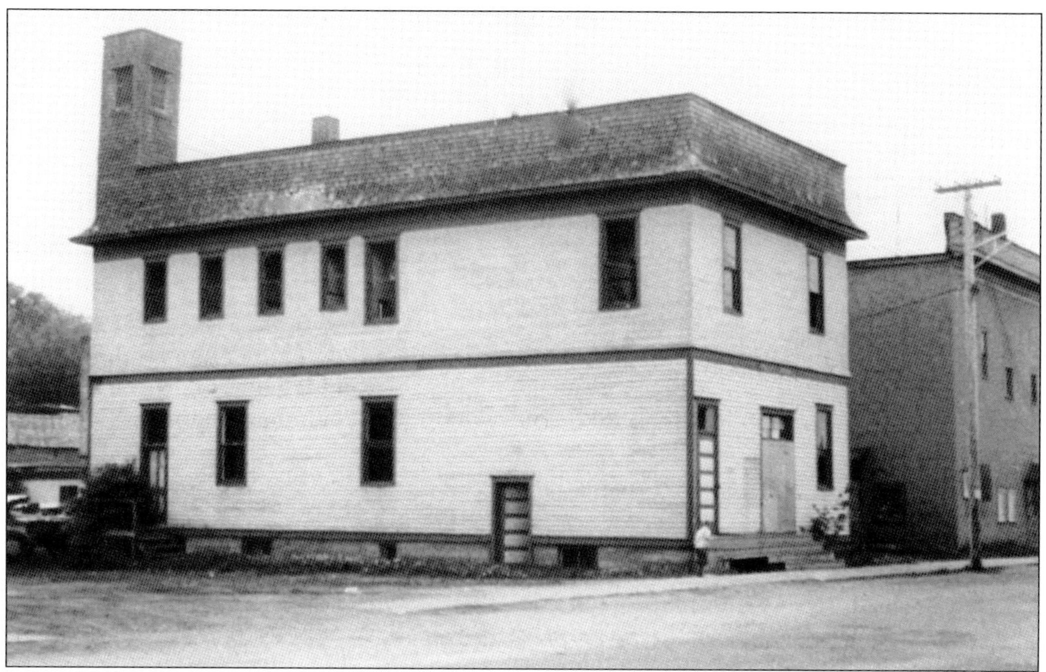

The town hall, a two-story framed building, stood between the Sportsman's Spot and the hotel. The first floor contained a meeting room for the town officials and also a one-cell jail. The top floor functioned for housing larger meetings as well as a movie hall. The basement had a three-lane bowling alley, five pool tables, a few slot machines, and a bar. The building was torn down in 1969.

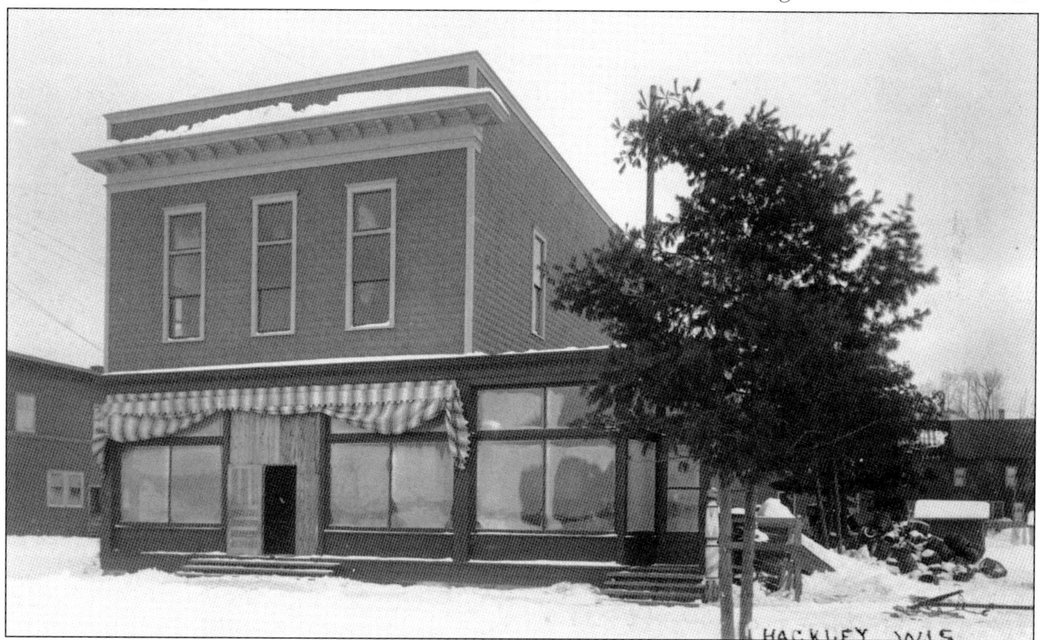

Appearing here is the opera house and saloon in the winter of 1909. In the background, to the left, is the company store. The hotel is located in the back right. The opera house later transitioned to become the Sportsman's Spot. With the expansion of State Highway 17 in 2006, "the Sportsman" was required to be torn down.

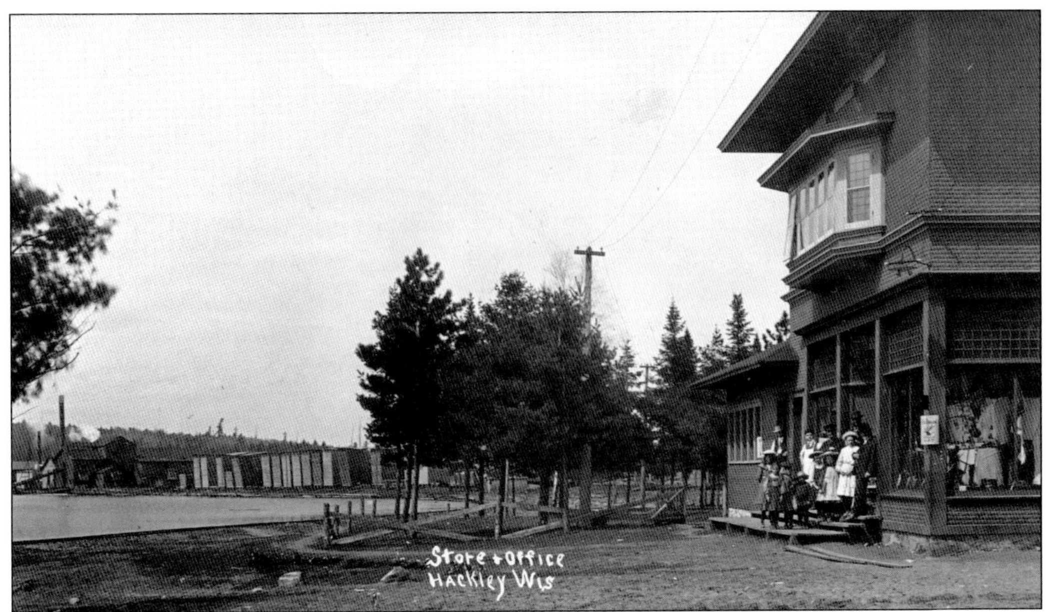

Finely dressed children and adults are having their photograph taken in front of the company store and office. The store also contained the post office. In the background to the left is the sawmill with stacks of finished lumber along the shore.

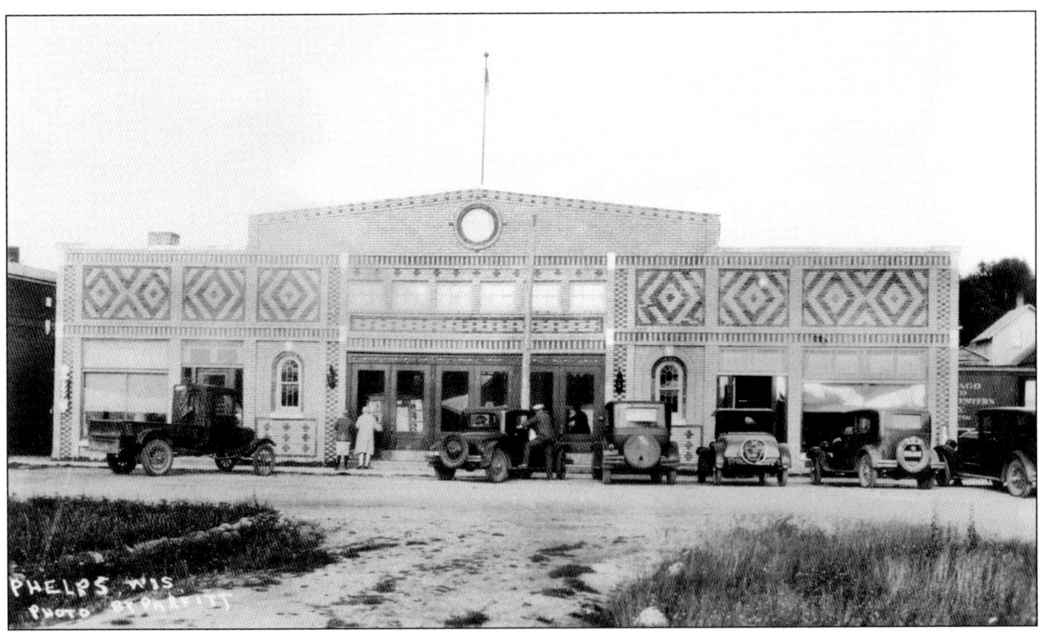

The Northern Lakes Theater was built in 1926 in the same location that the pole yard for the mill was once located. Among the incorporators were C.M. Christiansen, Homer Galpin, and Charles McCullough, all of whom were members of the Eagle River Fishing and Shooting Club. In later years, the building became a hardware store. Two ladies in this 1929 photo postcard show their curiosity about what movie is on the billboard.

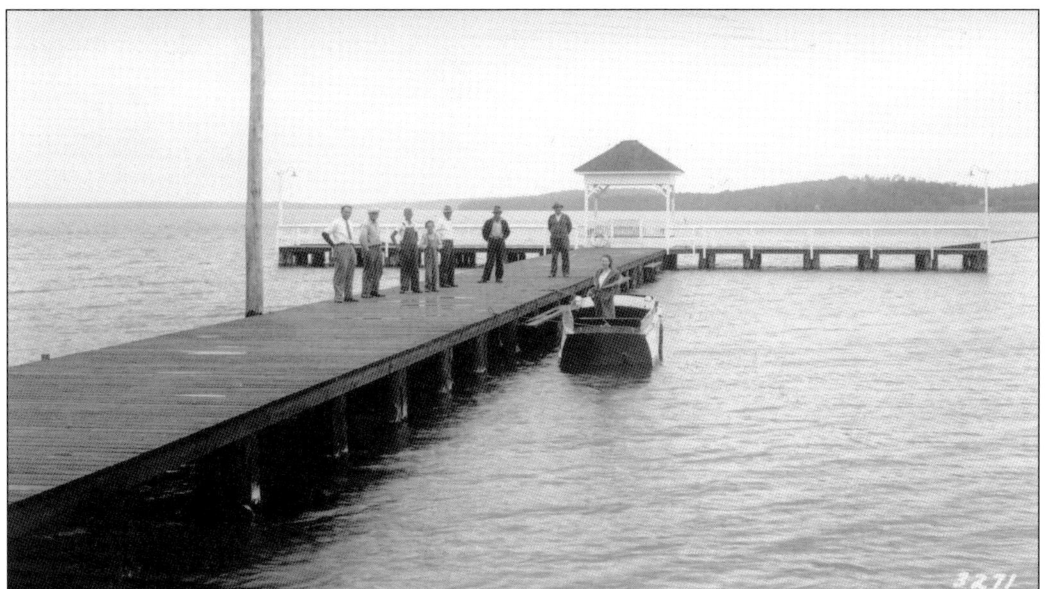

In later years, a gazebo replaced the old bandstand and was located on the end of the municipal dock. An inboard motorboat, as seen here, would take tourists on excursions around Big and Little Twin Lakes.

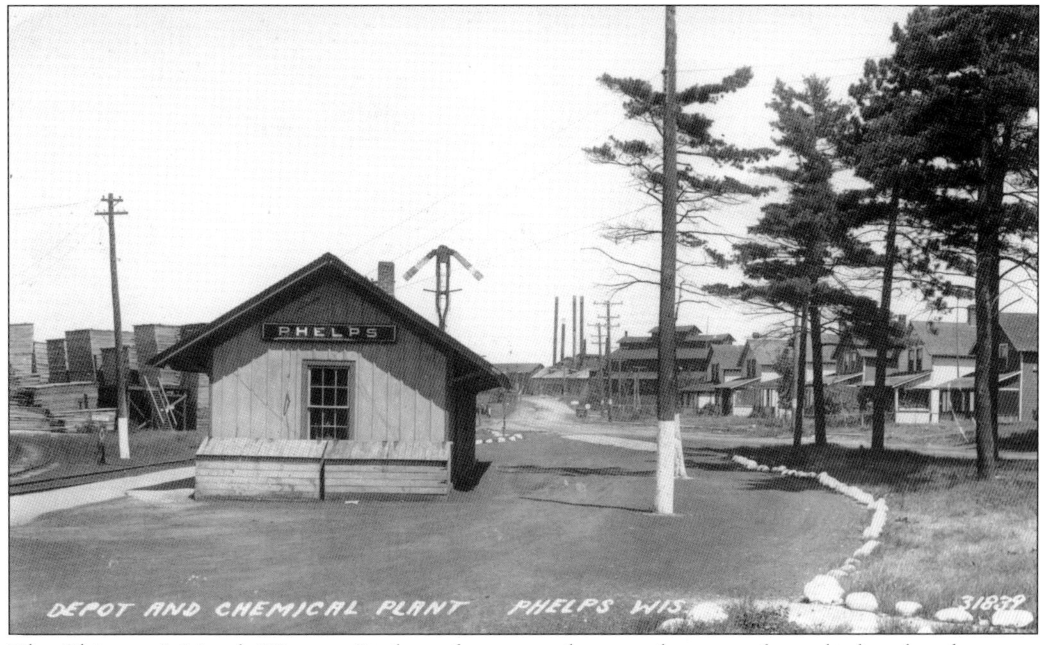

The Chicago & North Western Railway depot stood across the street from the hotel and next to the railroad supply depot to the left of this photograph. The main room of the little depot held benches and a wood stove, which also burned coal. This photograph dates prior to 1940, when the chemical plant seen in the background was still in operation.

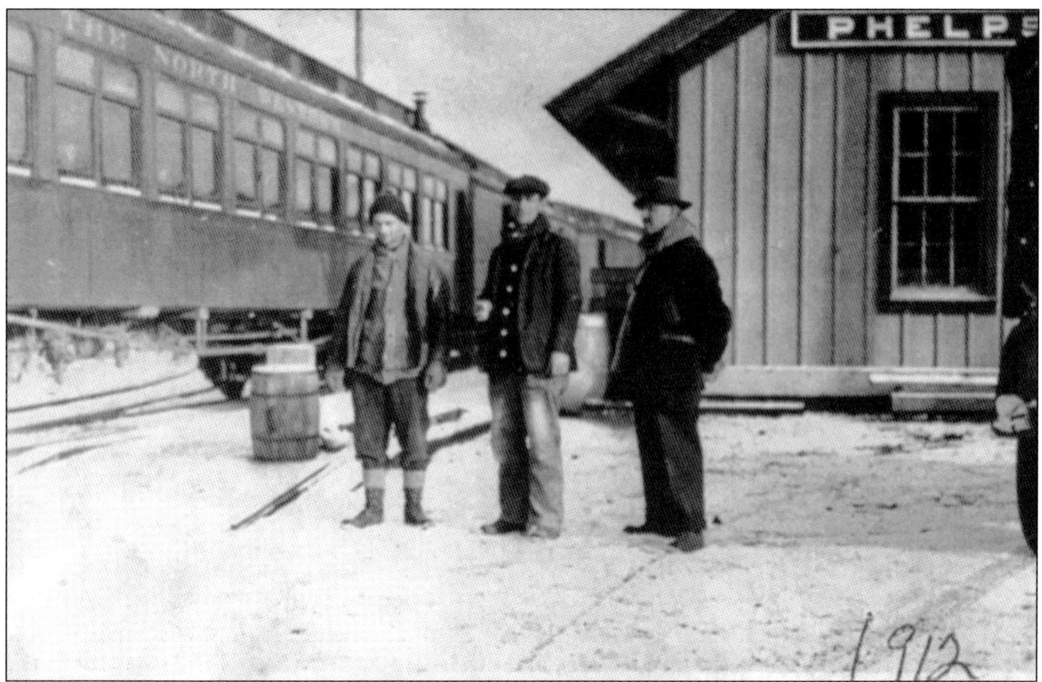

Charles Hazen of the Long Lake Lodge (right) and two other men are at the depot, apparently waiting for supplies or guests to take to the resort. The lower right dates this photograph to 1912. (Courtesy of Donna Lapisto.)

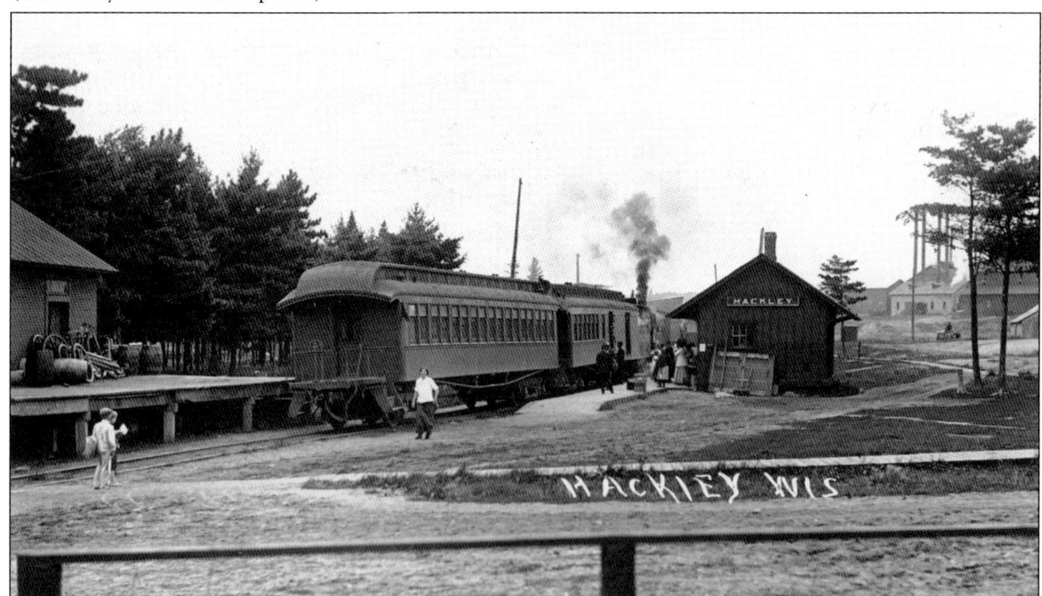

The Chicago & North Western Railway came from the south. A spur from Conover ran parallel and north of Highway E to Phelps. Passenger service was discontinued in 1931. A bus then ran between Phelps and Eagle River for train connections. After World War II, this service also came to an end. This photograph was taken prior to 1913, when the town was called Hackley, and shows passengers getting on the train heading home again. To the left is the supply depot with the loading dock.

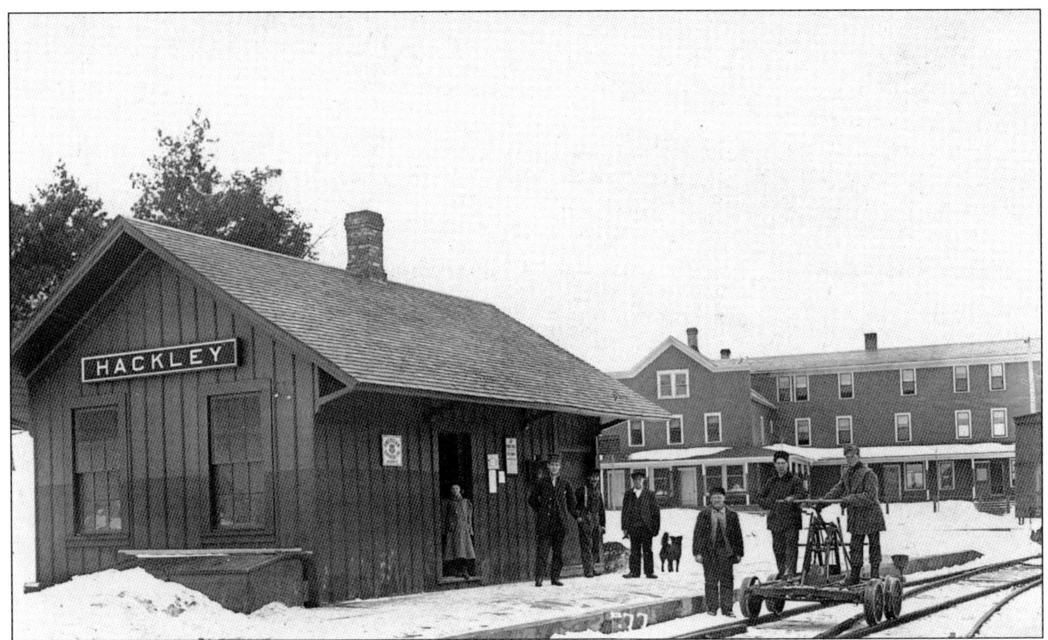

Al Fanton, a depot agent (second from left), and others are seen in front of the depot, with the hotel in the background. The pump handcar, operated by two men, was used for railroad inspection and maintenance. Handcars were assigned to a section of track approximately 10 miles long.

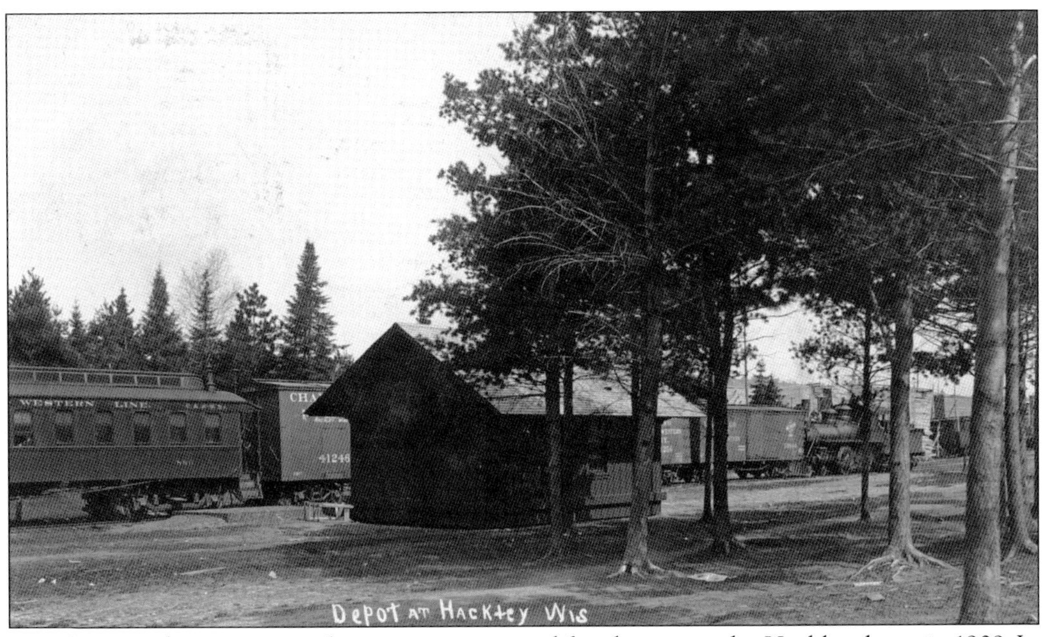

Seen here is a locomotive with a passenger car and freight cars at the Hackley depot in 1909. In later years, freight service had dwindled to about one train a week to bring material to the Pallet Corporation and Sylvan Products. In the late 1970s, all service ceased. Eventually, in 1980, the tracks were removed.

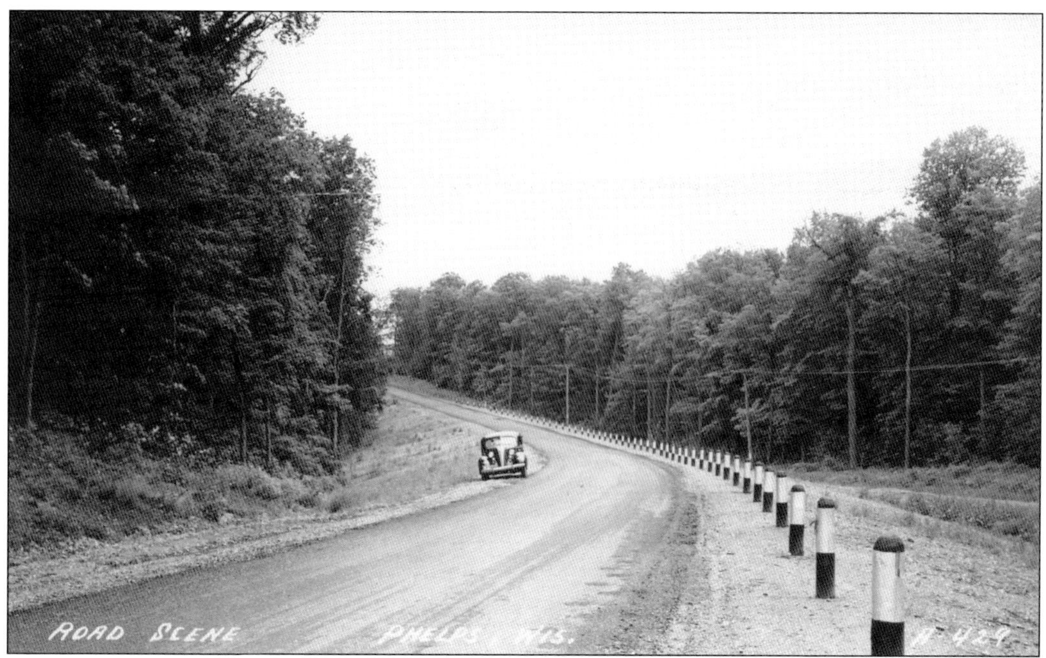

This photograph, taken in 1941, shows a 1937 Hudson Terraplane parked on the side of the road on Highway 17 near Phelps, Wisconsin. A 1930 article in the *Chicago Herald and Examiner* mentioned a trip to northern Wisconsin could take all day—and sometimes two. Few major highways were paved. Most were packed gravel roads like the one shown here.

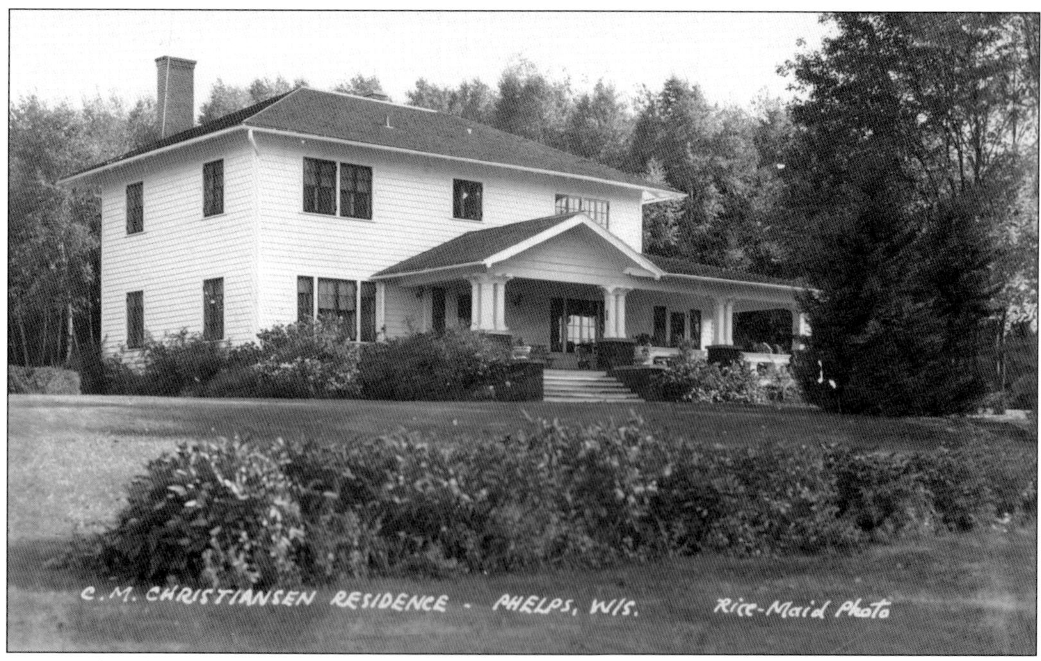

Depicted in this 1941 postcard, the C.M. Christiansen residence, on the shore of Big Twin Lake in downtown Phelps, was built in 1921–1922 on the property where the first Congregational church stood. The house was enlarged over the years and is still in the Christiansen family.

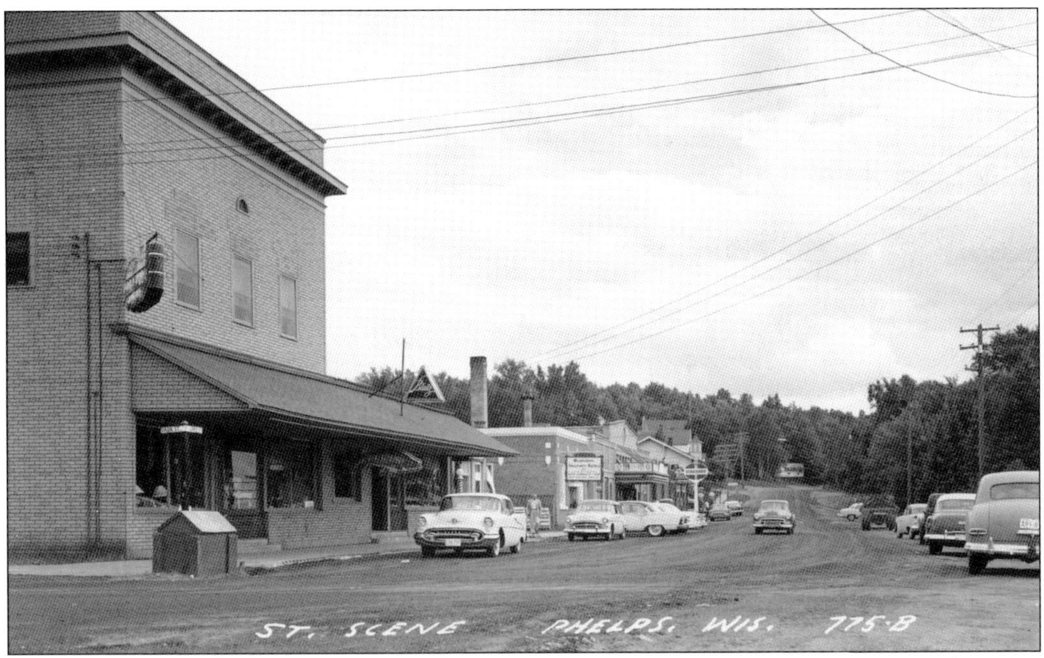

The Phelps business district is seen here about 1957. Highway 17 shows a packed gravel road or a road grated for blacktopping.

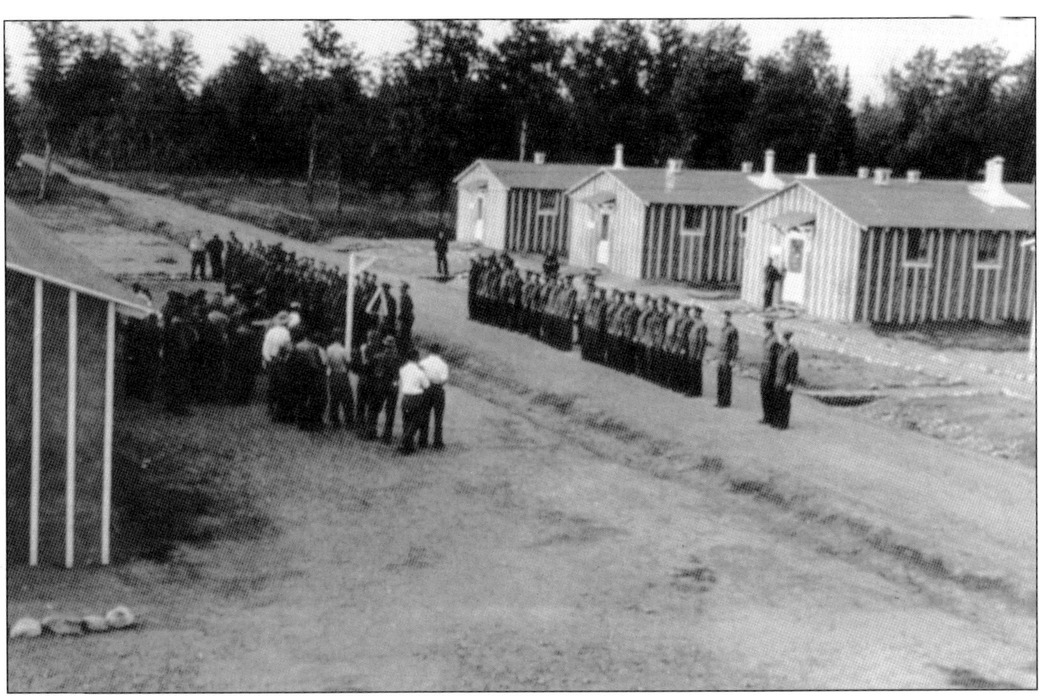

The Civilian Conservation Corps (CCC) was a public work relief program from 1933 to 1942. The program's goal was to conserve the country's natural resources while providing jobs for young men. This camp, Project No. F-26, 3638, was built in 1935. A historical marker locates this camp on Warvet Trail about two miles northwest of Phelps. (Courtesy of Phelps Historical Museum.)

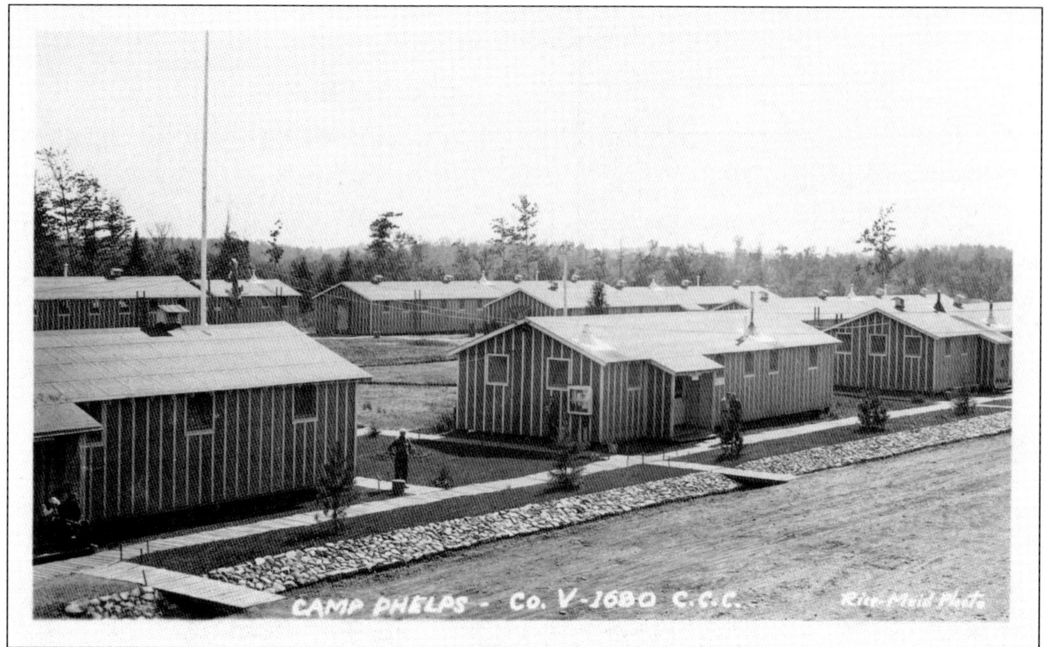

Two camps were listed in the Phelps area. This Camp F-26, 1680, built in 1935, was located two miles northeast of Phelps past the end of Coveyville Road. No research has been done on its exact location.

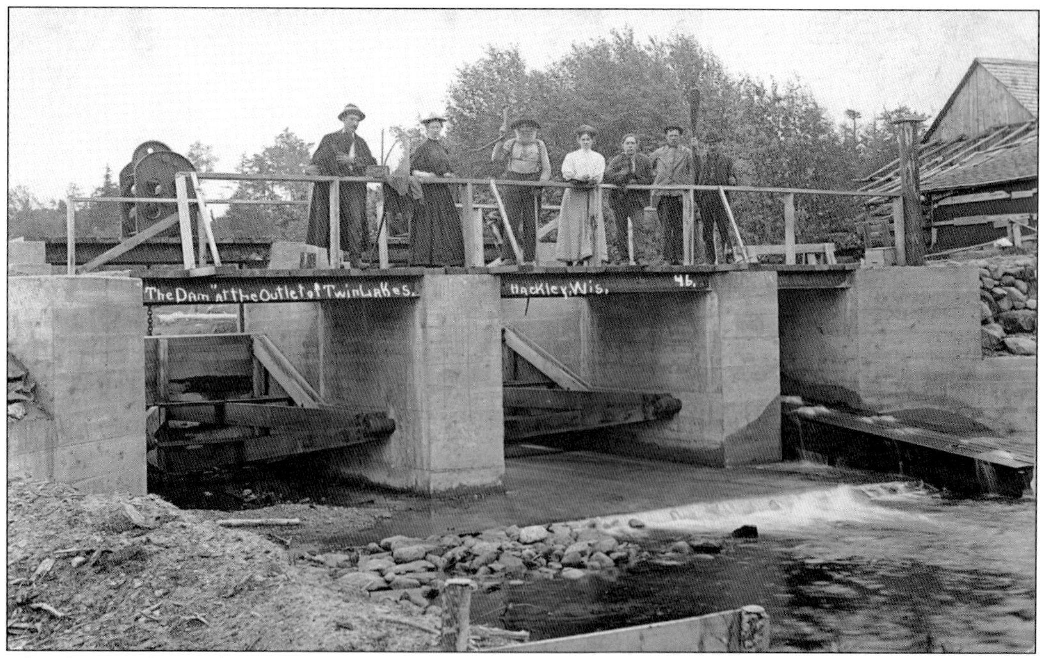

The dam at the outlet of South Twin Lake, shown in this 1909 postcard, was built in 1907 and operated by the Wisconsin Valley Improvement Co. They were responsible for organizing the flow for most of the upper Wisconsin River tributaries.

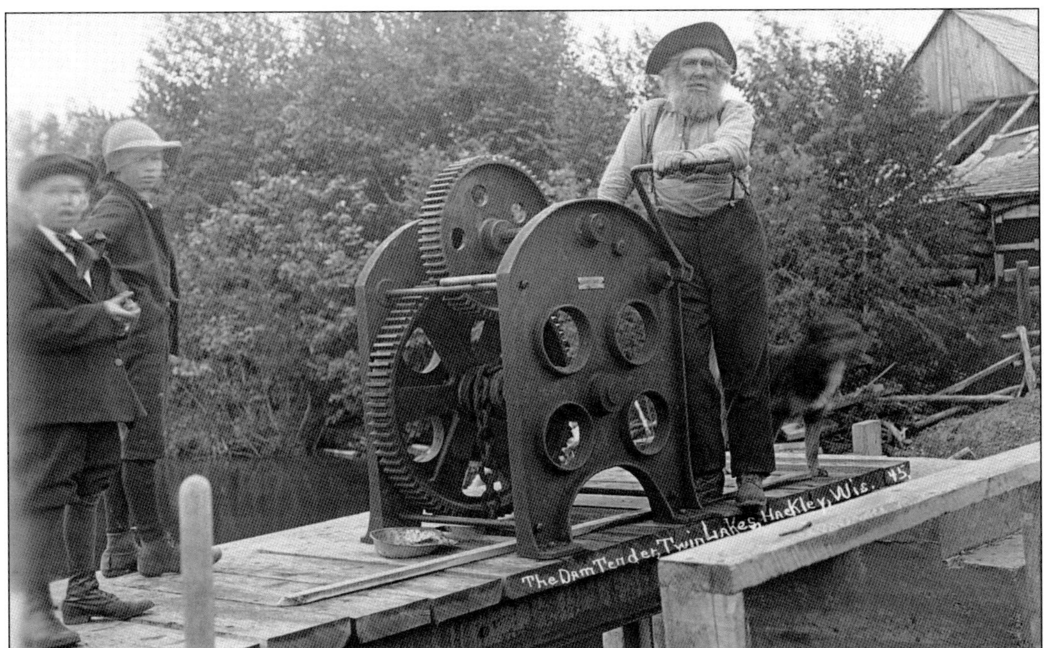

Two boys all dressed up are watching the gears rotate as Bill Stanton, the dam tender, operates the machinery that raised and lowered the locks, which controls the water flow on Twin Creek.

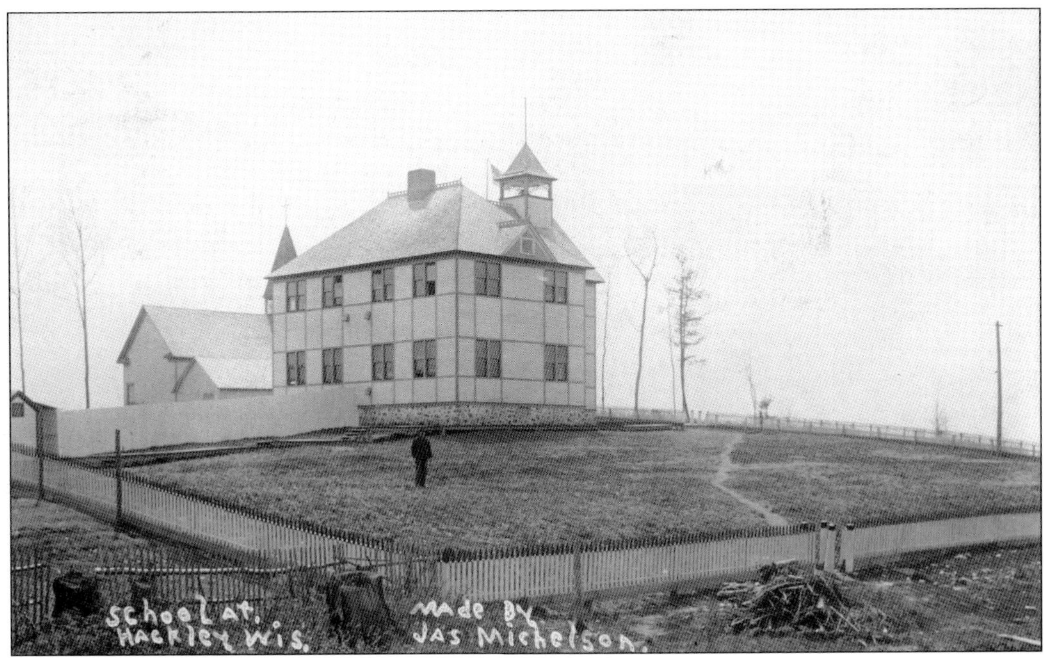

School House on the Hill, as it was called, was built around 1910 on the hill in the vicinity of the present school. It was a four-room two-story building with two grades to each room. This postcard dated 1912 shows a fenced-in area and the Catholic church in the background.

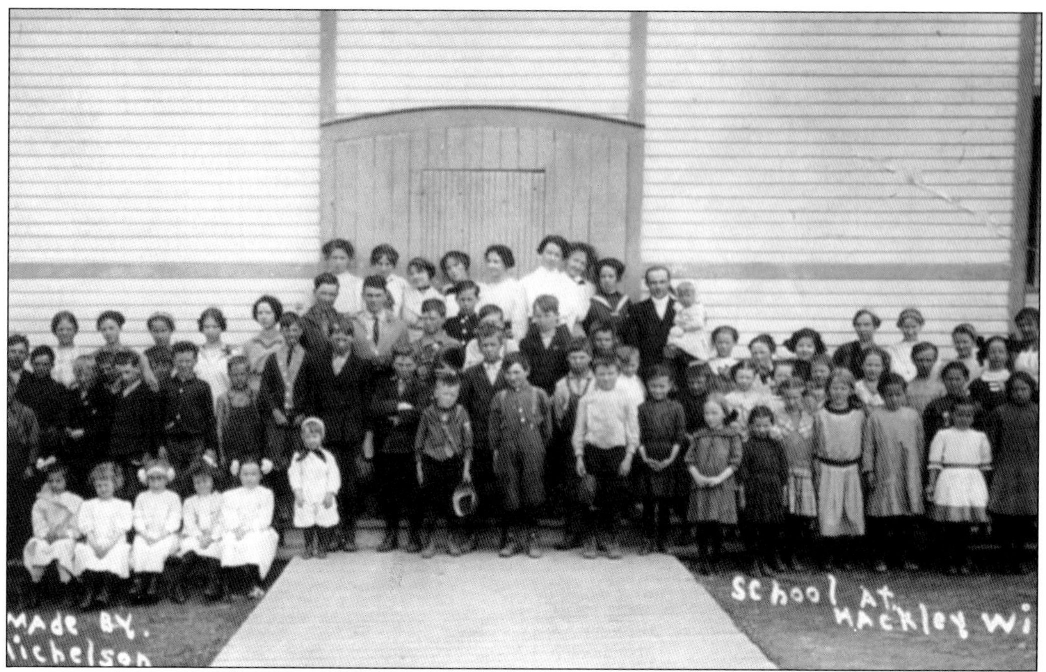

Students seen here are posing for a class photograph at the School House on the Hill in Hackley, Wisconsin. In later years, a new schoolhouse was built to accompany the growth of the town. The School House on the Hill was then used by the Crandall Boat Company to manufacture boats.

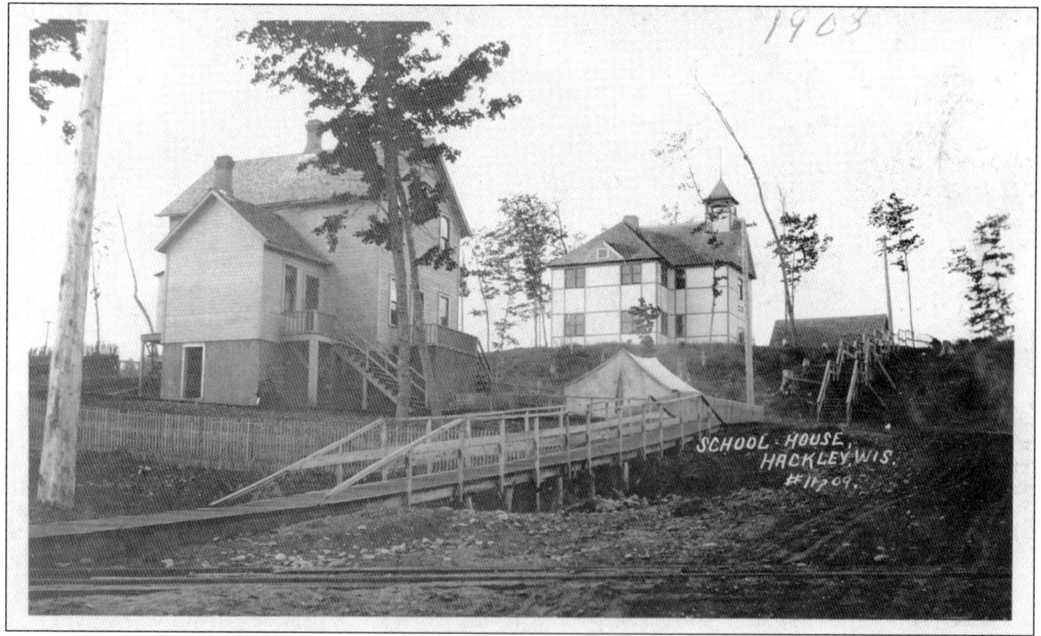

From this view, the school can be seen in the background, and an unidentified building can be seen in the left front. Note the boardwalk, the tent, and the staircase leading to the school. Eventually, the school building was condemned and sold to the Crandall Boat Company. Crandall Boat Company used that building until they went out of business in the early 1930s, at which time the building was torn down.

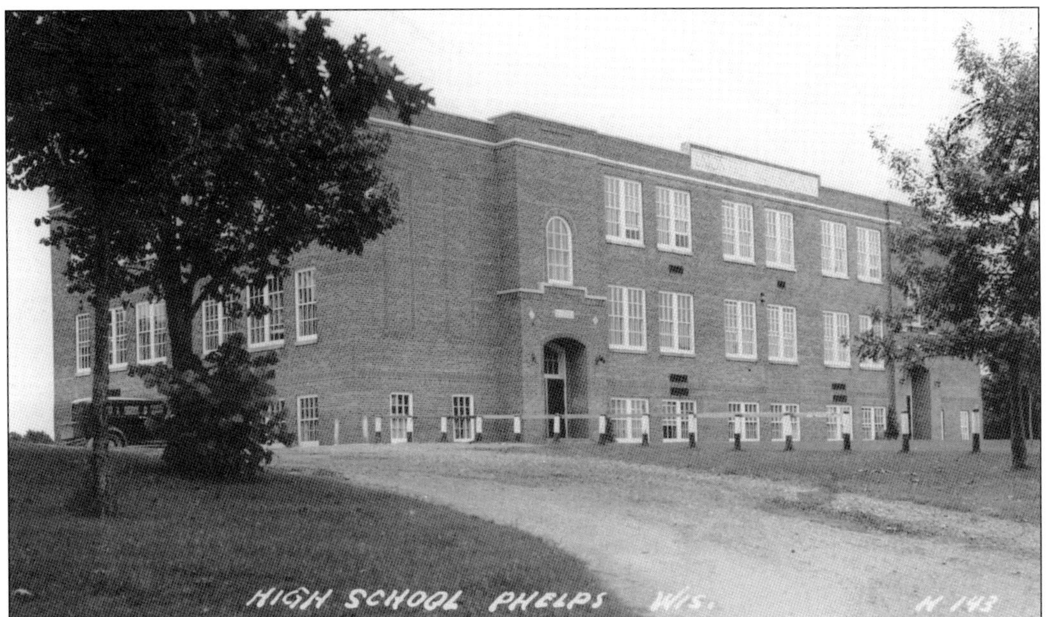

A new school was completed in time for the 1930–1931 school year. The first graduating class from the new school had 13 seniors. This postcard shows the building in about 1945. Additions and improvements, such as classrooms and a gymnasium, were added to the school over the years.

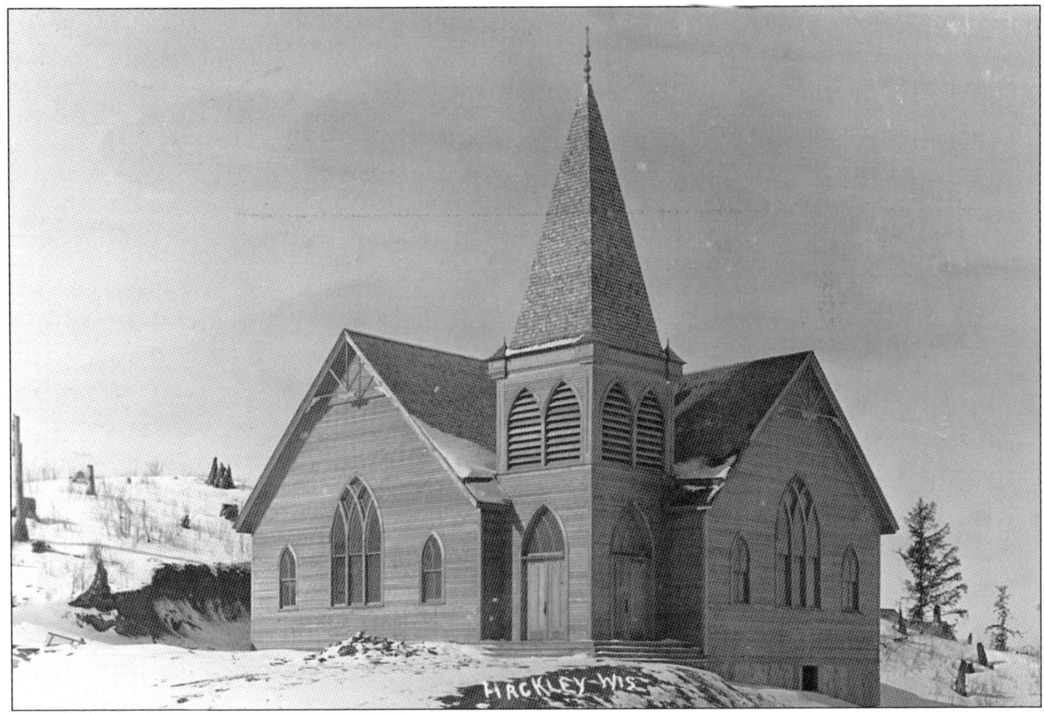

The First Congressional Church was built on the lakefront in 1909. The Hackley-Phelps-Bonnell Company donated the land. In 1919, the church burned down, and a new church was constructed in 1921 across the road from the old one. About the same time, C.M. Christiansen built a large house on the site of the old church.

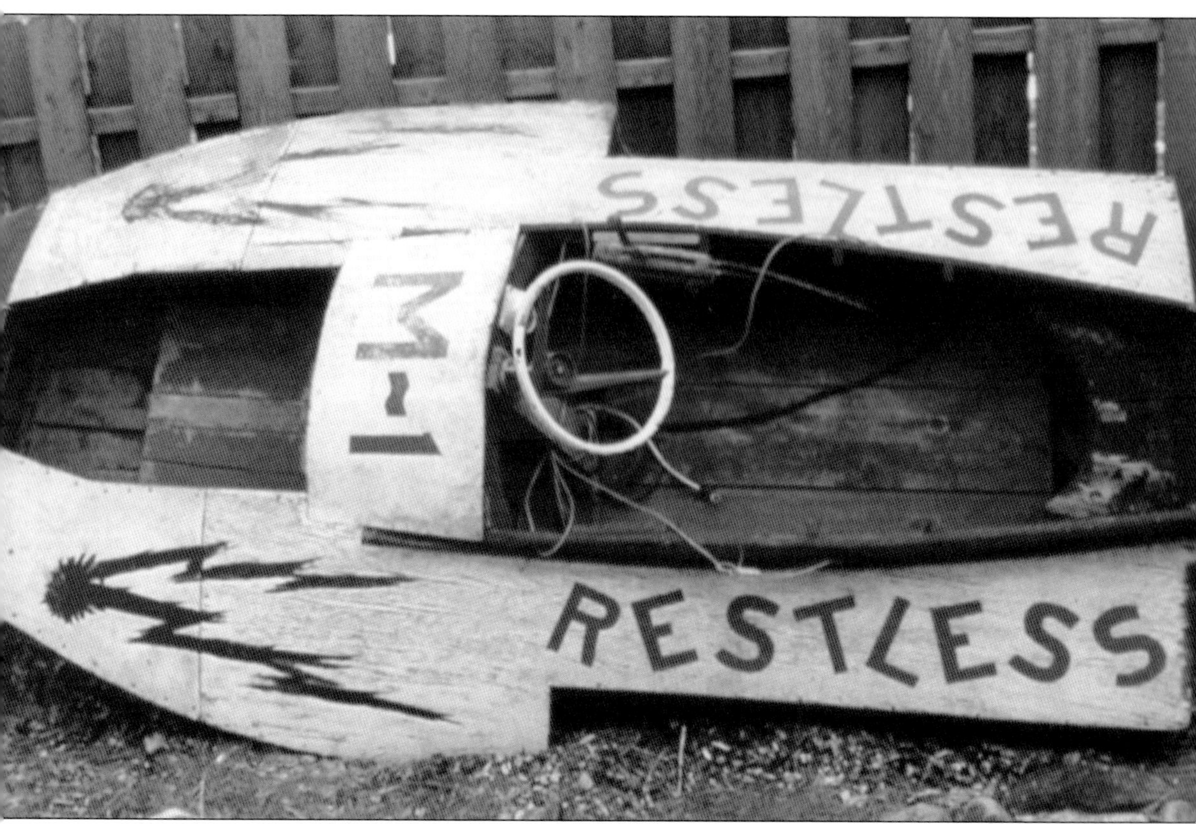

Depicted here is a Comet racing boat (in need of restoration) manufactured by the Crandall Boat Company. This boat currently resides at the Land O' Lakes Museum just outside of Phelps. The Crandall Boat Company was a firm that appeared on the scene from 1928 to 1933. Bruce Crandall, the owner of the Crandall Boat Works, was born in Chicago, Illinois, in 1904. He was a boat designer and, later, a naval architect with the Bureau of Ships. Crandall boat designs were published in *Motor Boating*, *Popular Science*, and other prevalent magazines. The company's largest outboard was a 19-foot boat, which was also offered with a hardtop. The main plant, general offices, and experimental lab were in New Port, California. However, boats were mostly built at their assembly plant and branch office in Phelps. To try the new boats out, races were also held on the lakes. A 1931 *Vilas County News* article mentioned boat races on Big Twin Lake, with Crandall Boats winning many races.

Two

Continued Expansion of Phelps

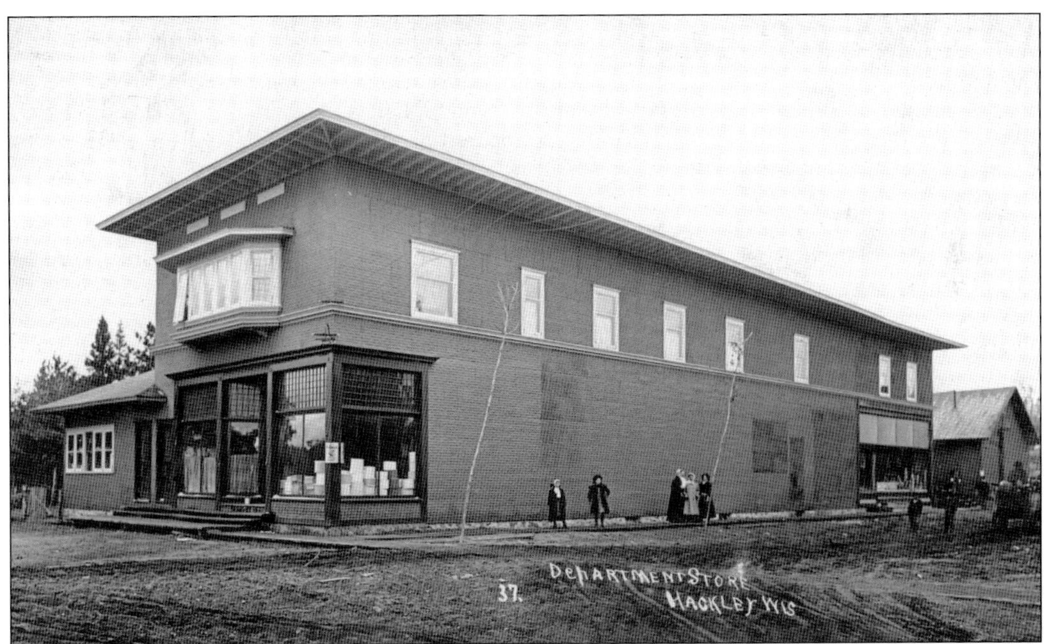

Women and children are standing in front of the Hackley-Phelps-Bonnell store in 1909. The supply depot and a horse-drawn wagon can be seen at the far right. Mill workers and other locals, as well as tourists, frequented the store for all their shopping needs because the "Big Store" carried everything, including groceries, hardware, clothing, toys, hunting gear, fishing gear, and even furniture.

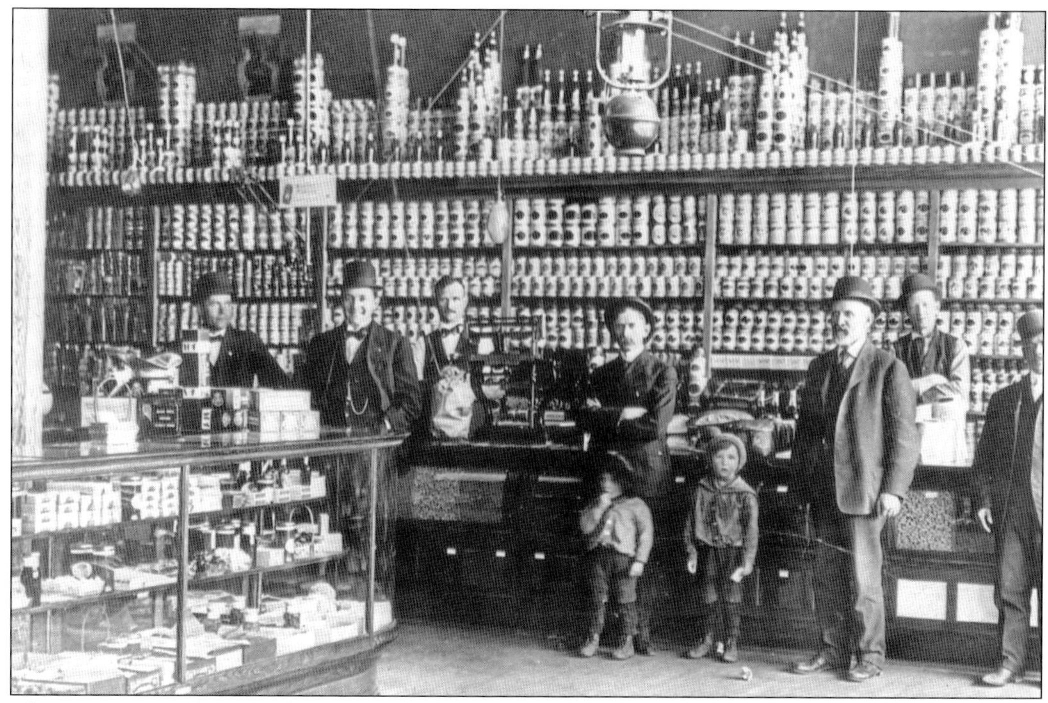

This scene was photographed at the company store in Hackley in about 1903. The third person from the right is William Phelps, whom the town was renamed in later years. Also pictured behind Phelps and the counter is Bill Irwin, the store manager.

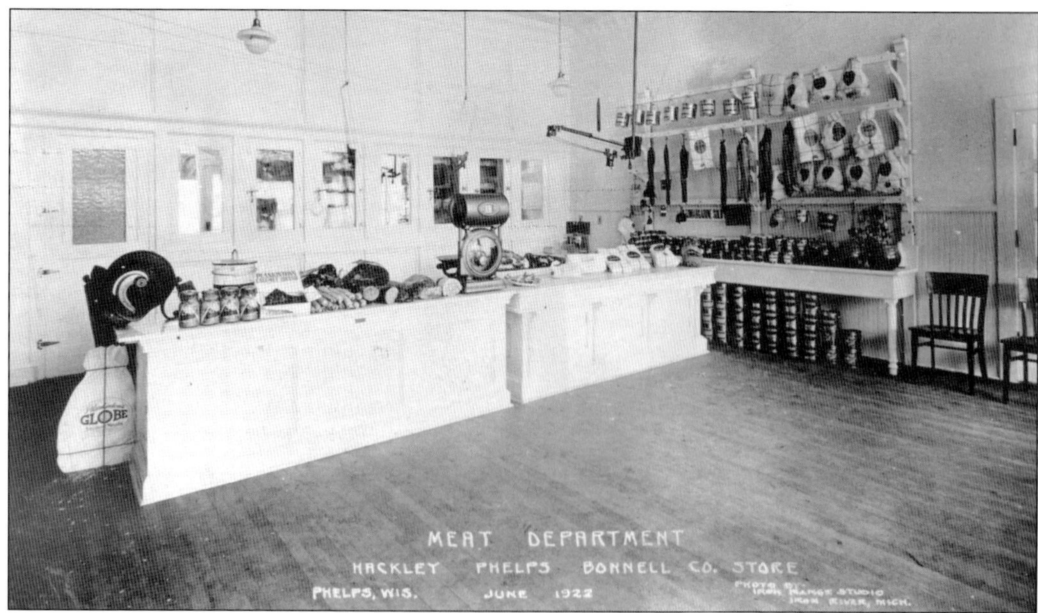

A large addition was added later on the east end of the general store, which contained a butcher shop, shown in this 1922 photograph, and a walk-in cooler, located above the meat department. Ice was the coolant in those days.

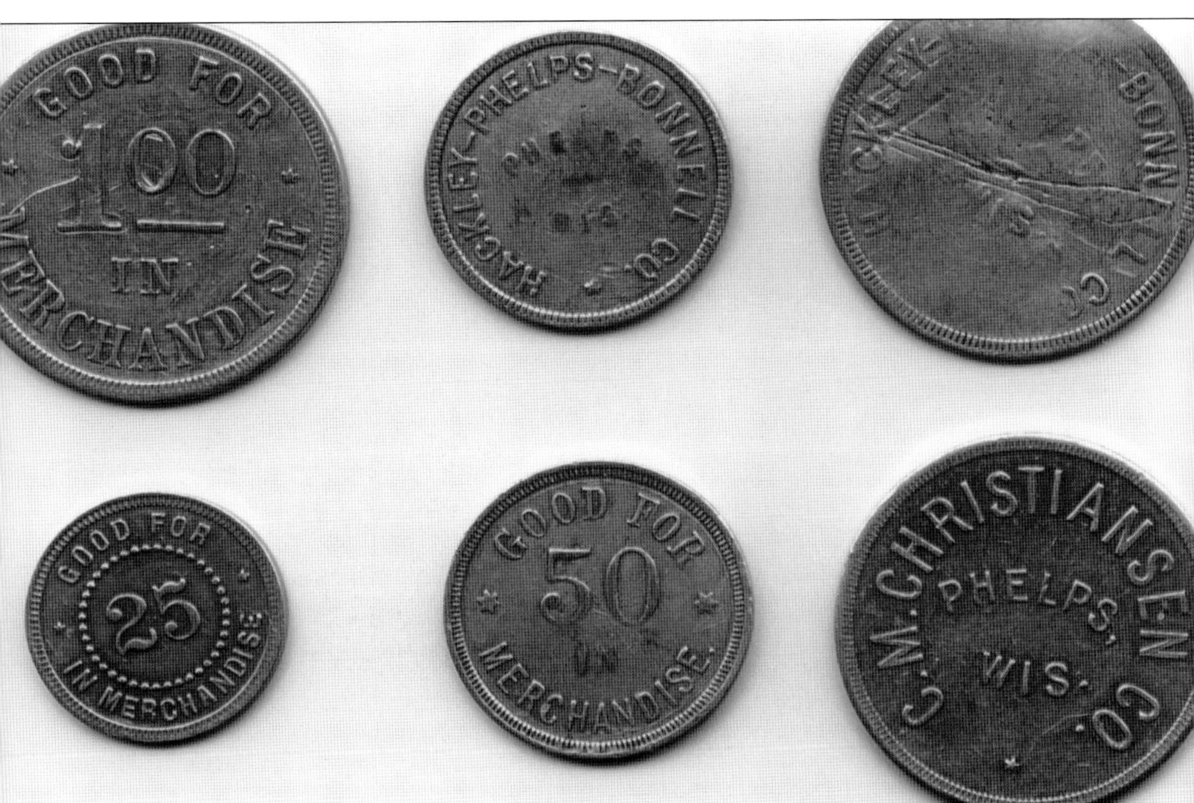

Lumber companies frequently paid their employees in scrip, which is substitutional currency that replaces legal tender. In Wisconsin, lumber companies specifically were exempted from the state laws requiring wages to be paid in cash. Most tokens were stamped with the value and name of the company that issued them and were only redeemable at the same store for goods or even for lumber. This was also the case with the Hackley-Phelps-Bonnell Company and, later, the C.M. Christiansen Company. Locals called the aluminum tokens "chink money" because of the metallic rattle when carried in their pockets. In the bottom row are, from left to right, C.M. Christiansen scrip shown in denominations of 25¢, 50¢, and $1; in the top row, from left to right, are scrip from Hackley-Phelps-Bonnell Company: $1, 50¢, and the back of the $1 token. Scrip was phased out in the 1950s, as many states outlawed the use of it to pay wages to employees.

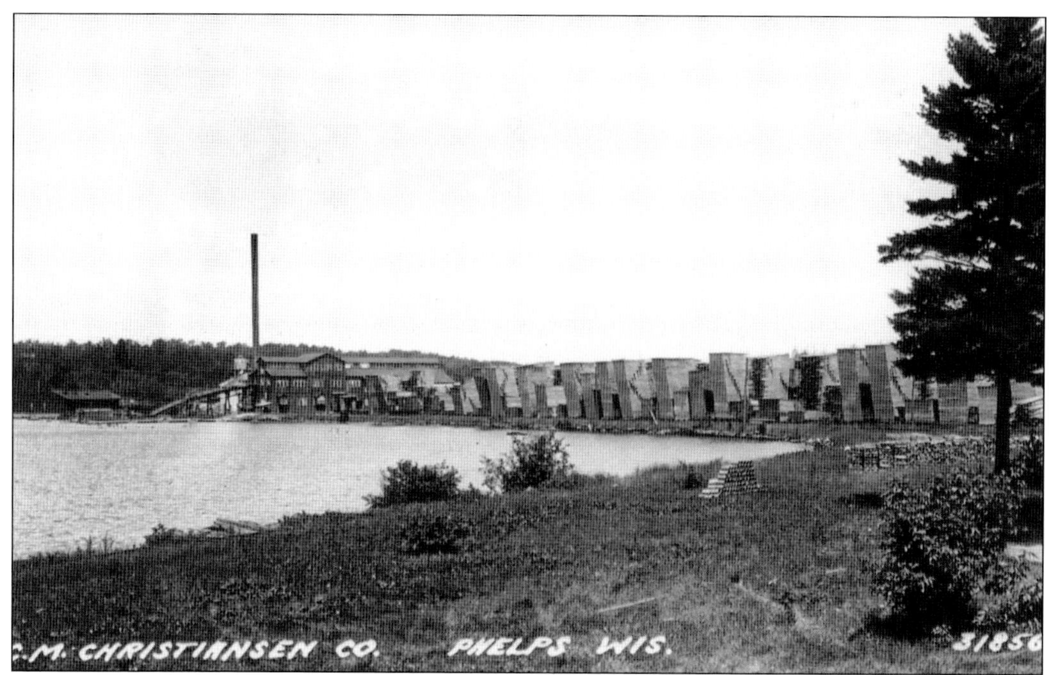

In 1903, three of the largest lumber firms in the state were merged into a new company to be known as the Hackley-Phelps-Bonnell Company. They were the Wisconsin Lumber and Bark Company, the Grand Rapids Bark and Lumber Company, and the Hackley-Bonnell Lumber Company. In 1928, the Hackley-Phelps-Bonnell Company was dissolved, and its assets were purchased by C.M. Christiansen. The mill is shown here on the shores of Big Twin Lake with stacks of finished lumber.

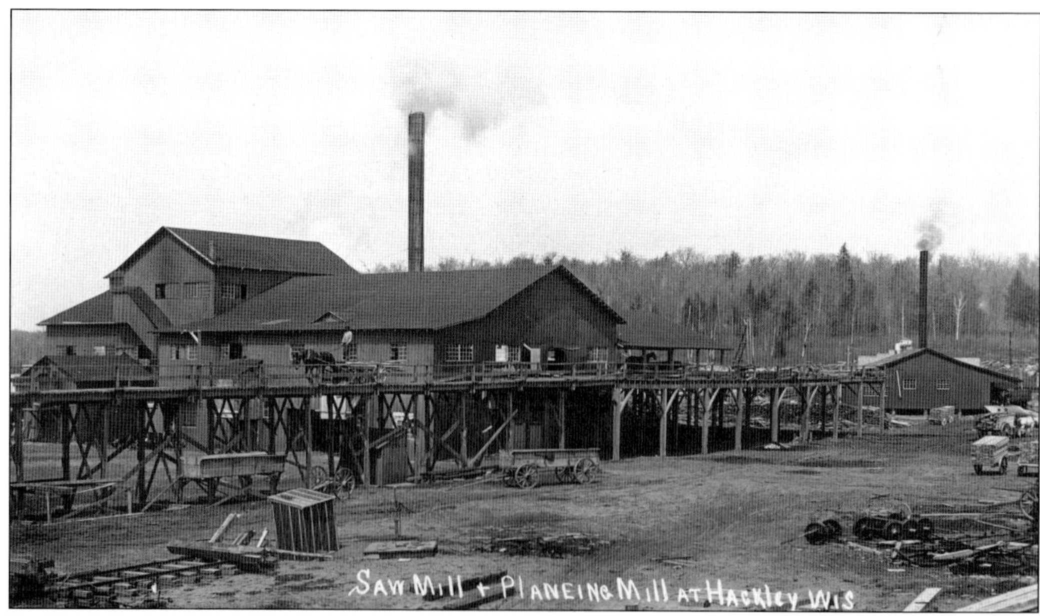

A mill worker, leading a horse-drawn flatbed wagon with finished lumber, is on one of six elevated tramways that led from the mill to the yard along the lake. The lumber was stacked to dry here. Featured in this 1914 postcard is the sawmill, with the planing mill in the far background.

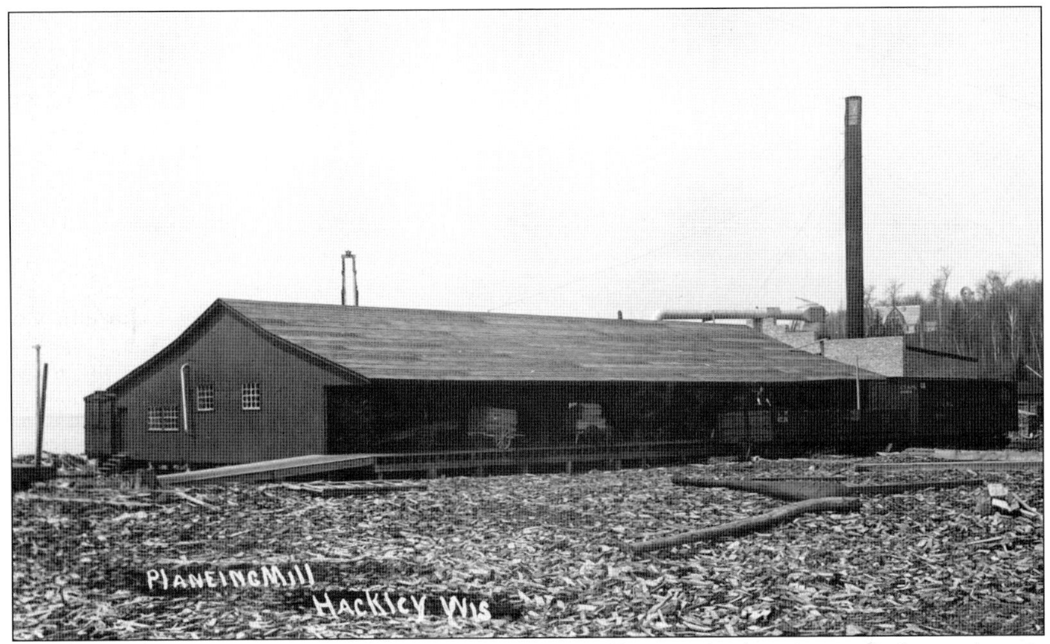

The planing mill, located north and next to the sawmill, was a facility that took the cut boards from the sawmill and turned them into finished dimensional lumber. Sawdust and other by-products were used to insulate ice blocks stored in icehouses. Wood shavings, shown strewn all over the yard in this photograph, were used for horse and cattle bedding. The planing mill and drying sheds were destroyed in a 1956 fire and never rebuilt.

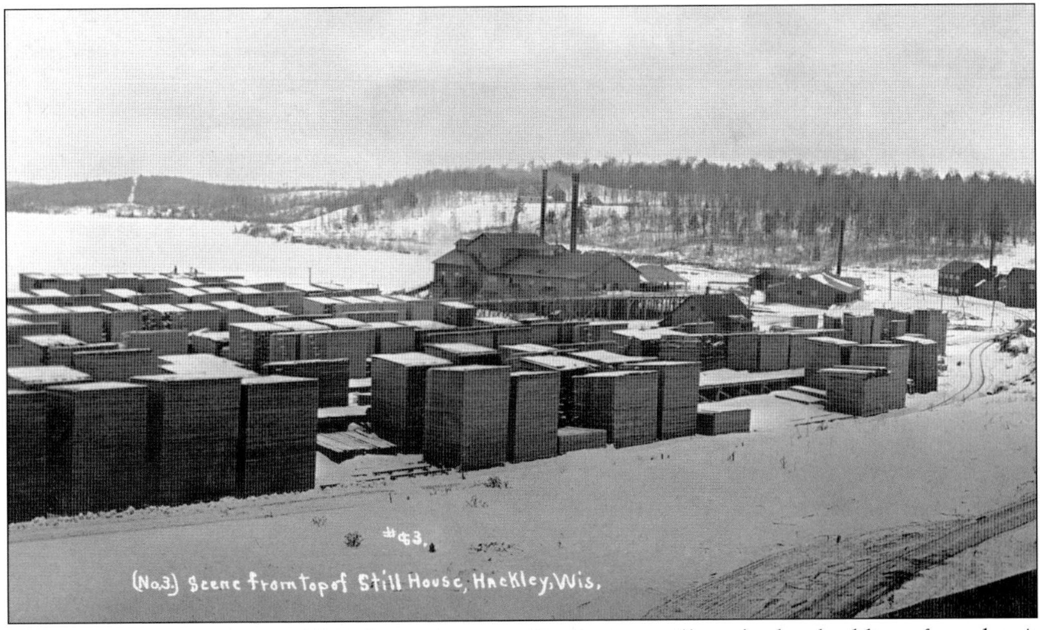

This winter scene taken in 1909 shows the sawmill, planing mill, and other buildings far right. A railroad spur can be seen leading to the piles of finished lumber stacked high in the drying yard. Note the area cleared of timber on the north shore of Big Twin Lake.

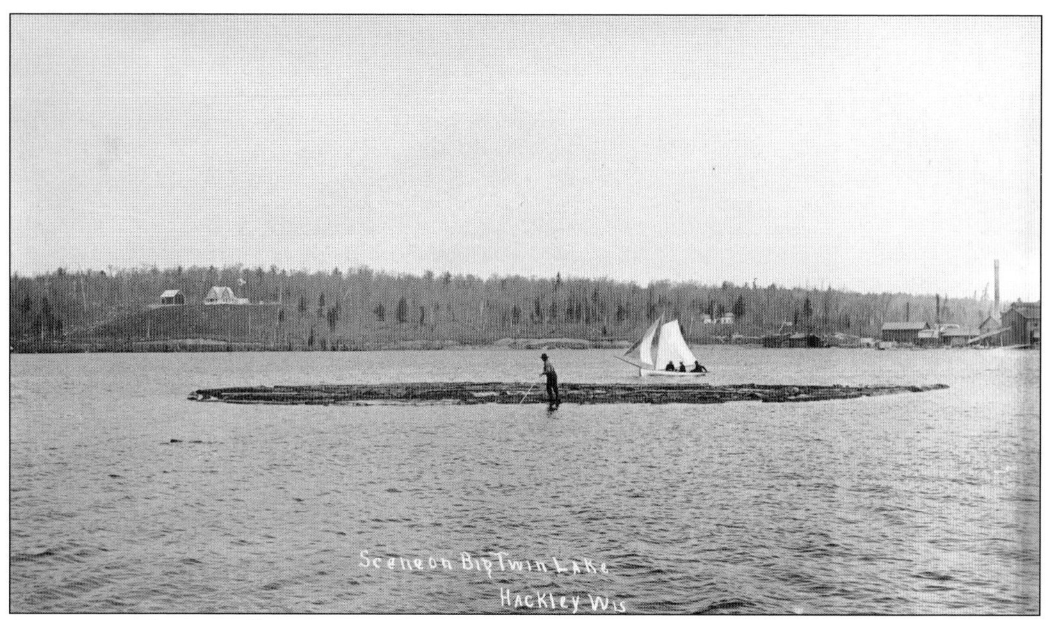

Curious people in a sailboat are watching a log driver guiding his raft downwind. With the breeze blowing in the general direction, he is able to steer the raft to the mill seen on the far right.

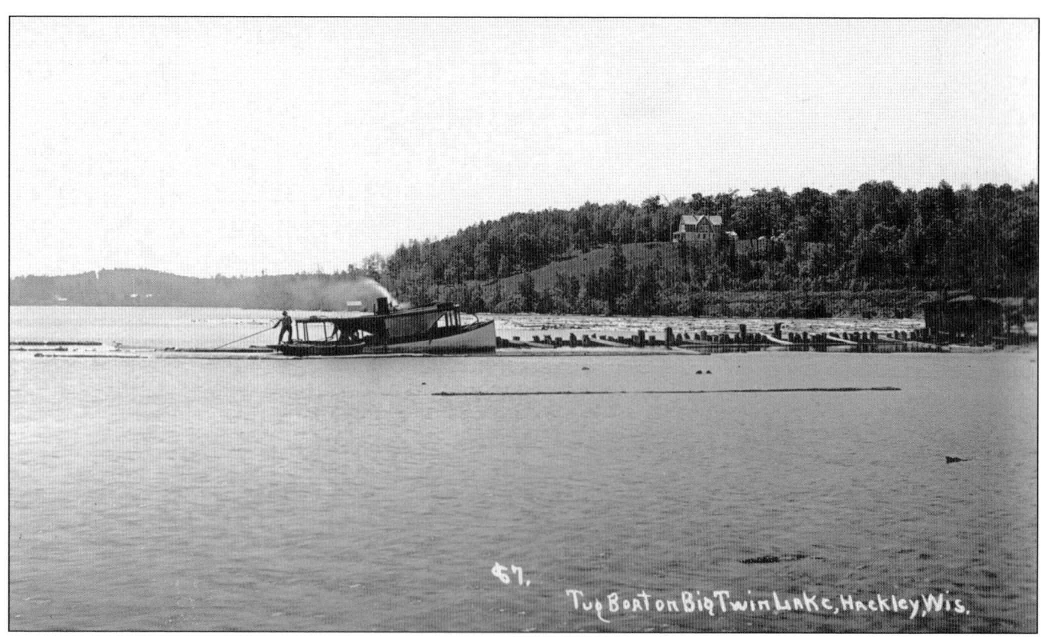

A tugboat is pulling logs toward a holding pen located at the mill. These logs, as well as those in the previous photograph, were probably cut near the Twin Lakes and launched near Lakota Landing.

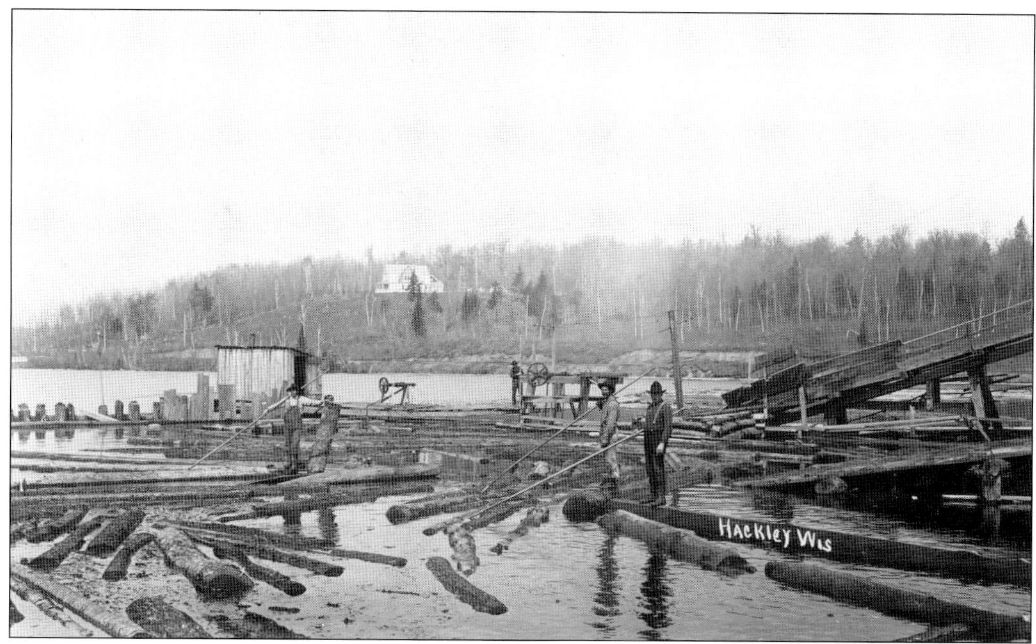

The "Hot Pond" was a body of water dugout near the base of the sawmill. Coldwater was piped from the lake into the boiler room, where it was heated and then piped back into the pond. The logs were soaked in the warm water and rolled, as shown here by the crew using pike poles. Ice and other debris melted away from the logs. This was done to prevent the saw blades from dulling.

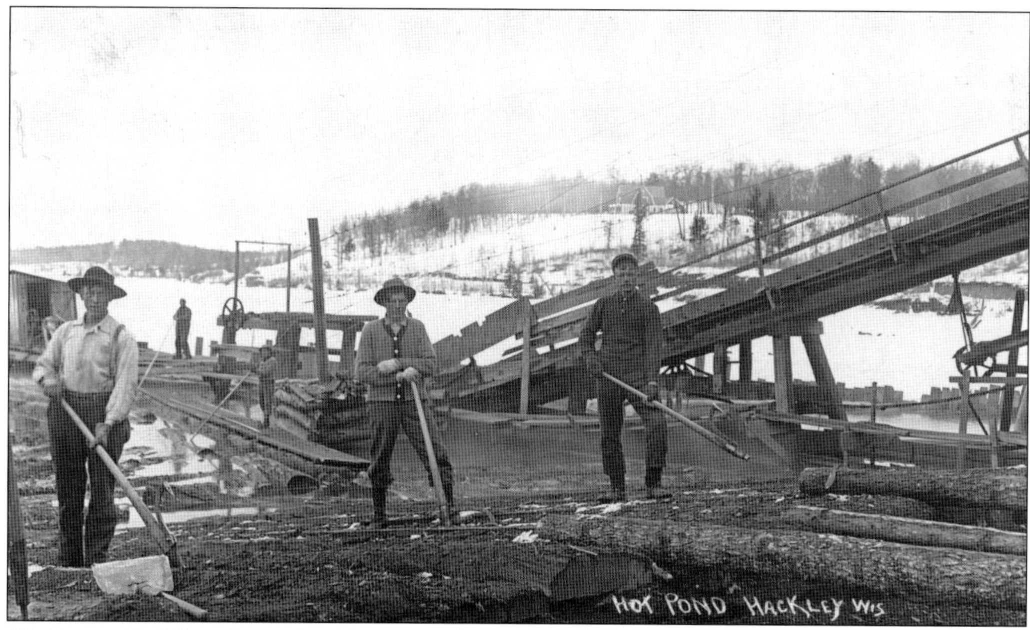

Workers called "pond monkeys" use cant hooks to roll the logs into the millpond for washing. After, they were guided up the chain-driven "bull slide," seen in the background that took them to the second floor of the sawmill.

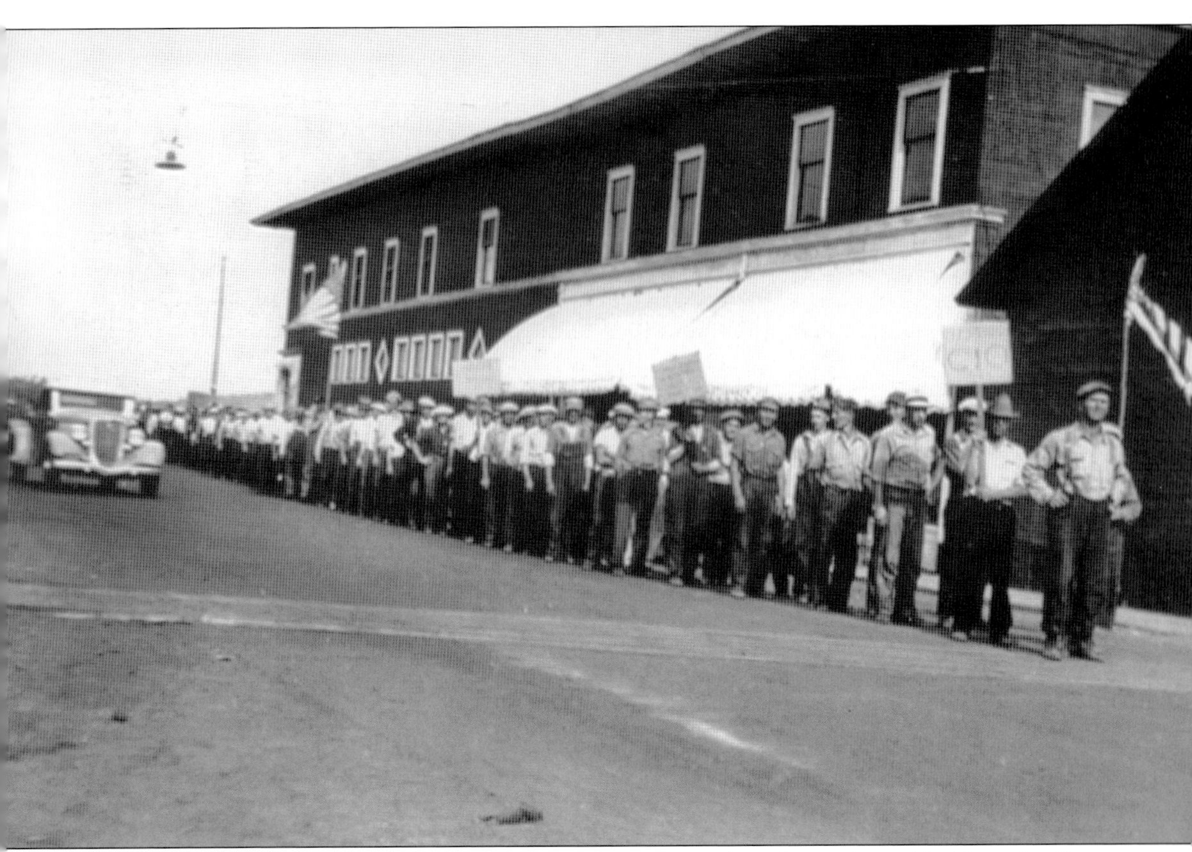

Mill workers are lined up in front of the company store. Leading the strike and holding the flag is Edward S. Monty, a resident of Phelps, who later became a civilian contractor working in Hawaii as a shipyard welder. He witnessed the bombing of Pearl Harbor in 1941 and helped cut openings in ships that were lying on their sides. In 1954, he visited his brother Russ in Phelps. On his return trip from Chicago to San Francisco, Edward was killed in a train derailment in Lomax, Illinois. Russ continued to live in Phelps, close behind his original childhood home on the north shore of Big Twin, near the Conover/Phelps railway tracks—the same ones that he used to walk to school. He also was employed by the mill during his lifetime.

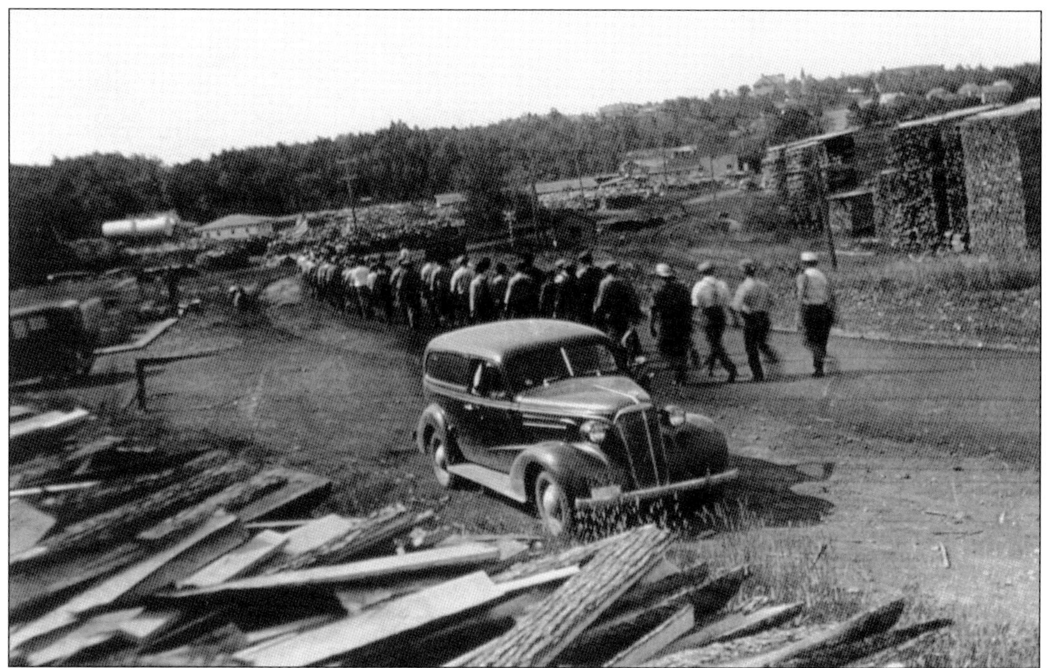

Striking millworkers in 1937 head from the sawmill to town on what is now County Highway E. Strikers were asking for a 7¢ per hour raise.

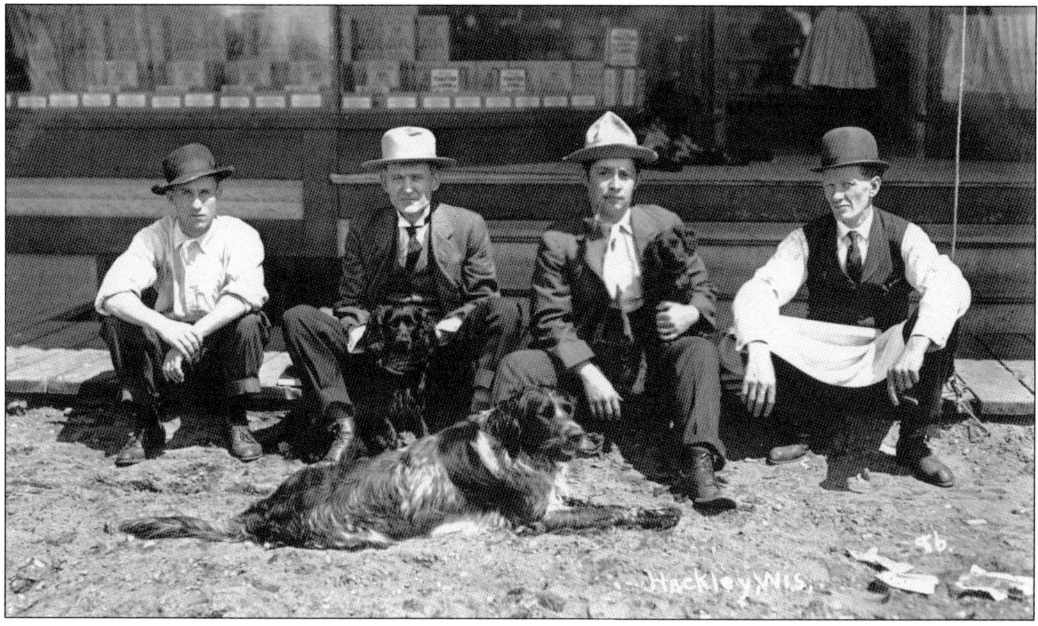

The location of this photograph is unknown. It just says Hackley, Wisconsin. It most likely was taken in front of the general store. The man on the right looks like a store employee, and the others may just be townspeople with their dogs.

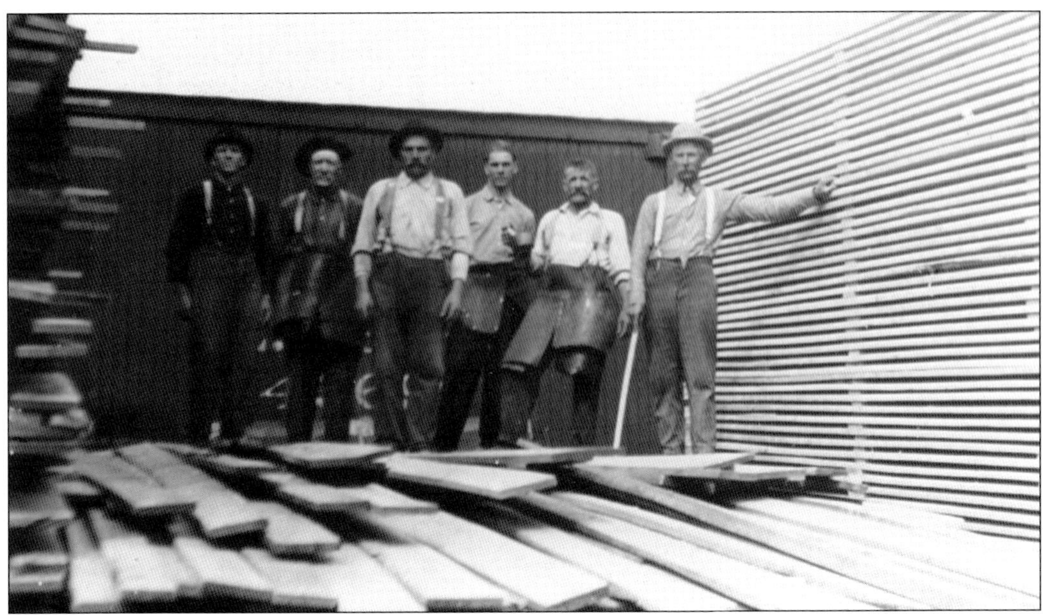

"Lumber pilers" are taking time off to have their photograph taken before stacking more lumber. Lumber pilers normally endured double shifts each day. They stacked the lumber in order to dry it prior to shipping by the rail. (Courtesy of Jack Carlson.)

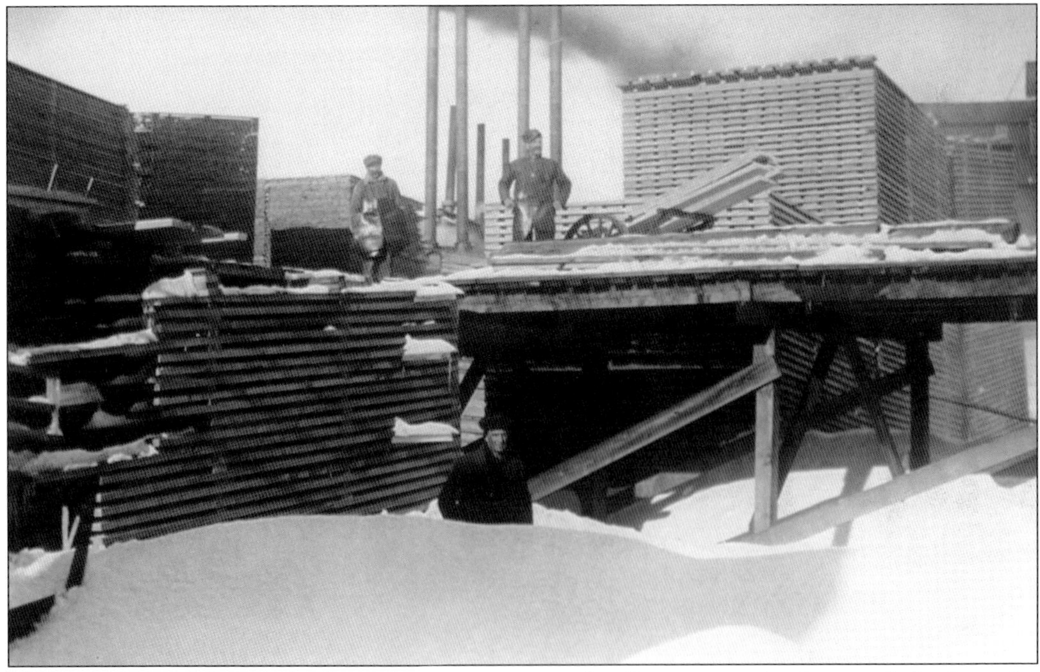

Three men are seen here with two on a tramway unloading a two-wheel cart of planks to be added to the pile. In the background are the chimney stags of the chemical plant. (Courtesy of Jack Carlson.)

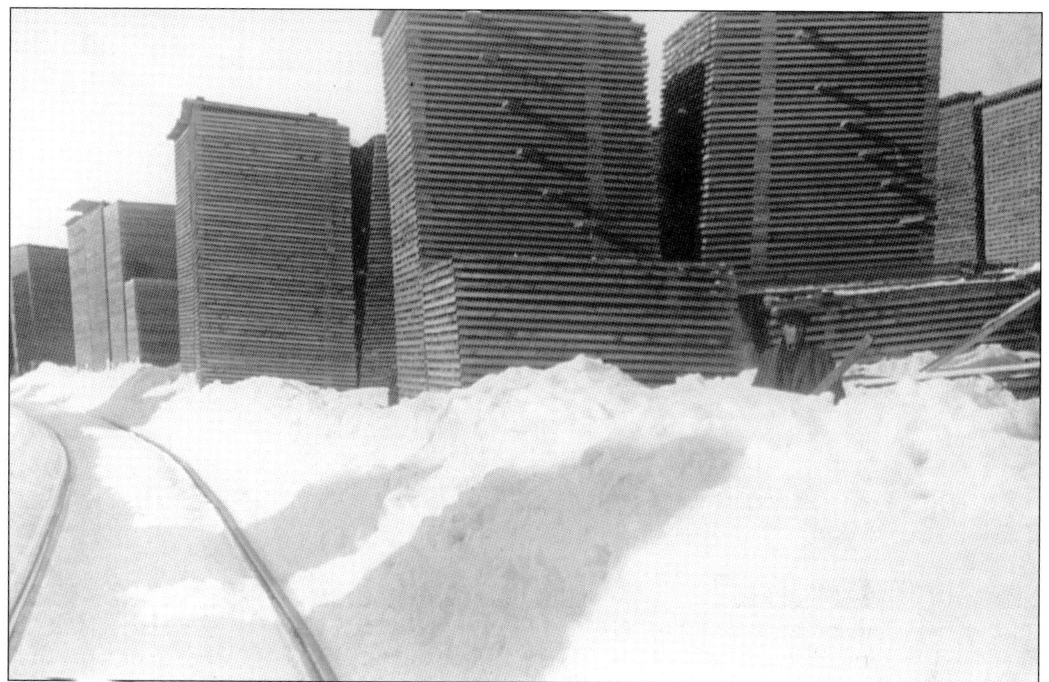

Railroad spurs were laid into the lumberyards to bring sawed lumber to be piled for drying. After a certain height, the "lumber pilers" would use the tramways and raise the piles tier on tier to a height of 25 feet maximum. The stacks were inclined slightly to provide maximum drainage.

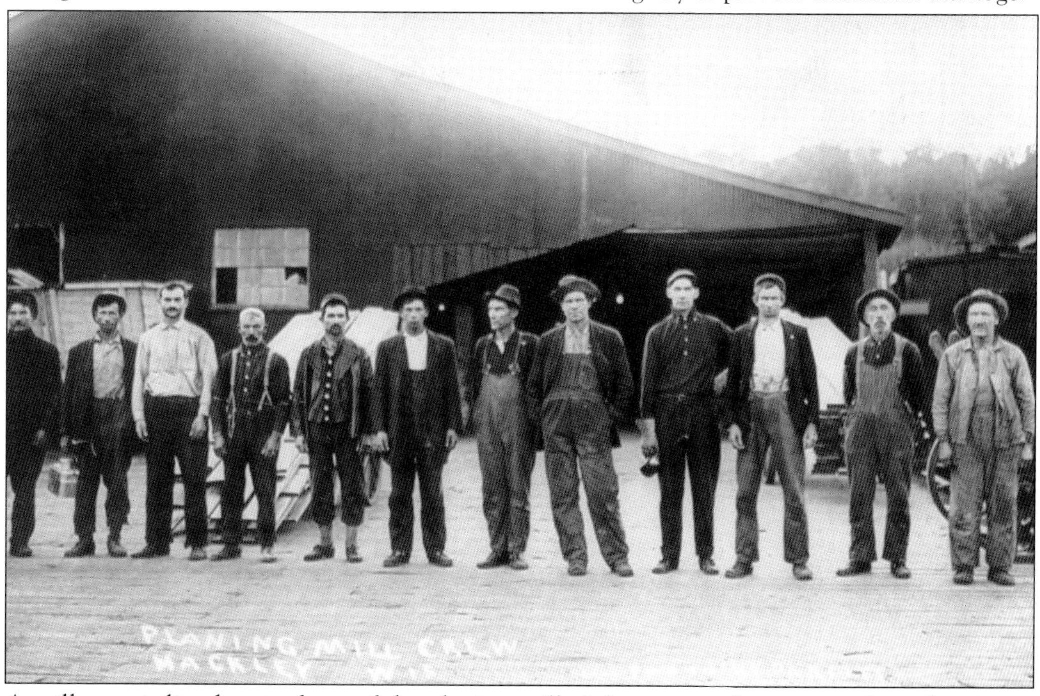

A mill crew is lined up in front of the planing mill. A boxcar can be seen on the railroad spur leading to the mill. This postcard references Hackley, so it must date back before 1913. (Courtesy of Donna Lapisto.)

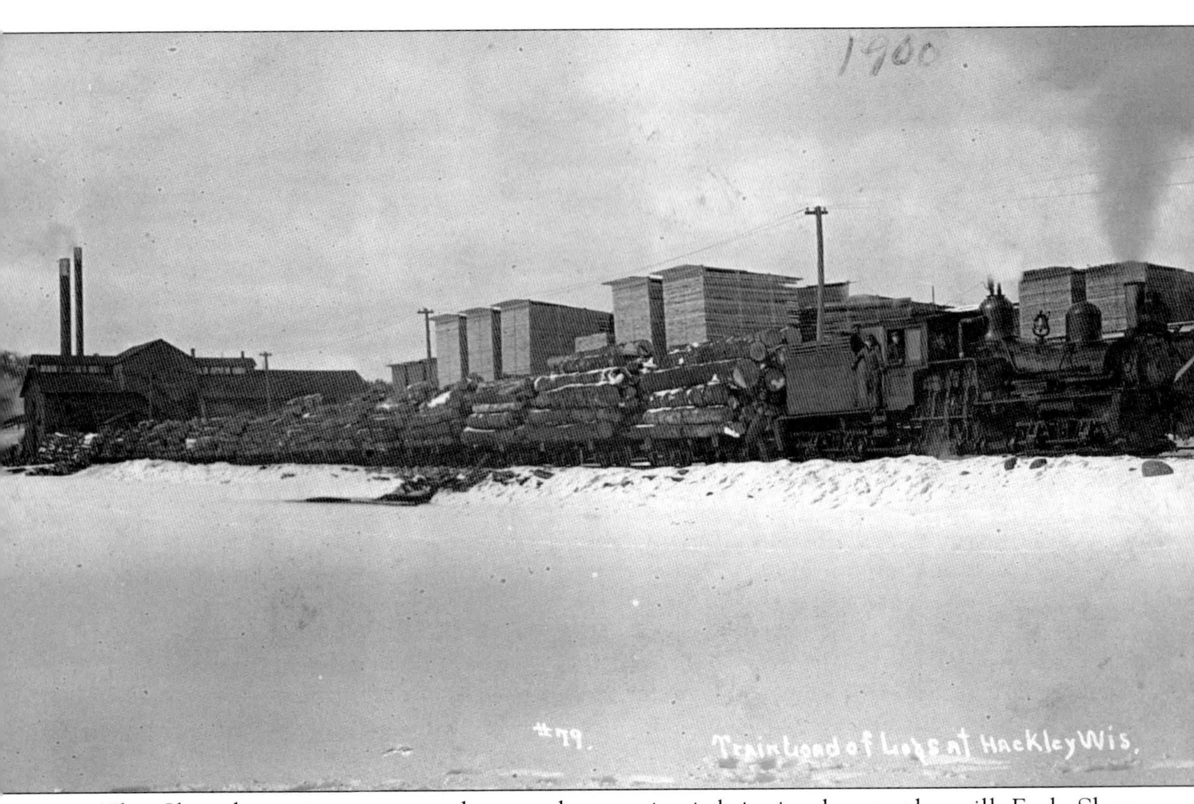

This Shay three-piston two-truck steam locomotive is bringing logs to the mill. Early Shay locomotives were popular with the logging industries, including Hackley-Phelps-Bonnell Company, as they typically could pull 10 times their own weight. The founder of this locomotive, Ephraim Shay, was a logger himself at one point in his life in the 1870s. He desired a more functional way to move logs to the mills instead of utilizing winter snow sleds. He then designed the geared locomotive, and his partnership with Lima Machine Works propelled its success. At least two locomotives, owned by Hackley-Phelps-Bonnell, were labeled Nos. 2 and 3. One was built in 1905 by shop 969, and the other was built in 1901 by shop 649, respectively, of Lima Locomotive and Machine Company.

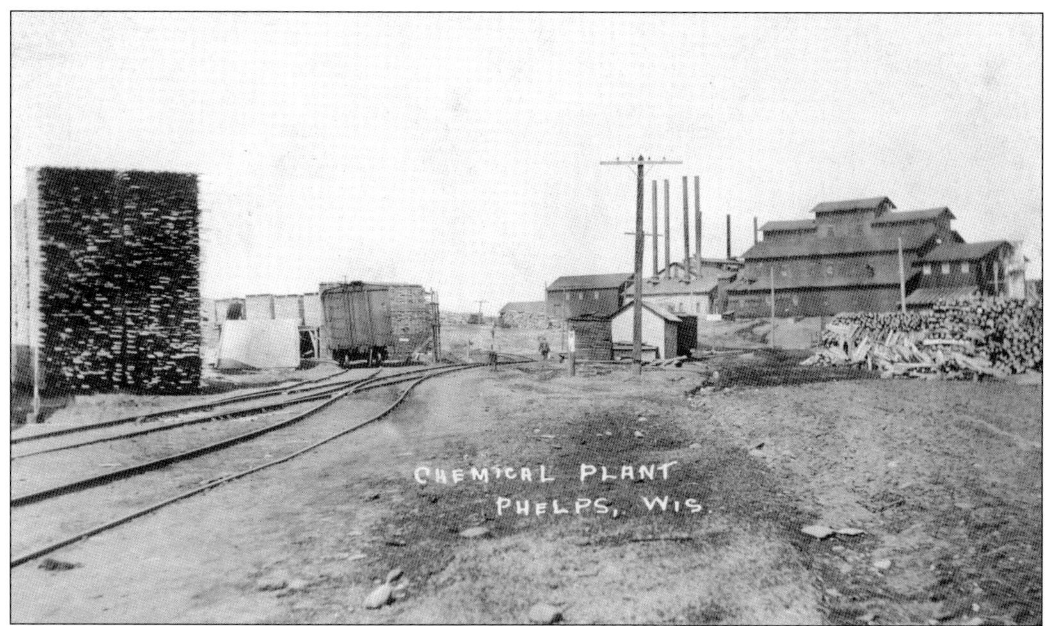

The Wisconsin Chemical Company built a plant across from the sawmill and east of County Highway E. It consisted of a large boiler room for steam and four retort boilers with chimneys (kilns) to produce charcoal. This postcard has a date of 1916.

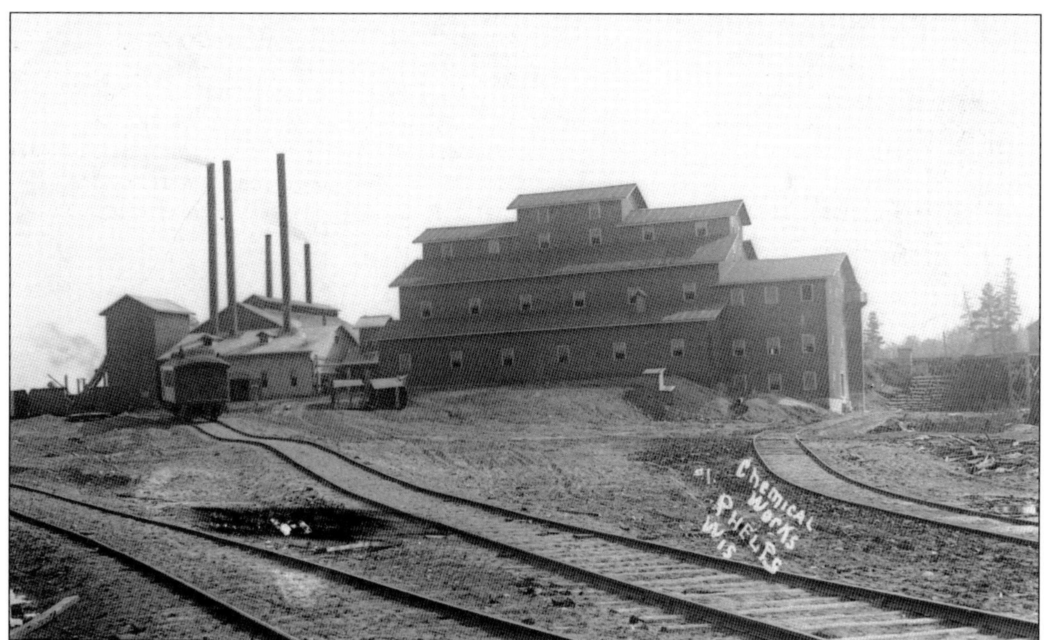

Railroad spurs connected lumber camps with the chemical plant and also the sawmill. Most of the charcoal was loaded into boxcars and shipped to smelters. In 1928, the Hackley-Phelps-Bonnell bought the plant and, in 1935, was sold again. The process was growing obsolete. In 1940, the plant closed its doors and the buildings were razed.

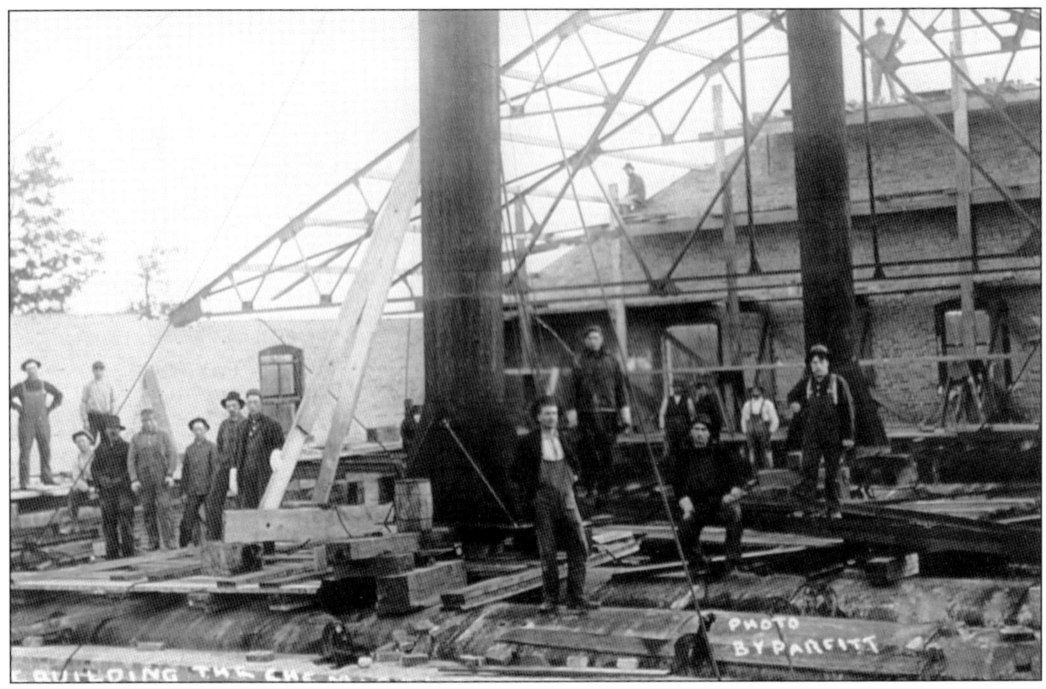

Tradesmen and laborers are seen here rebuilding the chemical plant. The chemical plant had been damaged by a fire. The plant produced wood alcohol, acetate of lime, charcoal, and other by-products. This photograph with the name Hackley, Wisconsin, had to be taken before 1912. (Courtesy of Jack Carlson.)

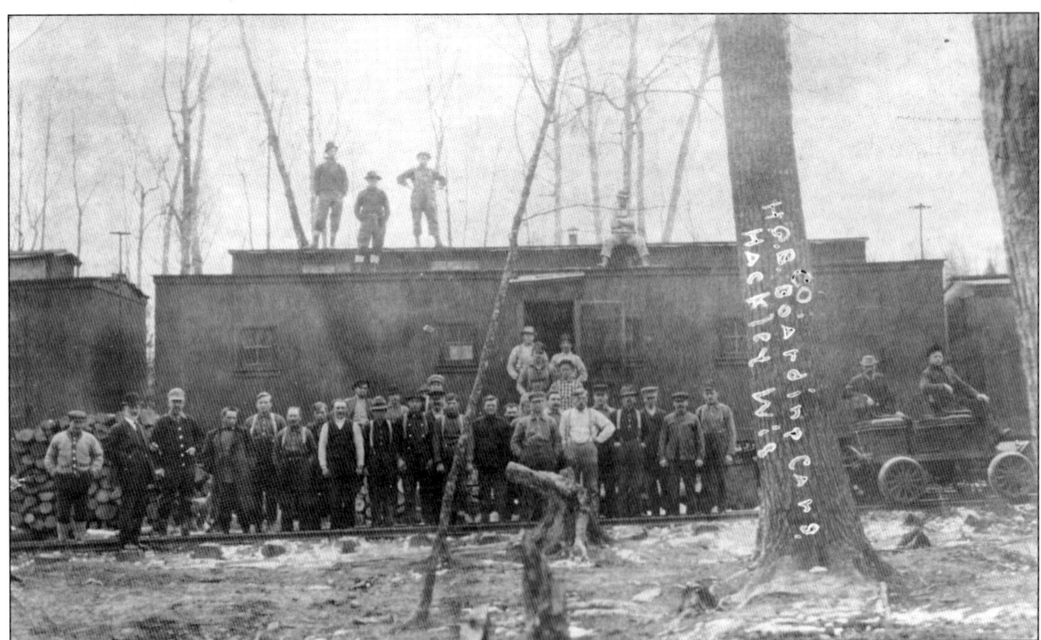

A logging crew is posing in front and on top of a bunkhouse converted from a boxcar. These conversions filled the bill replacing camp tents. These bunkhouses could easily be moved on the railroad spurs leading to other logging camps. (Courtesy of Jack Carlson.)

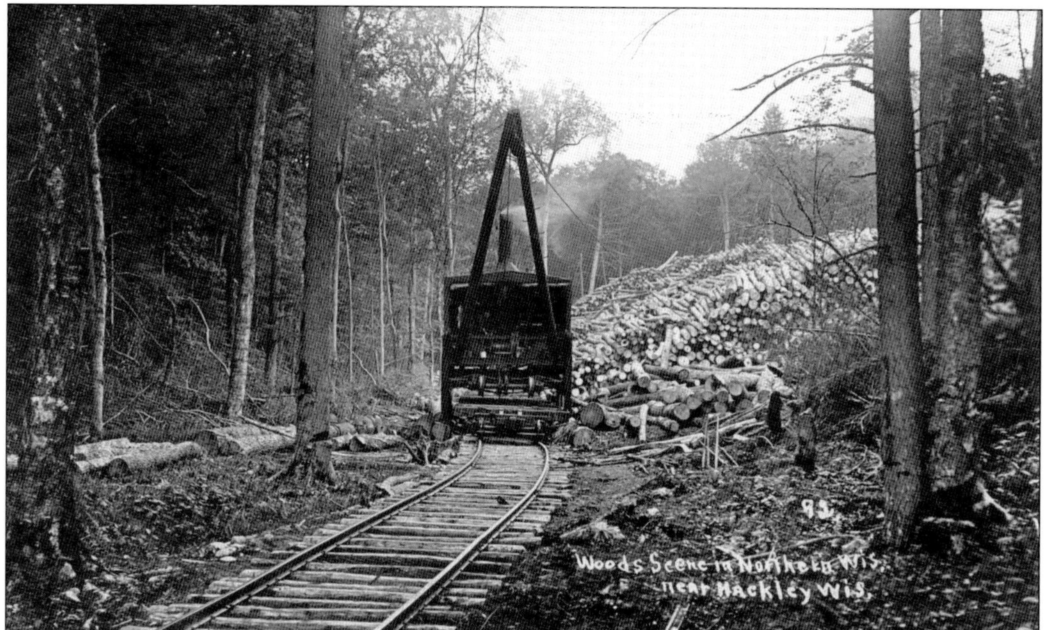

Logs were felled and bucked in the woods; skidded by horses and, later, by fully tracked steam tractors; and piled by the tracks, as seen here. From here, they are loaded on flatbed cars and hauled to the mill.

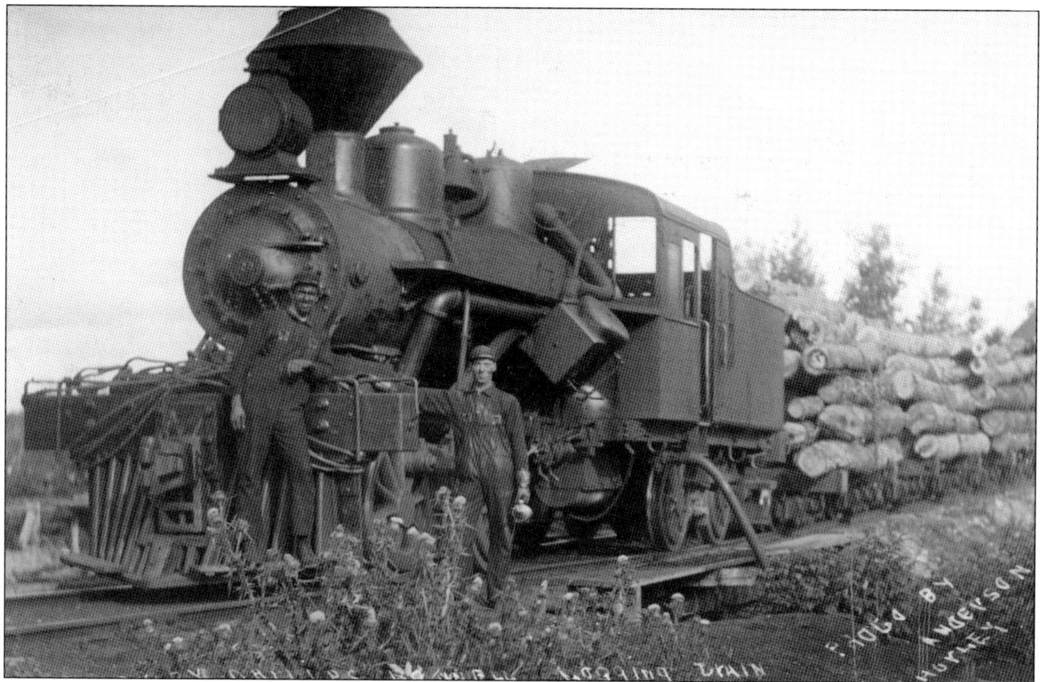

A Heisler steam locomotive is hauling logs from one of the lumber camps to the sawmill. The two men are Frank Rustler (left) and Albert Pray. The postcard reads "Hackley-Philips," but the caption should be "Hackley-Phelps." Phelps is often confused with Phillips, Wisconsin.

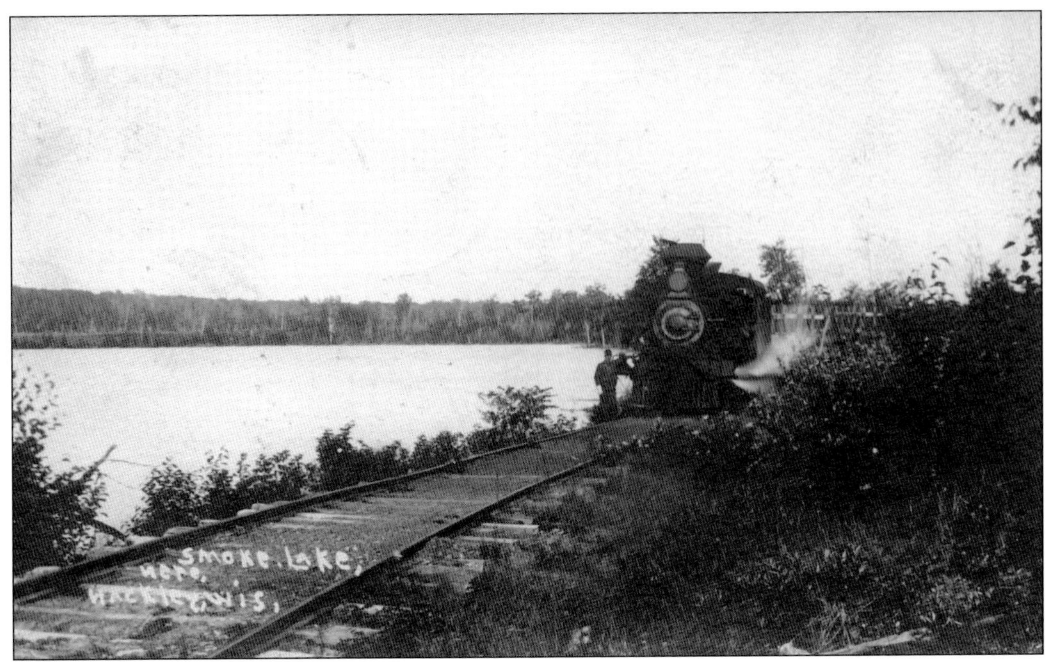

Several railroad camps were located near Highway 17 in the area of Big Sand Lake and Smoky Lake. This 1912 photograph, inscribed with "Hackley, Wis.," shows a locomotive skirting the south shore of Smoky Lake near Camp Eight. Logging was probably done in Michigan since only a small portion of the lake is actually in Wisconsin.

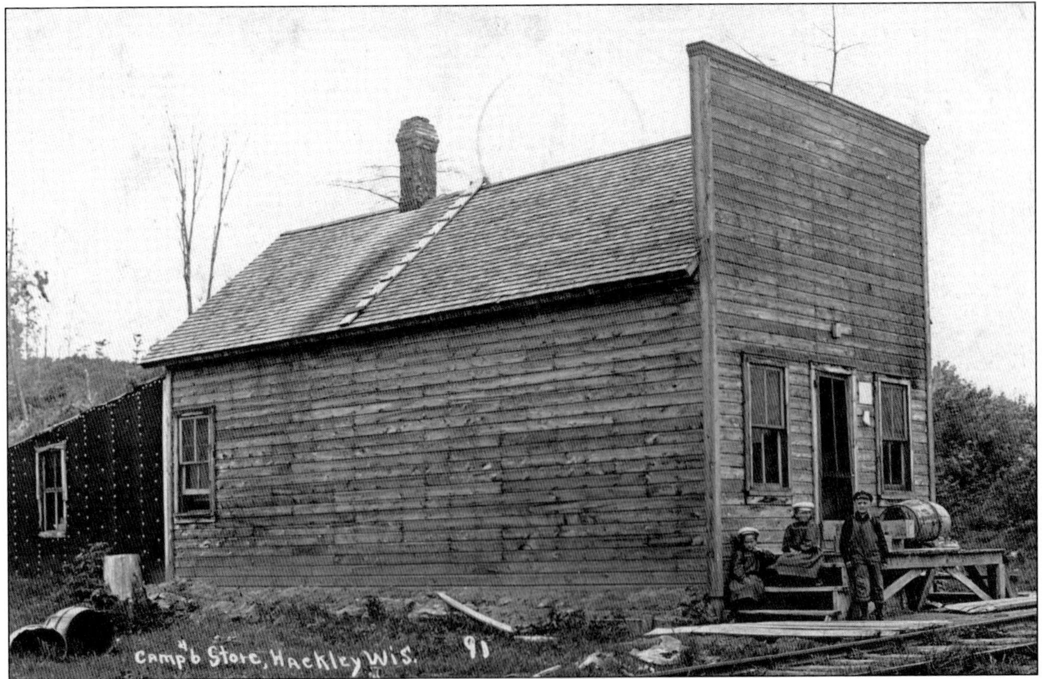

Camp Six was built in 1906 near Smoky and Big Sand Lake. The camp also had a store, as shown here in 1910. Goods and hardware were kept here to supply this and the surrounding camps. Note the tracks and the storekeepers.

Three

RESORT LIFE

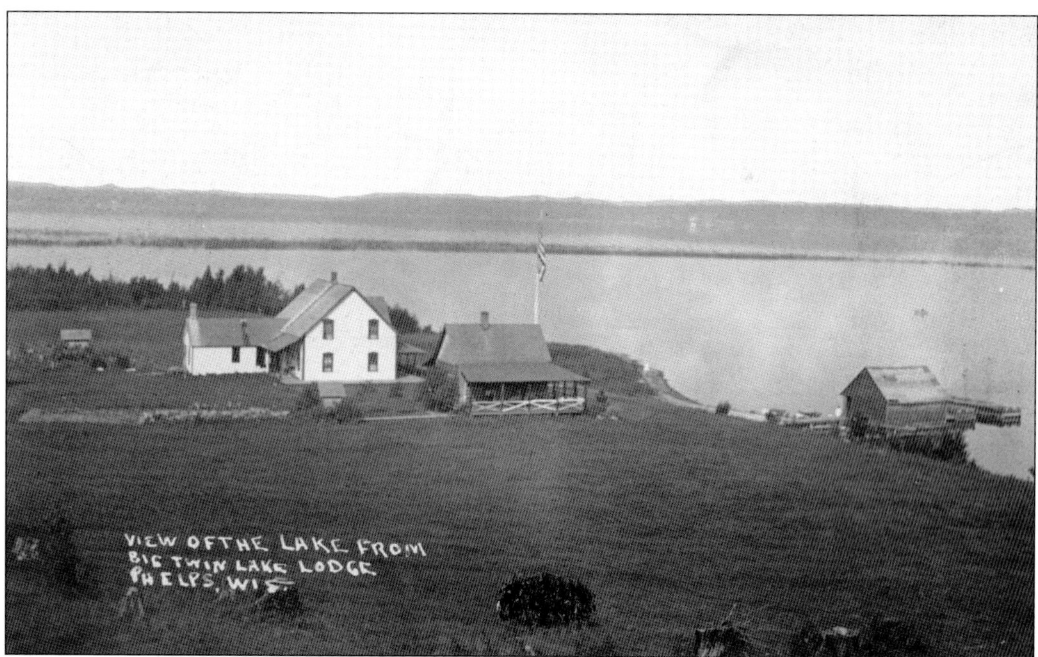

Axel Oberg came to Hackley, Wisconsin, and bought 58 acres on the southeast shore of North Twin Lake. Noting the increase of the summer tourism trade, he went into the resort business and built Big Twin Lake Resort (Lodge). Shown here is the lodge and a tree room cottage in 1922.

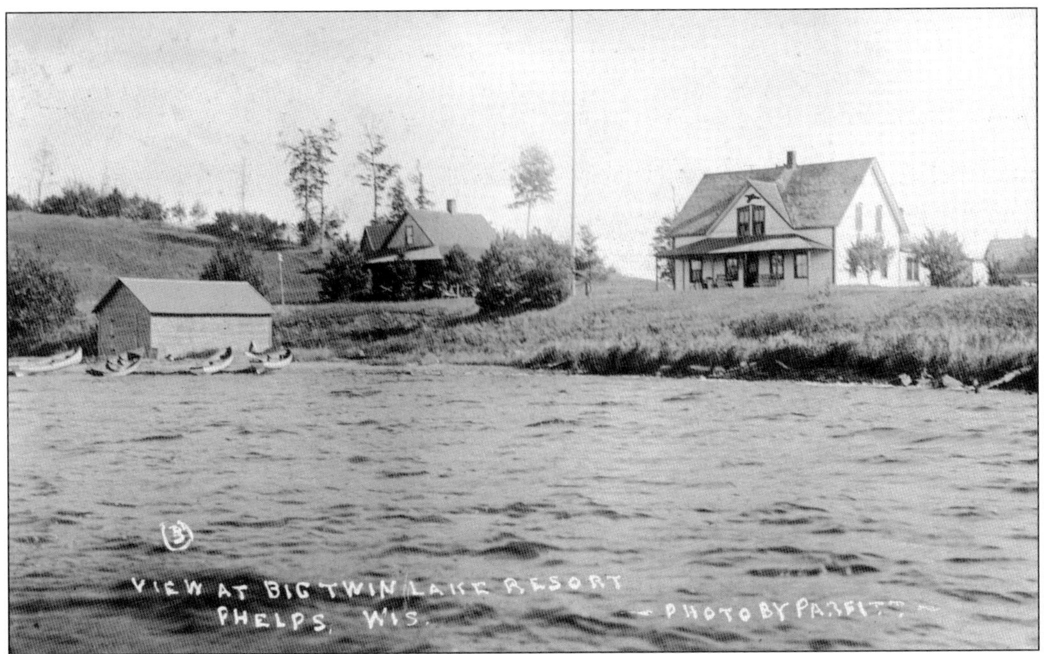

A view from North Twin Lake shows Big Twin Resort. The main lodge was remodeled and enlarged by 1923 to a two-story building able to accommodate 20 people. The cabin is seen to the left of the main building. The boathouse on the shoreline was common at resorts, as they stored outboard motors, oars, and gasoline.

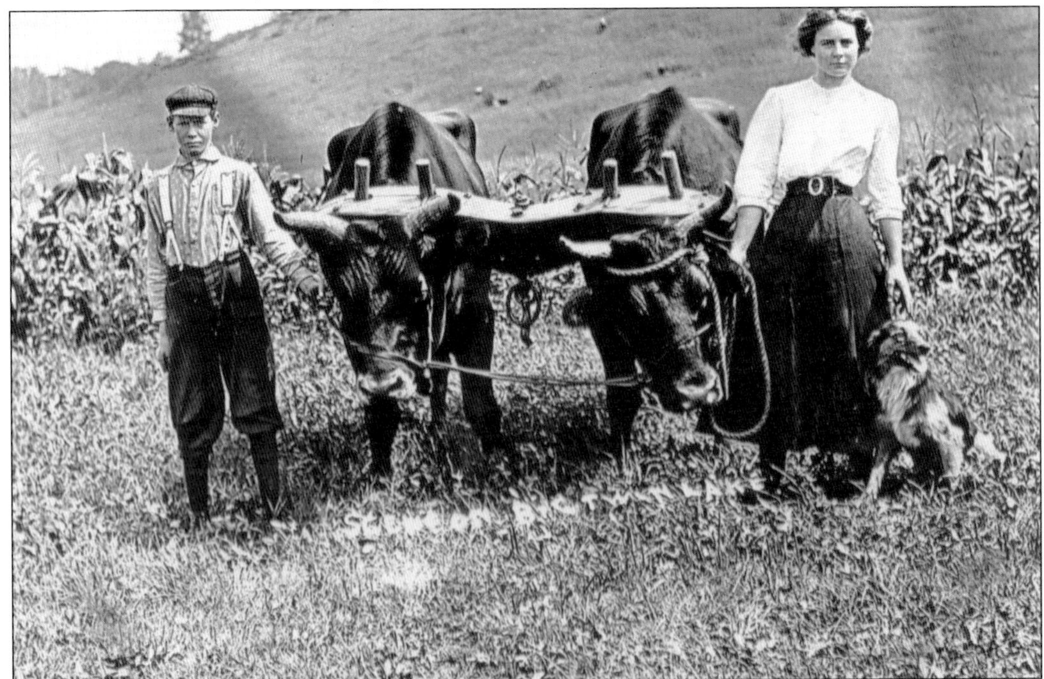

Axel Oberg's children, Harry and Mabel, lead a team of oxen, named Tom and Harry, in this 1913 photograph. Some of the land was cultivated at the flat near the lake of Big Twin Resort. Raising some of their own crops, like vegetables, fruits, and grain, helped sustain the resort.

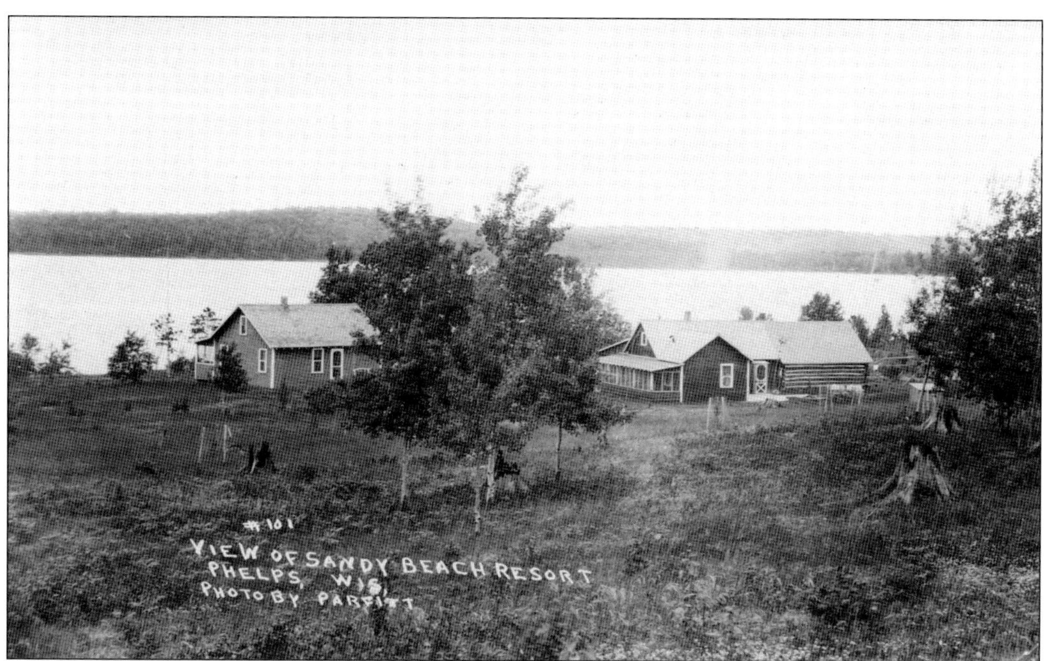

August F. Koeller came to Phelps in 1919 and settled on 17 acres that he purchased back in 1916. He developed this into a summer resort on Big Twin Lake and named it Sandy Beach Resort. This view shows the main lodge and one of four cabins.

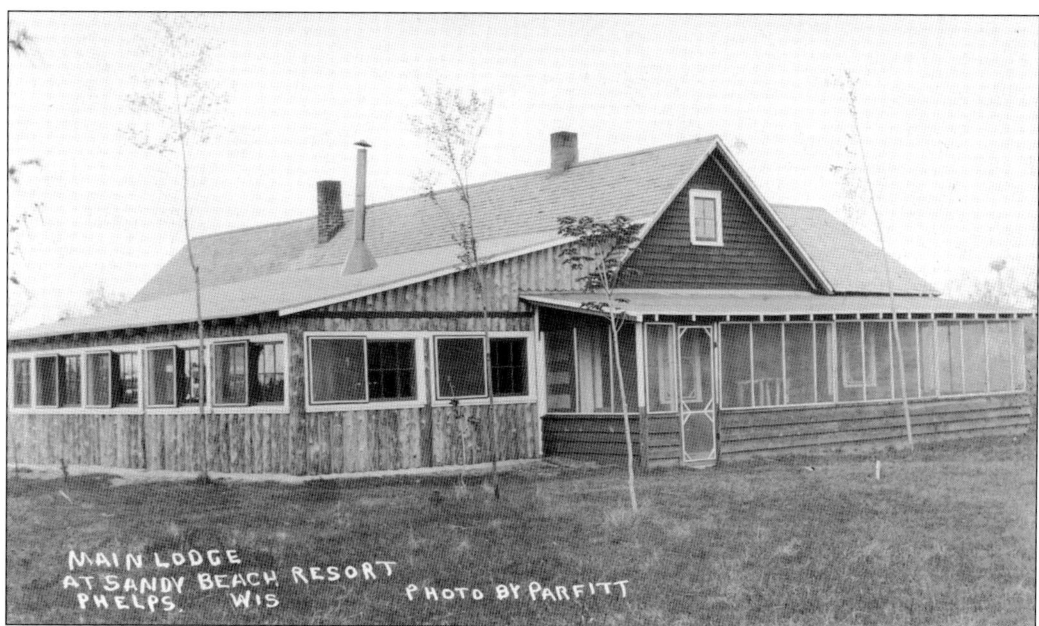

This is the main lodge of Sandy Beach Resort. A dining room, sitting room, and office were on the main floor. August Koeller, his wife, and some employees lived on the second floor. The porch overlooking the lake was common with the older resorts.

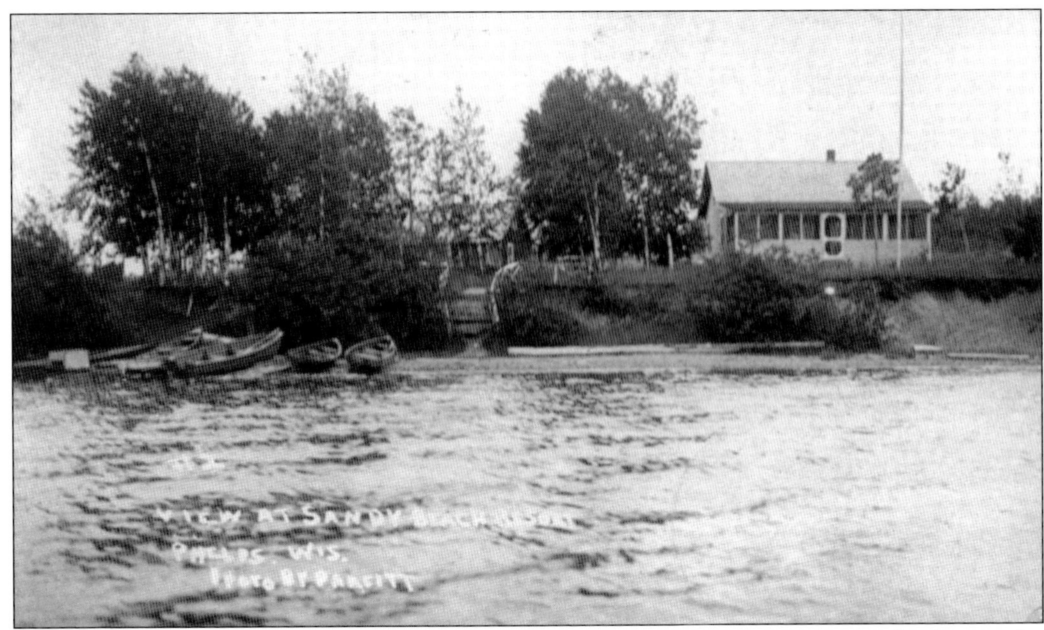

This undated photograph shows Sandy Beach resort on Big Twin Lake, with steps leading to the shore and boats pulled up on the sand beach. In later years, the resort was remodeled and became the Holiday Lodge, which then burned down on December 3, 2004. The Holiday Lodge is no longer in business; it is now a private residence.

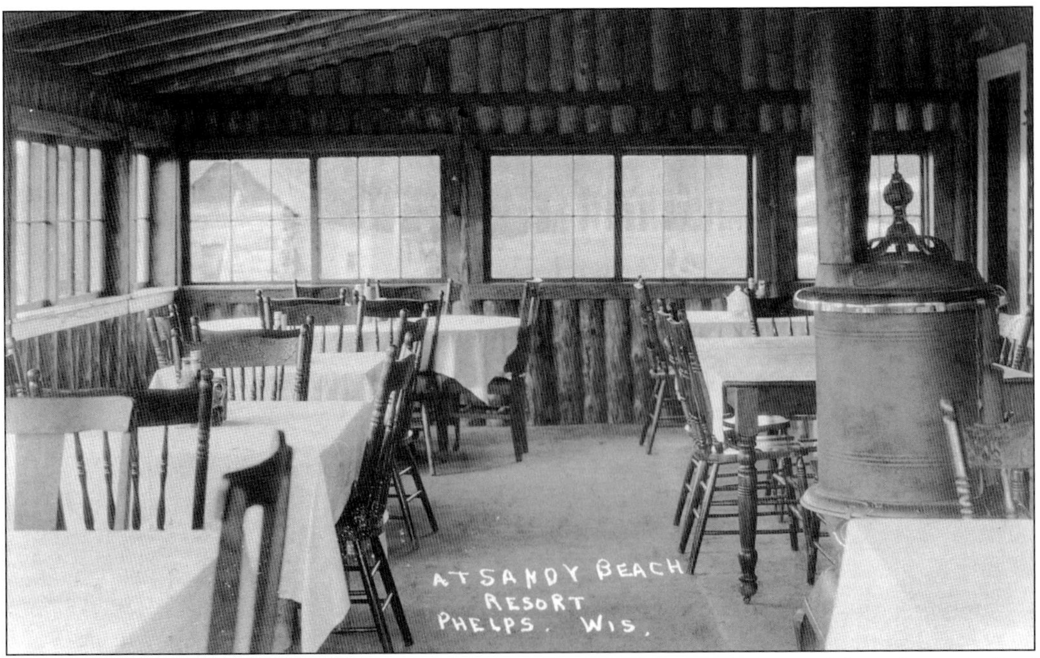

White table sheets are covering the dining room tables at Sandy Beach Resort. Note the potbellied stove and the screened-in windows on top of the vertical logs.

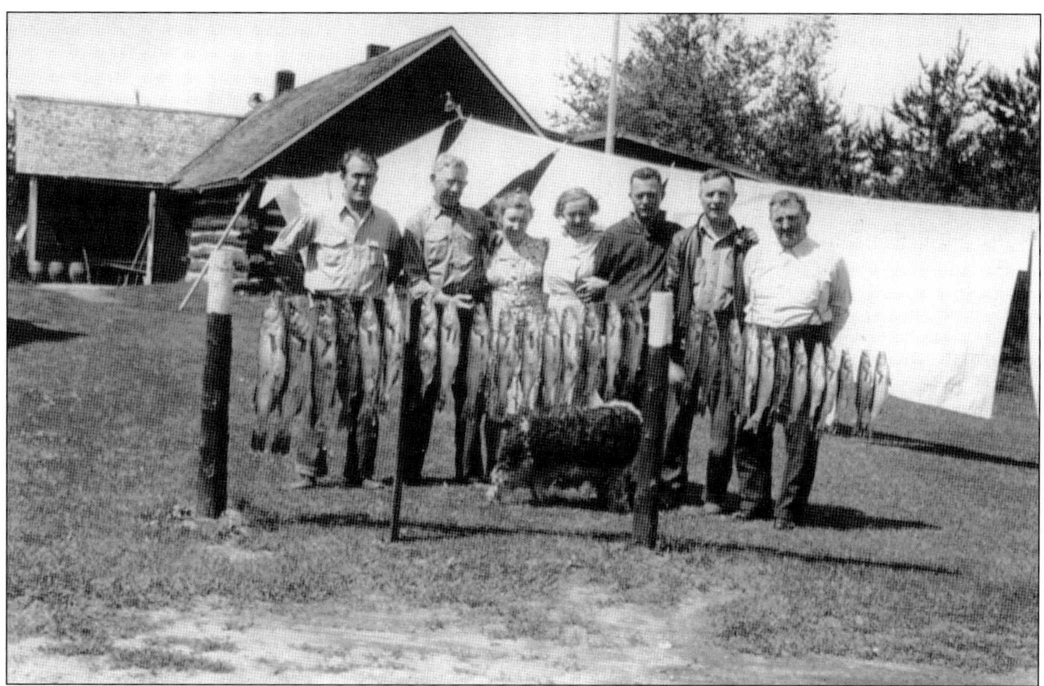

Guests at Sandy Beach Resort are showing off their catch. Bedsheets are hanging on the line to dry, as they were no washers and dryers in those days. (Courtesy of the Phelps Historical Museum.)

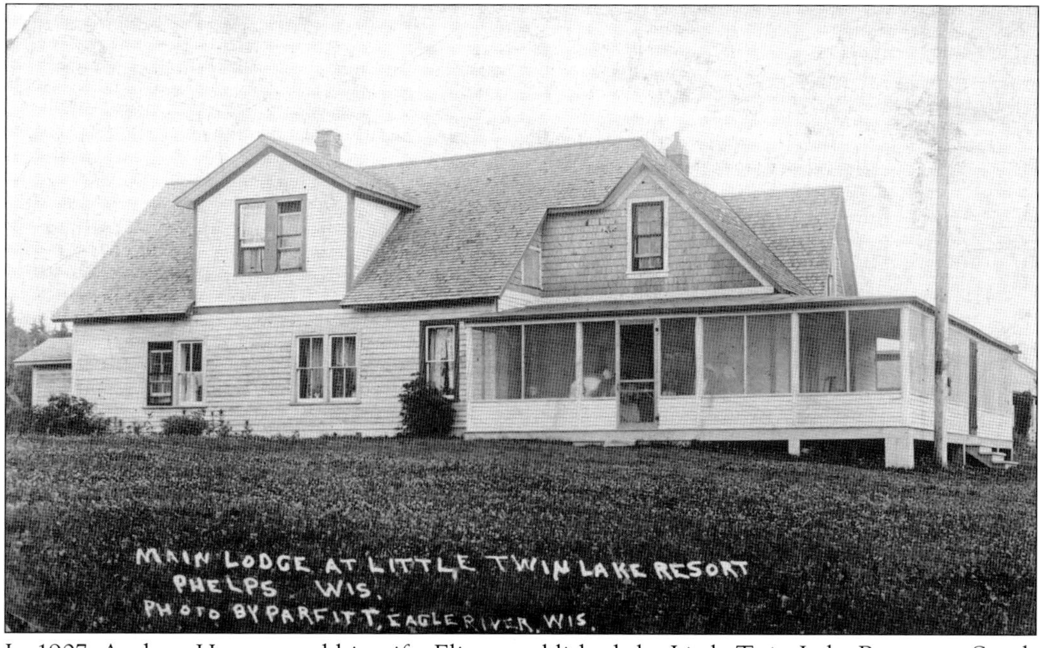

In 1907, Andrew Hansen and his wife, Elise, established the Little Twin Lake Resort on South Twin Lake. The resort had several cottages and could accommodate 40 guests.

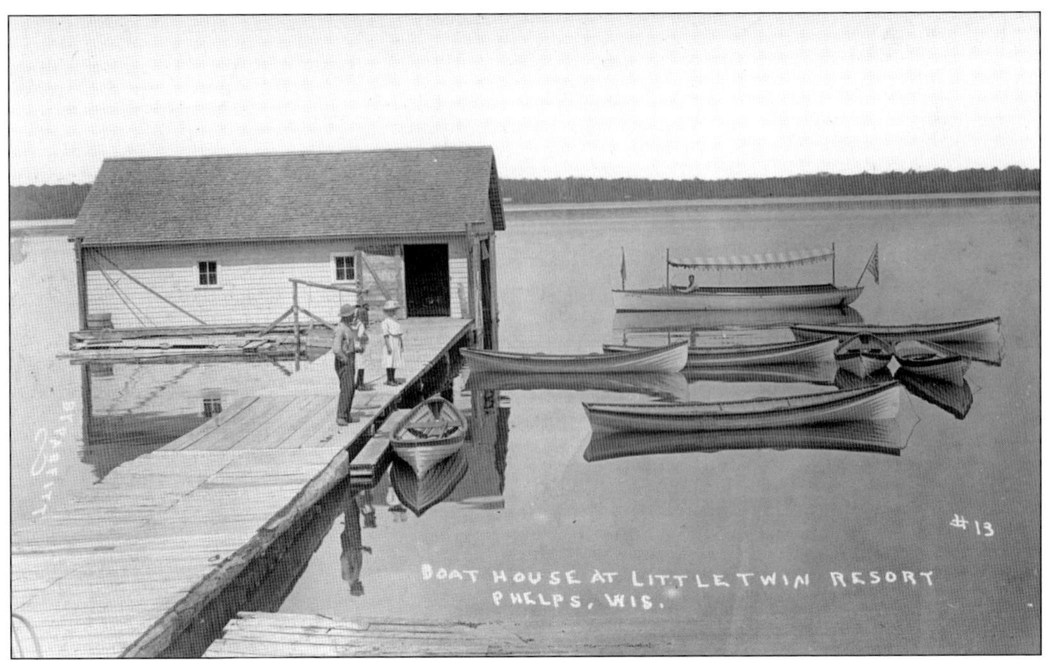

This postcard dated 1917 shows the pier leading to the boathouse at Little Twin Resort. It looks like the two girls are waiting for a ride while the harbormaster is thinking about it. The launch (as shuttle boats were sometimes called) in the background, *Kristine,* would go to Phelps to pick up vacationers.

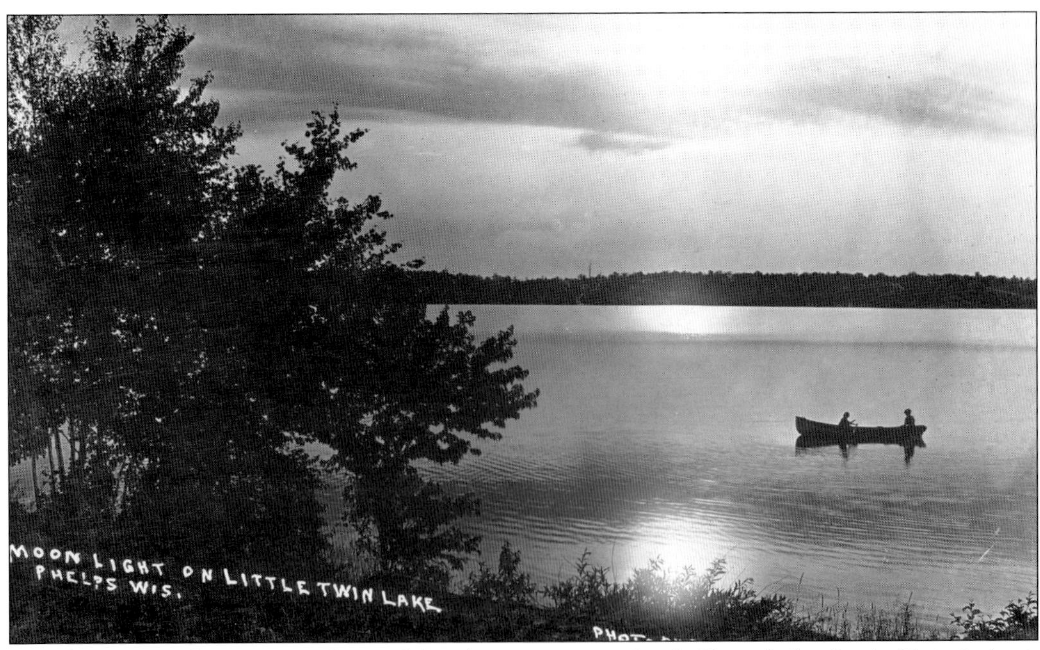

Couples in a rowboat enjoy a beautiful, calm evening on Little Twin Lake. Little Twin Lake is now commonly referred to as South Twin.

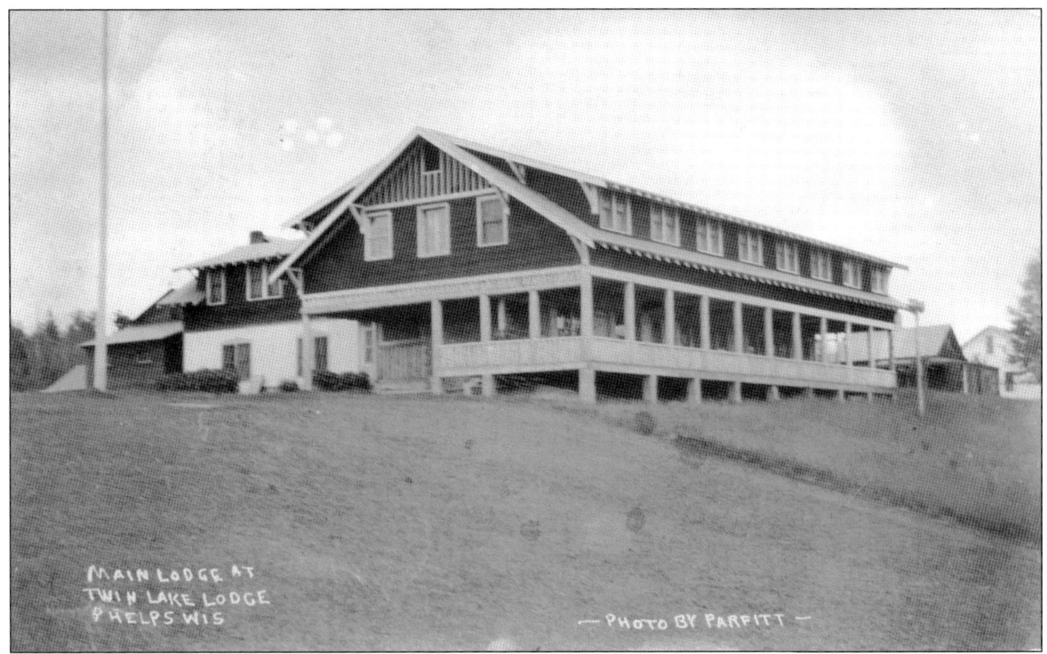

Abel St. Louis bought the Little Twin Lake Resort from Andrew Hanson in 1922 and named it Twin Lake Lodge. Part of the original lodge was destroyed by fire in 1923 but was rebuilt as shown here, with a screened porch running the full length of the building.

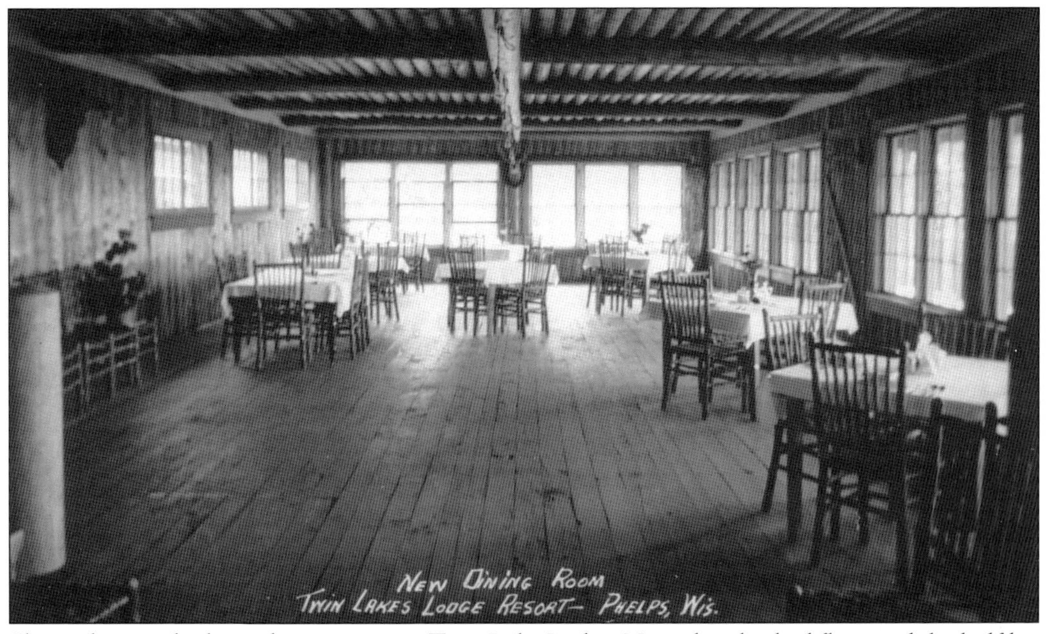

Shown here is the large dining room at Twin Lake Lodge. Note the planked floor and the half-log ceiling. Most resorts had the American plan, which included three meals per day provided to the guests. Most resorts also offered access to boats and bait.

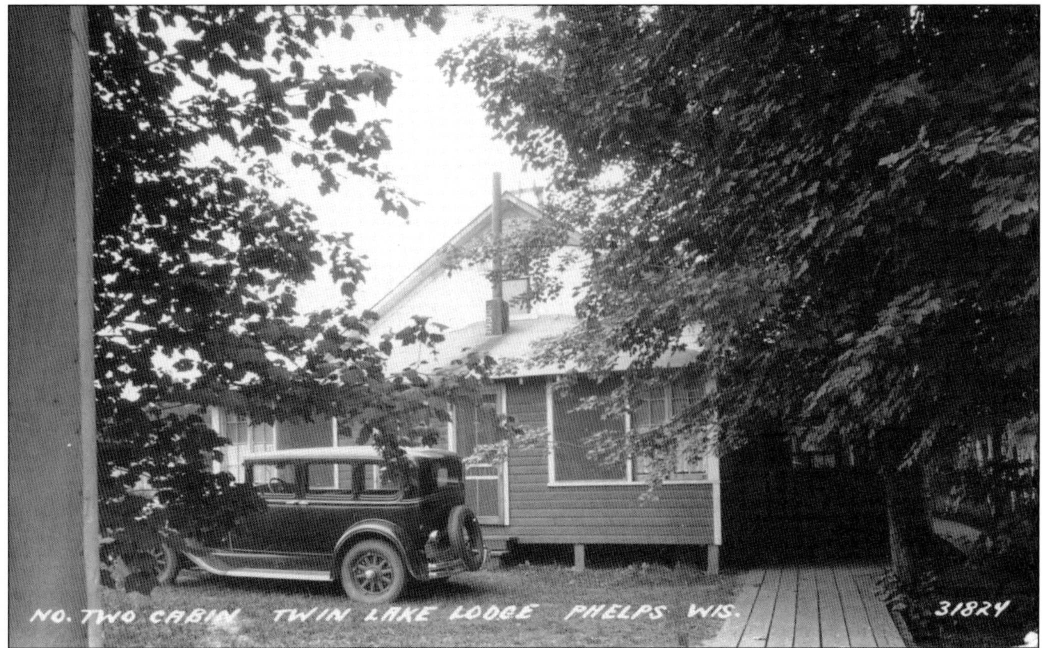

Hidden in the trees, the No. 2 cabin at Twin Lake Lodge can be seen. Most vacationers came to Phelps on the Chicago & North Western Railway in the early years. A few that had automobiles drove to their destination, as these guests probably did in the late 1920s.

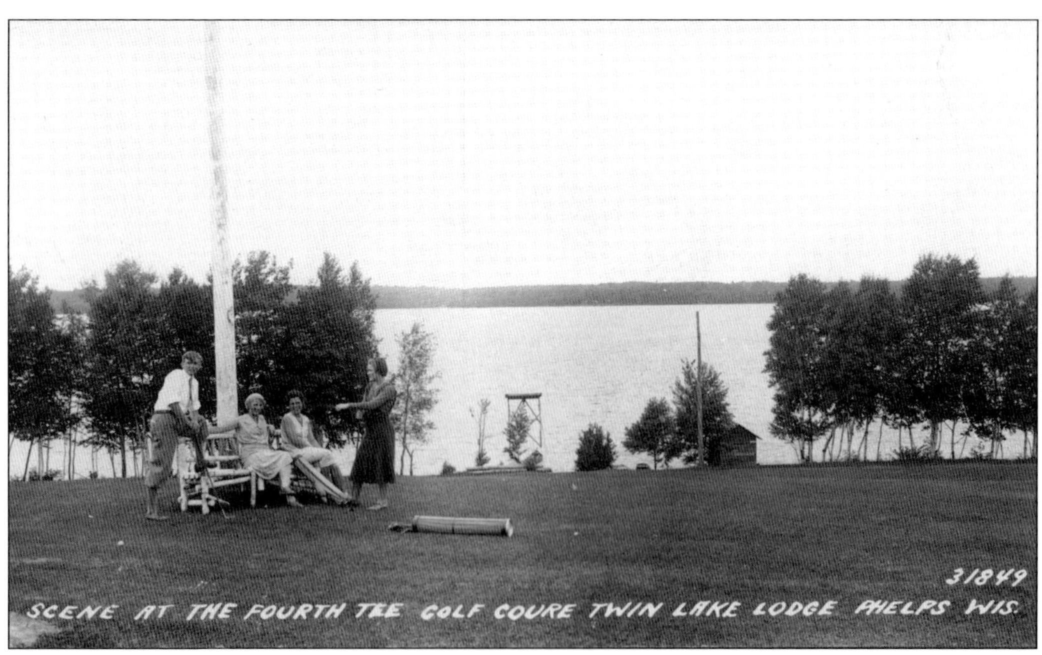

Twin Lake Lodge had a golf course on Little Twin. These folks are enjoying a little rest at the fourth tee.

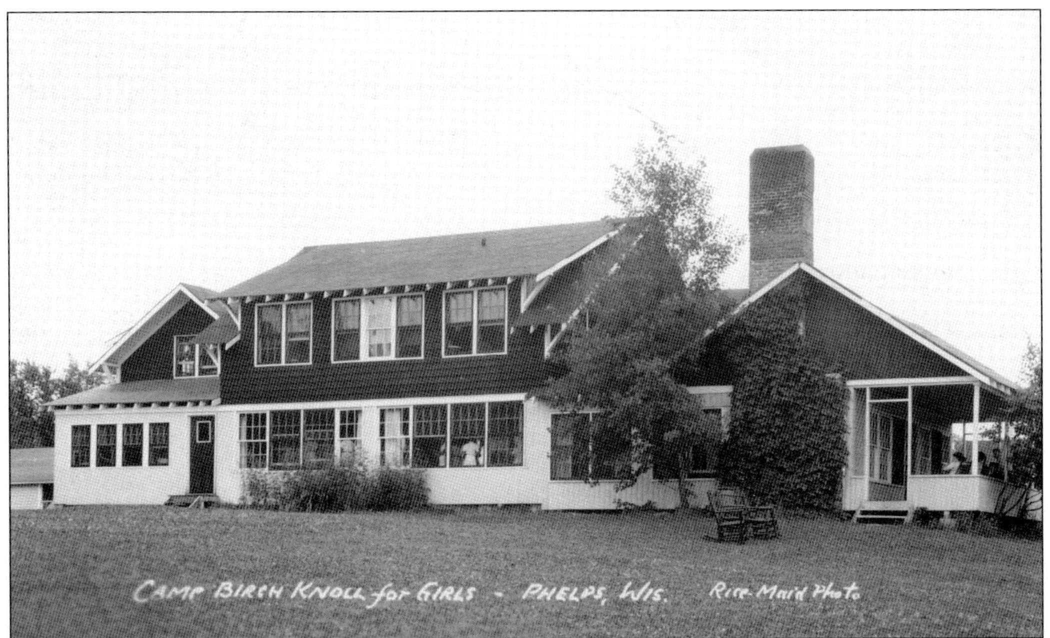

In 1946, Mrs. Abel St. Louis sold Twin Lake Lodge to Mort Levin from Chicago. Levin operated the business as a Jewish girls' camp until selling it to the Baier family, who still runs the business as Camp Birch Knoll for Girls.

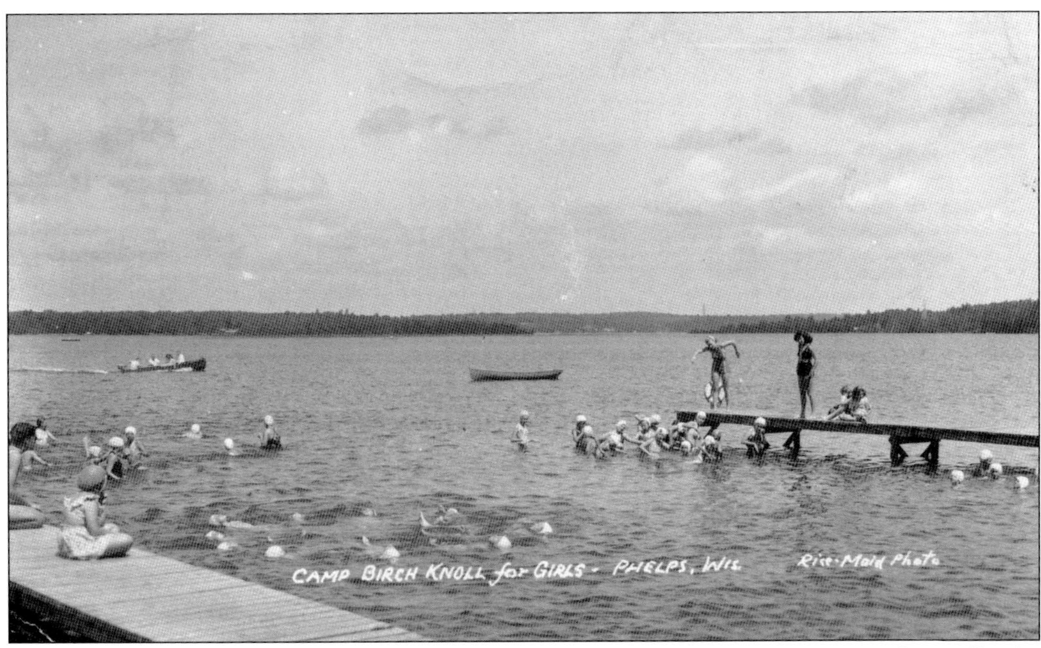

The girls in this 1949 postcard are enjoying the day out in the lake at Camp Birch Knoll. The shallow narrows can be seen in the center background leading into North Twin Lake.

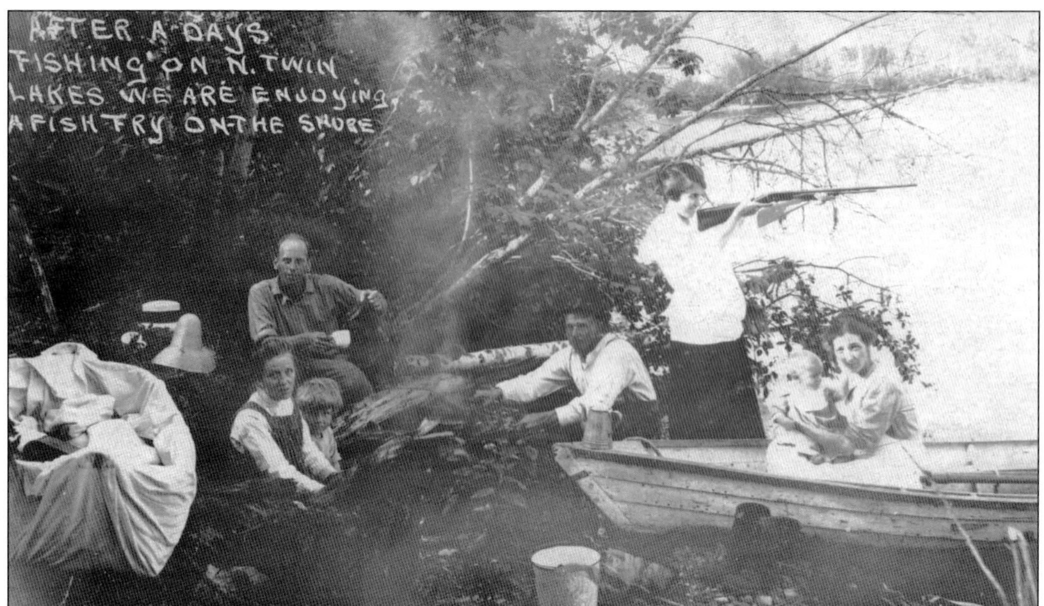

"After a day's fishing on N. Twin Lakes we are enjoying a fish fry on the shore," reads this undated postcard. The lady standing next to the boat poses as she aims a rifle at some waterfowl or a leaping muskie.

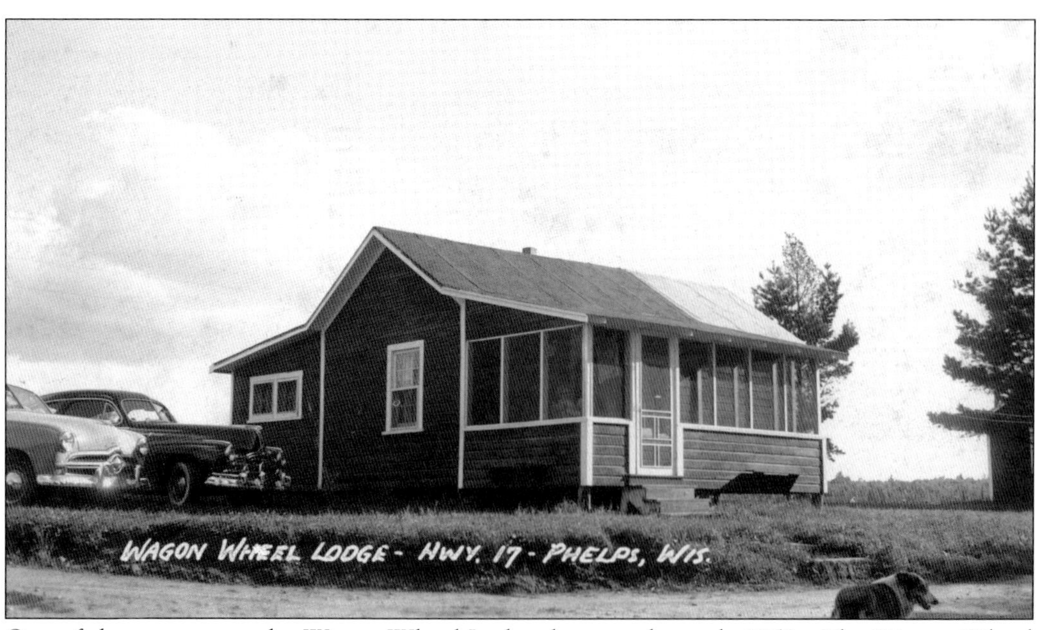

One of the cottages at the Wagon Wheel Lodge dates to the early 1950s. The Wagon Wheel Lodge was located on Little Twin Lake, just east of the dam on Twin Creek.

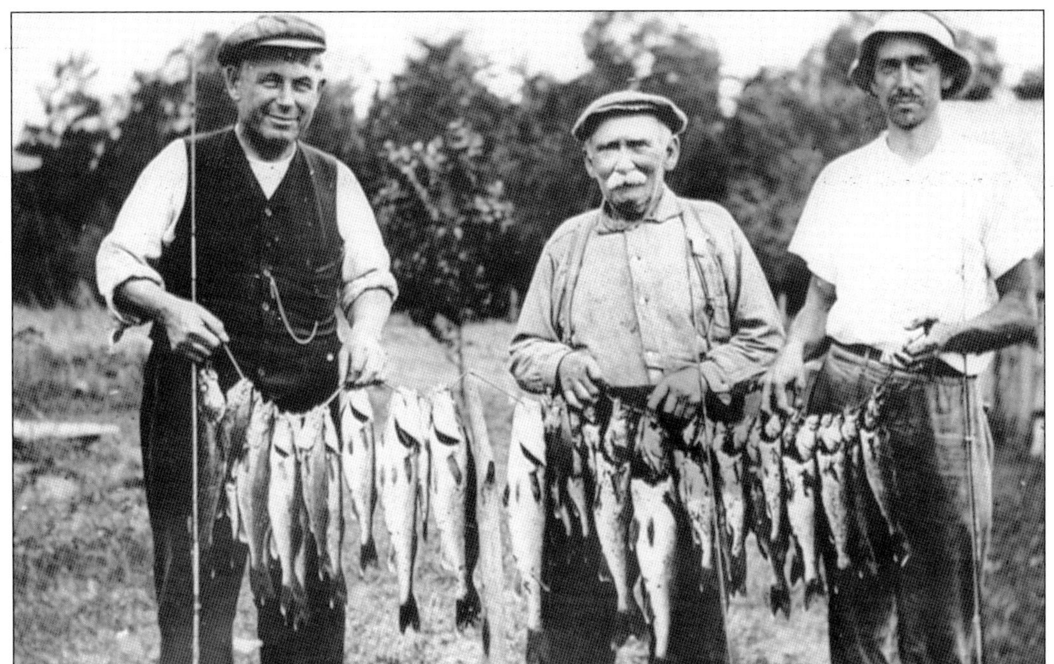

It looks like a good day's catch of walleyes on the Twin Lakes of Phelps, Wisconsin. Most likely, there was no limit on the amount of fish being caught in the early years like there is today. This is roughly the 1930s. (Courtesy of Phelps Historical Museum.)

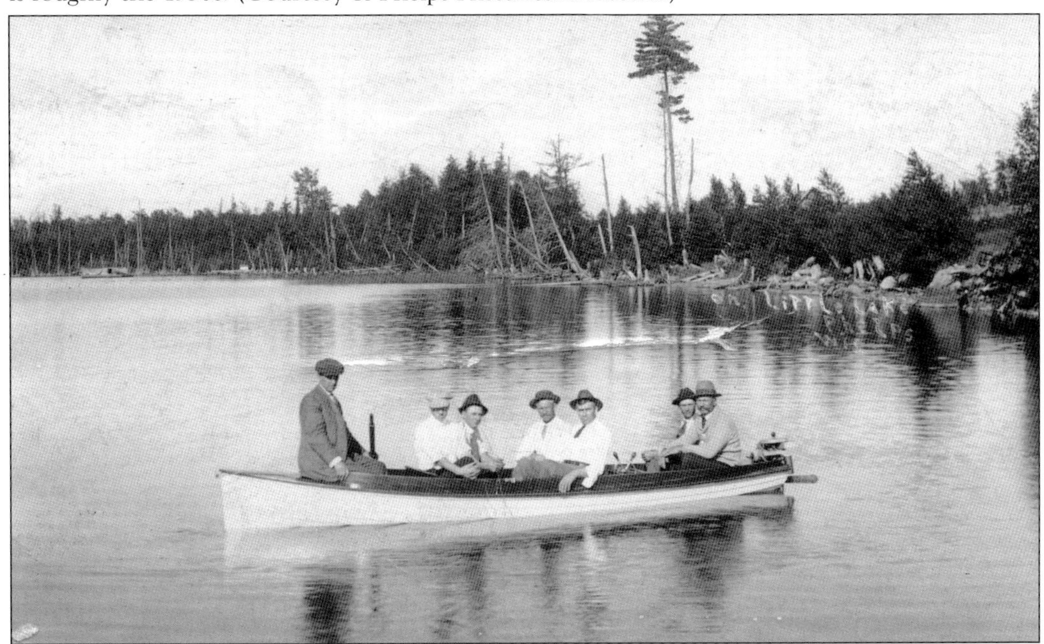

The caption barely visible along the shore to the right reads, "On Little Twin Lake Phelps Wis." These four men are either going for a boat tour or are being taken to one of the resorts. It does not appear like they are going fishing. Look very carefully and note the hand crank on top of the flywheel of the outboard motor plus the steering wheel. The type outboard motor was a Johnson, Evinrude, or Elto, manufactured in the mid-1920s.

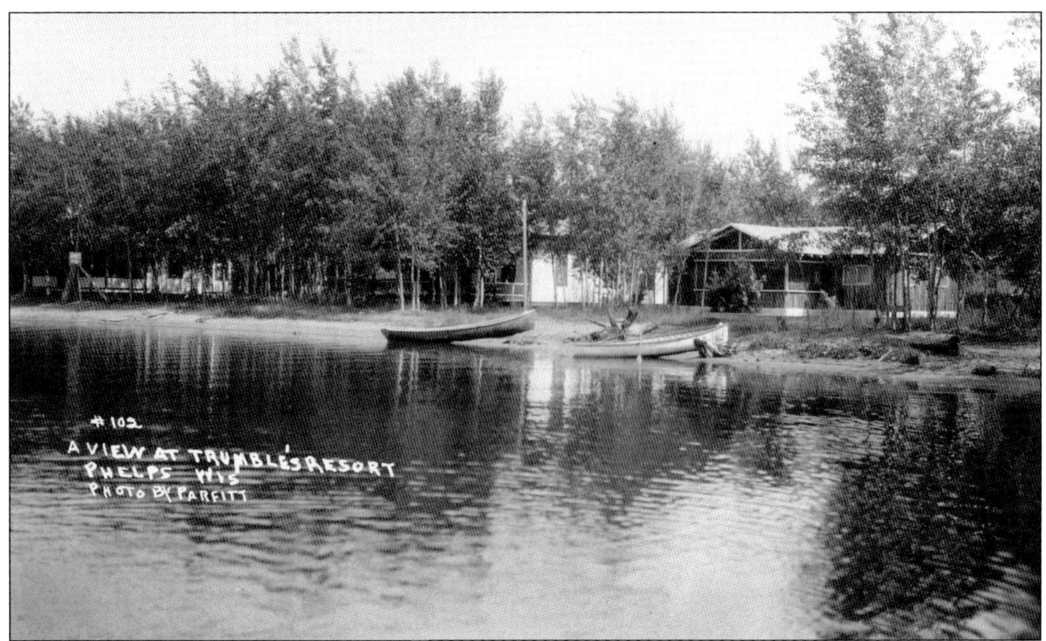

Trumble's Resort was located on the southeast shore of North Twin Lake, one and one-half mile from the village of Phelps. Robert Trumble built his resort in 1921. This establishment had a number of proprietors over the years. It was called the Lakeside and is now the Great Escape.

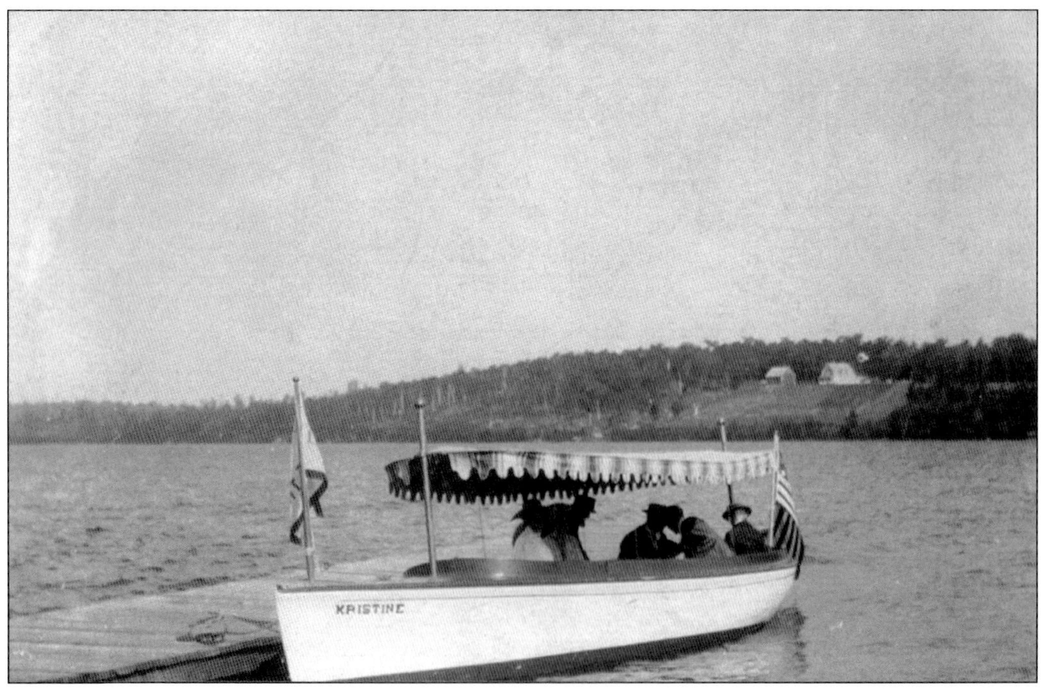

The *Kristine* again docked at a pier in Phelps to return or take passengers to Little Twin Resort. The house and barn seen on the northeast shore of Big Twin Lake appear in several other photographs.

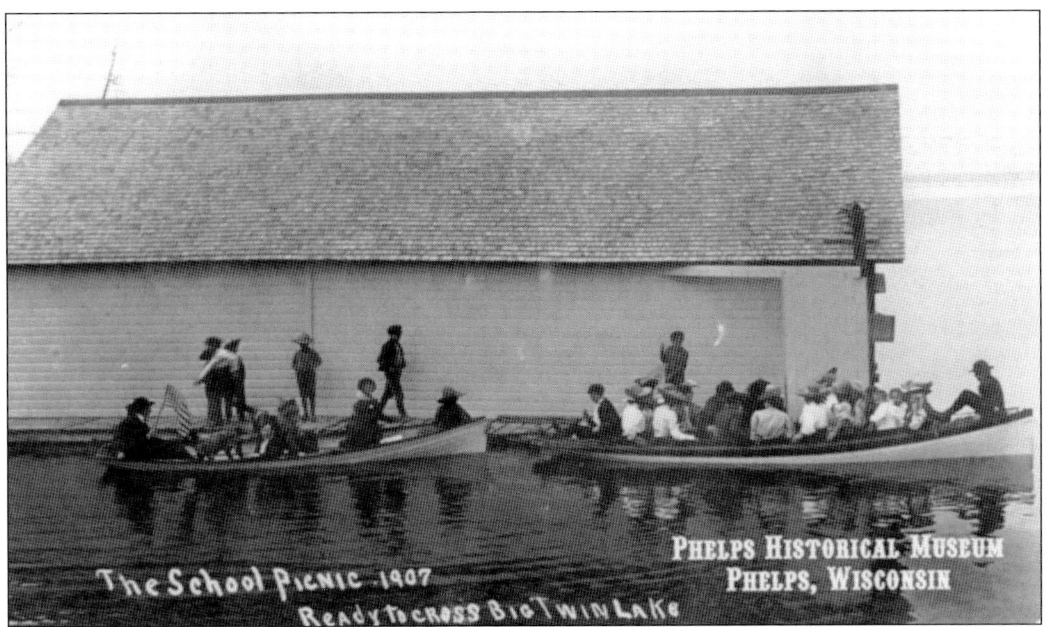

"The School Picnic – 1907 Ready to Cross Big Twin Lake" denotes a voyage across Big Twin Lake from the boathouse located near town. There is a large number of people in the boats and no life jackets. (Courtesy of Phelps Historical Museum.)

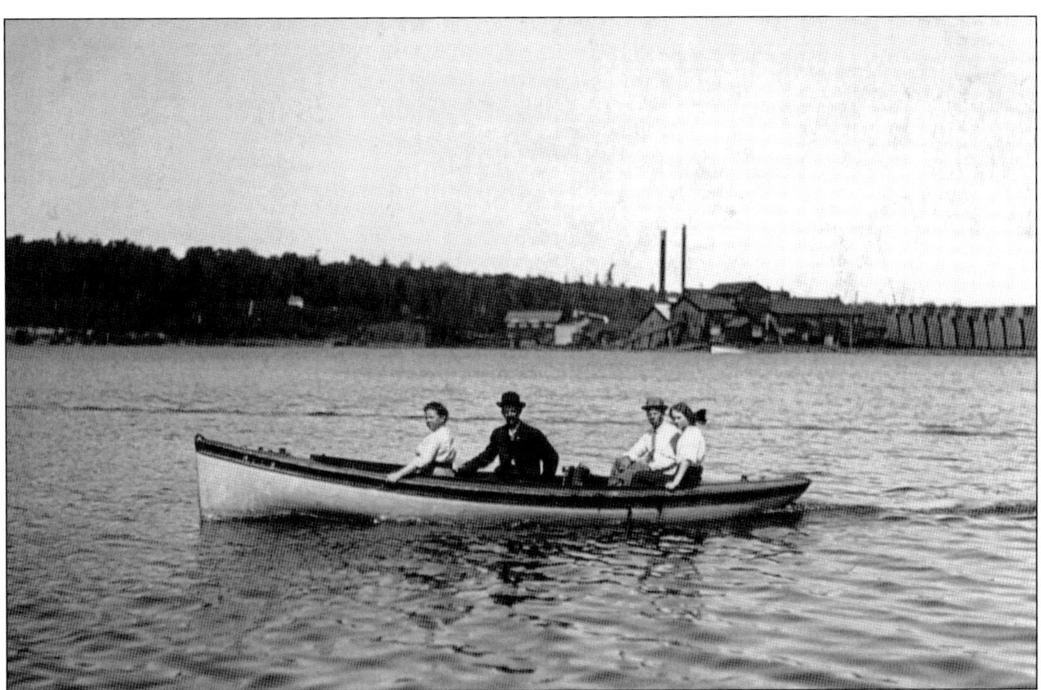
Some guests enjoy taking a boat ride on Big Twin. The lumber mill with piles of finished boards is seen in the background. It was common for guests to be transported by boat to their resort after arriving by train or car.

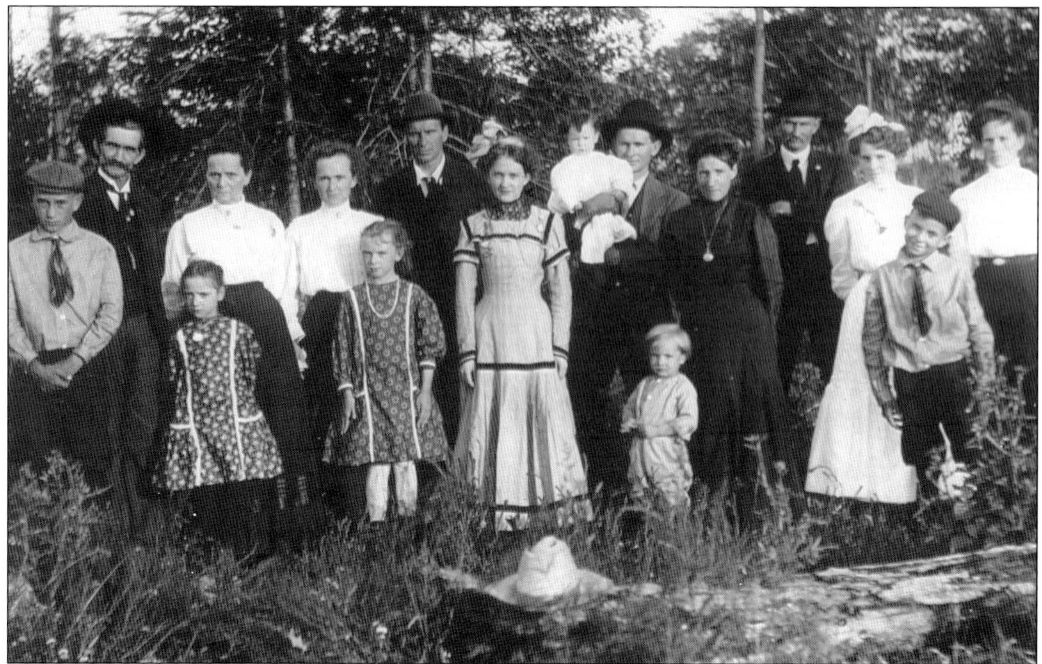

A group of people and children, perhaps families and relatives, are gathered near Phelps for this photoshoot. In those times, it would be more appropriate for people to have a somber look with no smile, as demonstrated in this postcard.

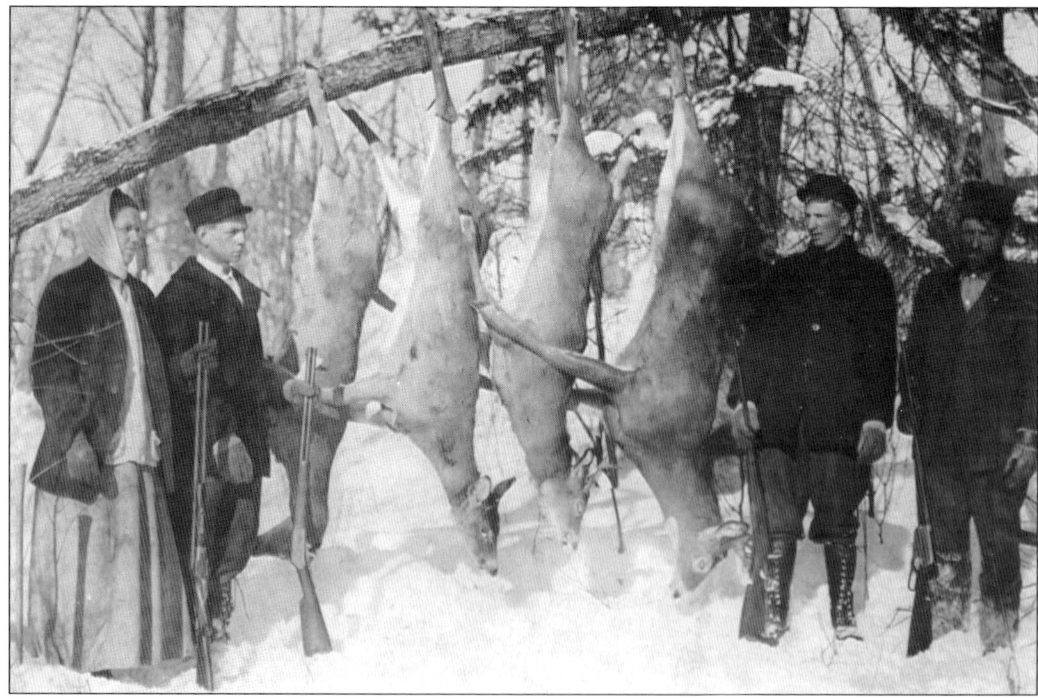

Some hunters display the day's harvest. The inscription on the back of this photograph reads, "Deer Hunting near Phelps." Hunting is a popular sport, as the vast forests are home to many wild game. Most hunting seasons run from fall to early winter. (Courtesy of the Phelps Historical Museum.)

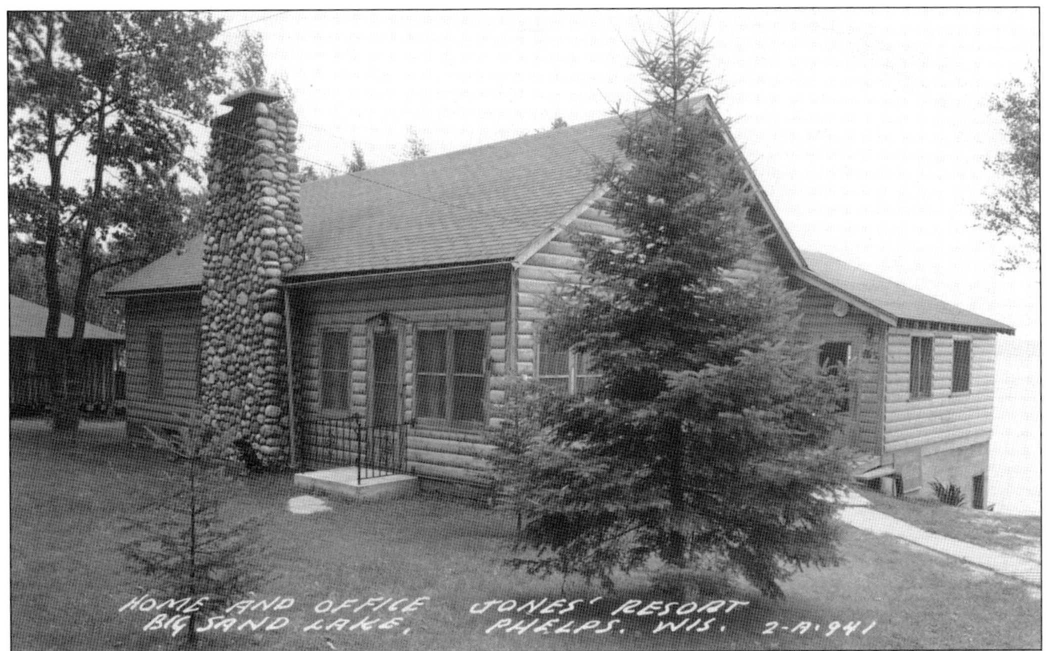

One of the earliest resorts on Big Sand Lake was founded by John Mitila in the early 1920s. Mitila built several cottages on the north shore of the lake. More notable owners in later years were Lueck's Resort and Jone's Resort, shown in this 1956 photograph. The cabins were sold and are now known as the Maple Crest Cottages. Some of the homes are available to renters on a limited basis.

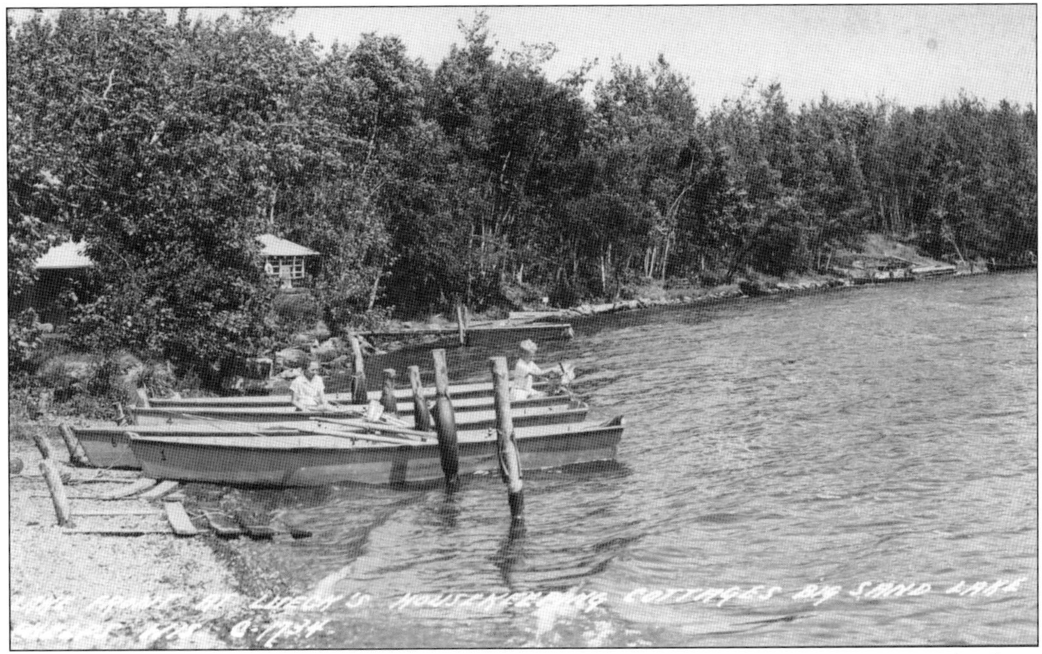

Probably a mother and her son are already in the boat and just waiting for someone to take them out on the lake. The postcard is dated 1941 at Lueck's House Keeping Cottages.

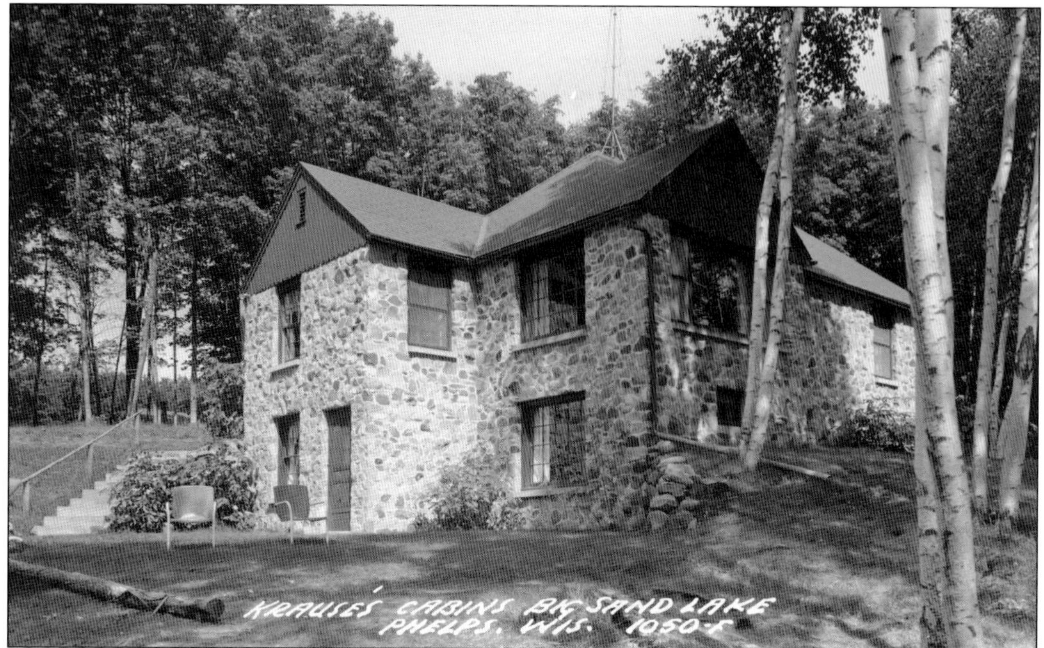

Early in the 1940s, the Krause family of West Bend, Wisconsin, bought property on Big Sand Lake just south of Lueck's Resort. Walter, Loraine, and their sons built six cabins in five years. The main house was made of fieldstones gathered along the shore of the lake and took three years to build. By the 1970s, they began selling the cottages and, shortly after, the Stone House.

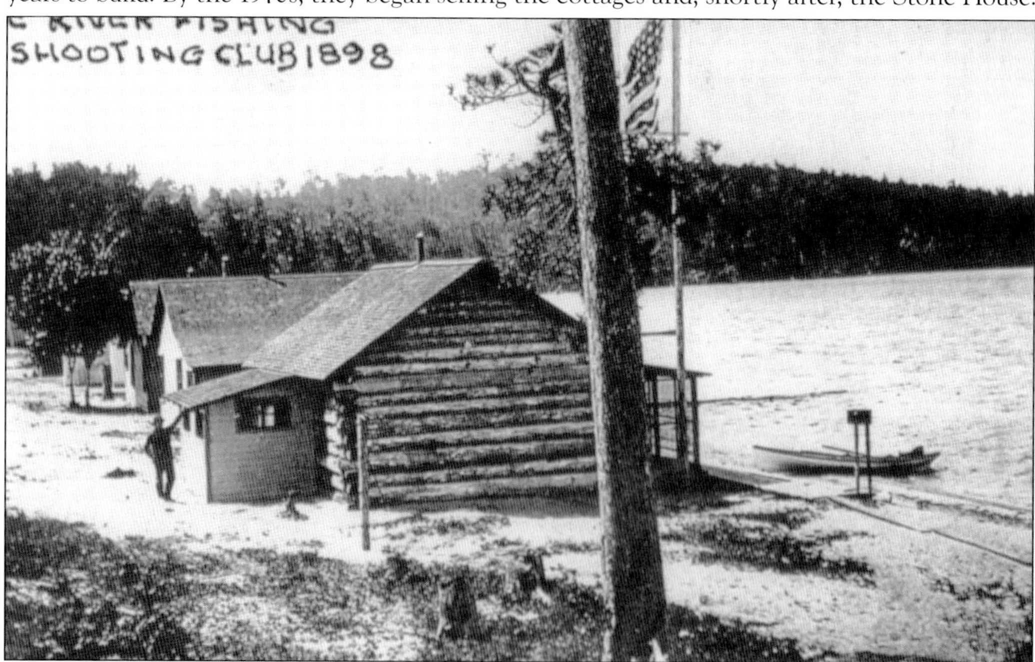

A group of businessmen from Chicago bought acres of logged out land on the north shore of Big Sand Lake, and in 1891, they formed the Eagle River Fishing and Shooting Club. This is one of the earliest photographs showing some of the first cabins along the shore. (Courtesy of Big Sand Lake Club.)

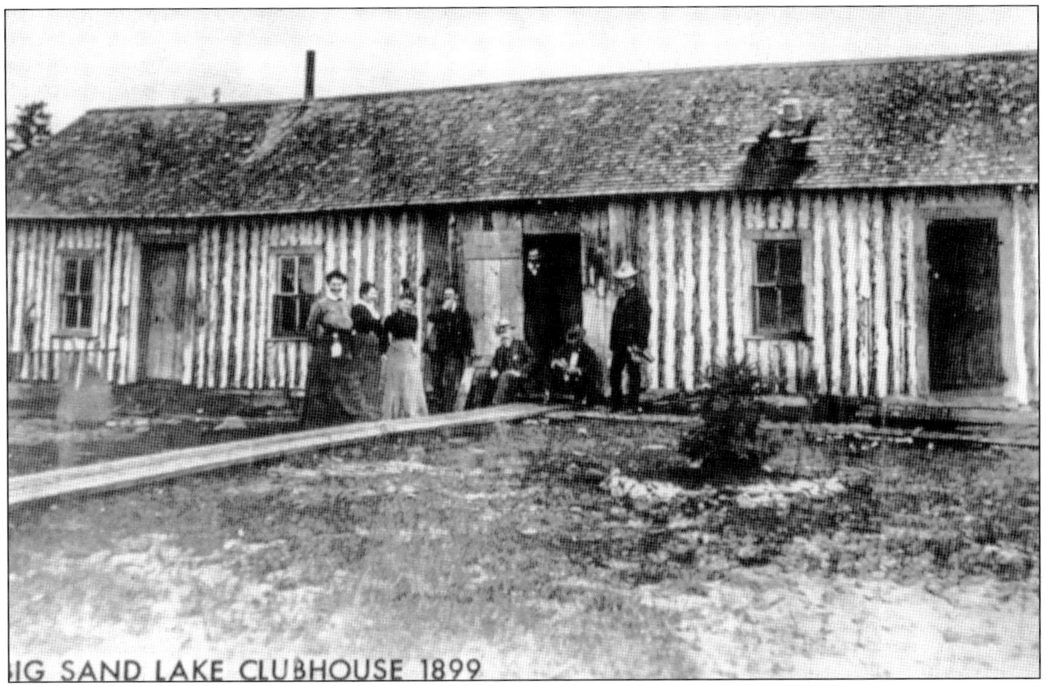

This is the original Eagle River Fishing and Shooting Club House on Big Sand Lake in 1899. Although a few wives made the arduous trip before the turn of the century, the club remained essentially a male enclave until later years, when women and children shared the club's experience. Note the vertical logs with concrete chinking. (Courtesy of Big Sand Lake Club.)

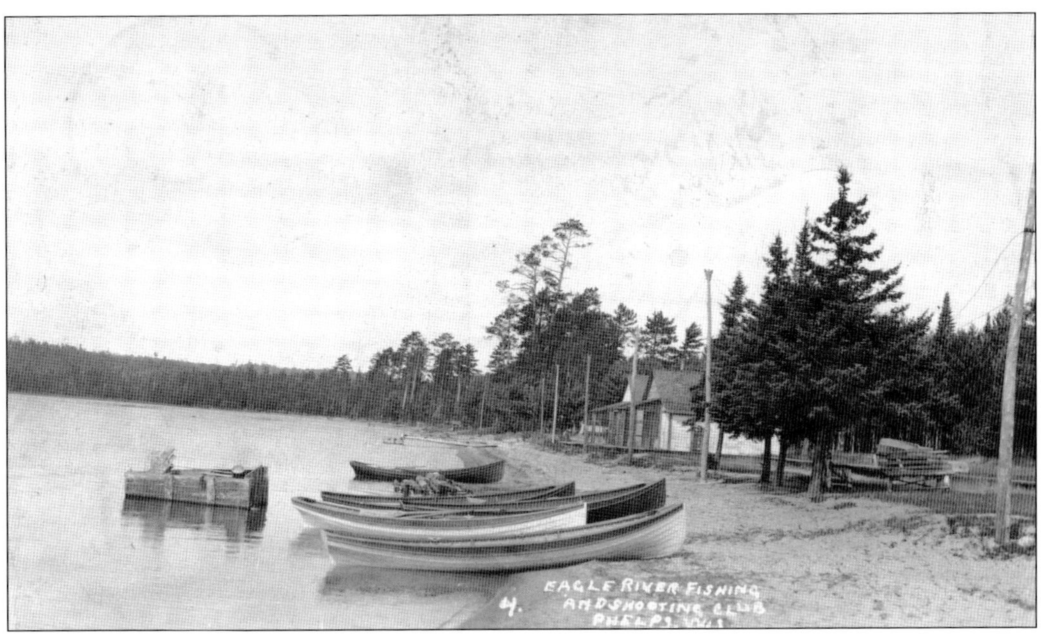

Rowboats are pulled up on the sandy shoreline, and a fish or storing crib is seen in the water. It looks like this scene with two cabins and a pier were located at the south end of the Eagle River Shooting and Fishing Club.

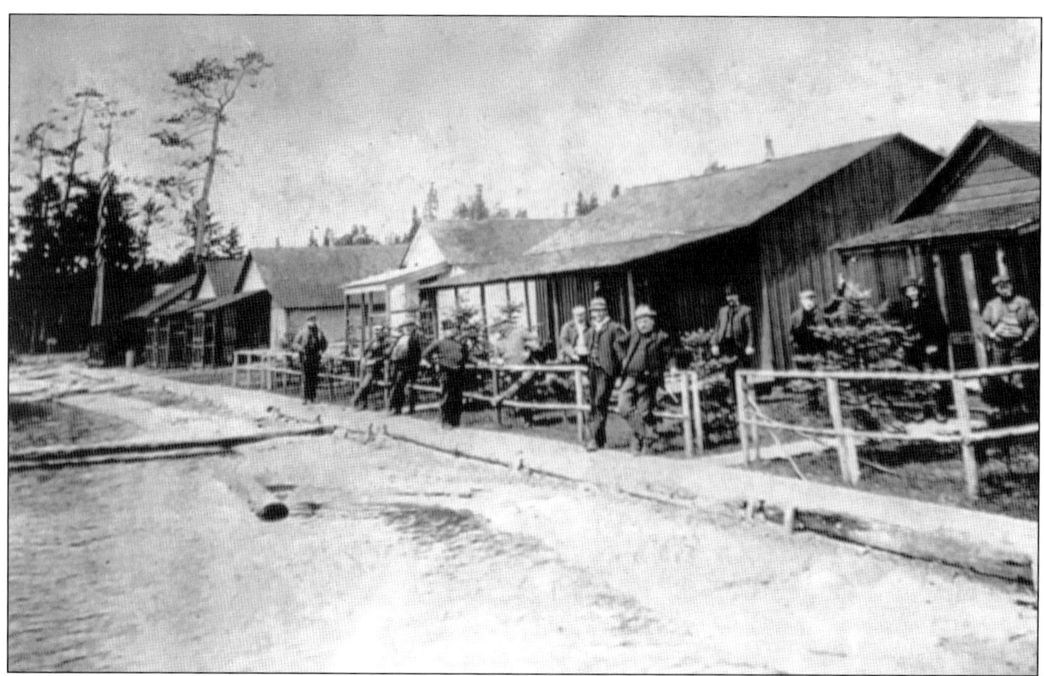

Here are some of the men looking for adventure far enough away from Chicago. They took a train to Eagle River, Wisconsin, and, from there on, headed with horse and wagon to Hackley (Phelps). Following a trail led them to Hazen's Long Lake Lodge, where they acquired some boats and rowed through the connecting channel to the north side of Big Sand Lake. (Courtesy of Big Sand Lake Club.)

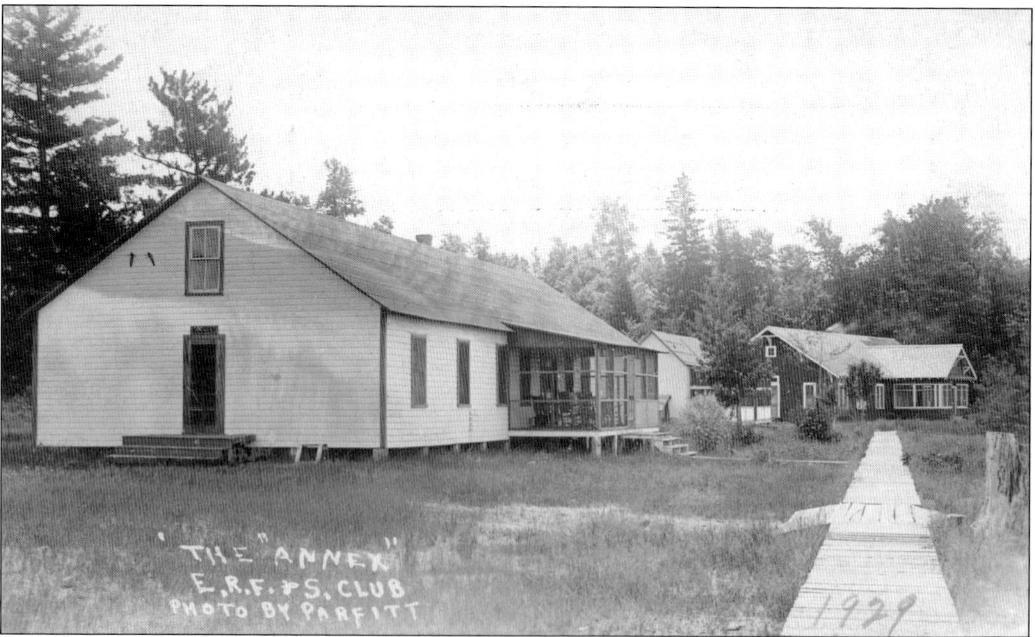

The annex of the Eagle River Fishing and Shooting Club housed the staff. It stood next to and east of the clubhouse, as shown here in 1929. Eventually, it was torn down to make room for the "Blackstone" housing for members. In the 1960s, that housing was replaced by six chalets.

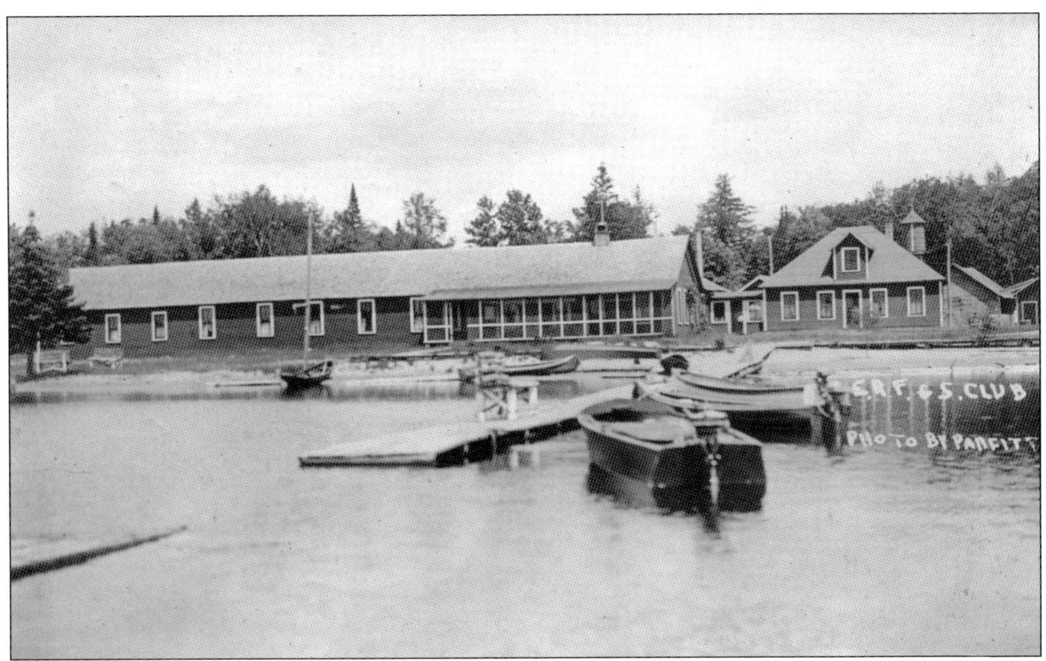

This image of the second clubhouse in 1921 shows boats with outboard motors docked on the main pier. This clubhouse, affectionately known as "the Flop," burned to the ground in 1924. That event led to the construction of the present building.

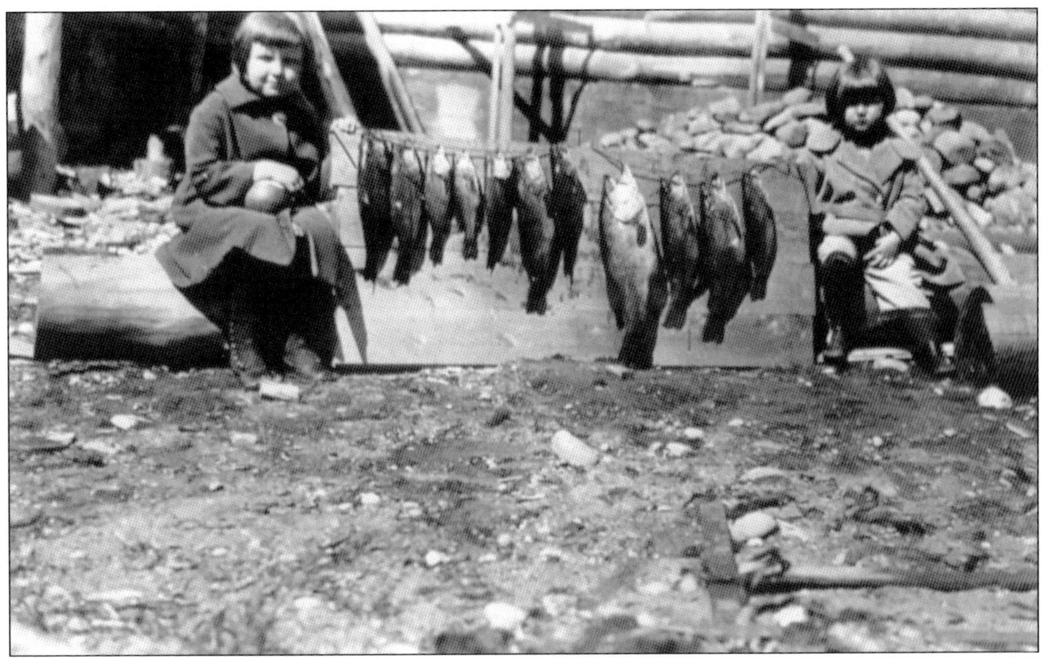

Helen (left) and Ruth Bohnsack sit on a log with a stringer of largemouth bass in 1925. In the background is the new clubhouse under construction. (Courtesy of Big Sand Lake Club.)

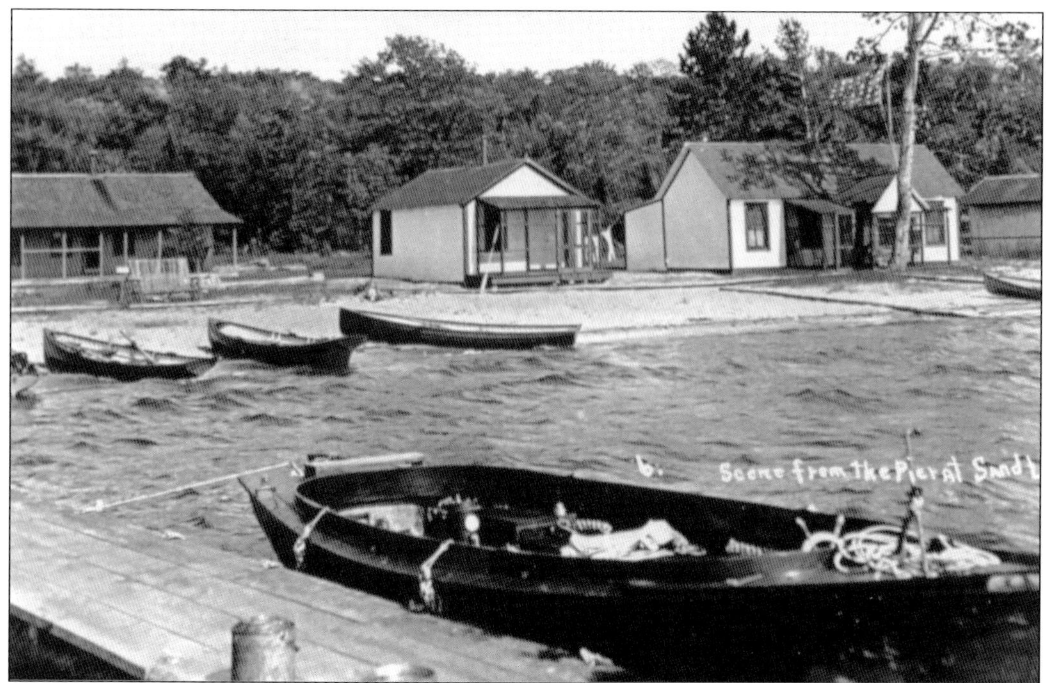

Rowboats are pulled up on the sandy shoreline while the inboard gets preference, being tied up at the pier. The second clubhouse is just visible at the far left, with cabins strung out along the shoreline. (Courtesy of Big Sand Lake Club.)

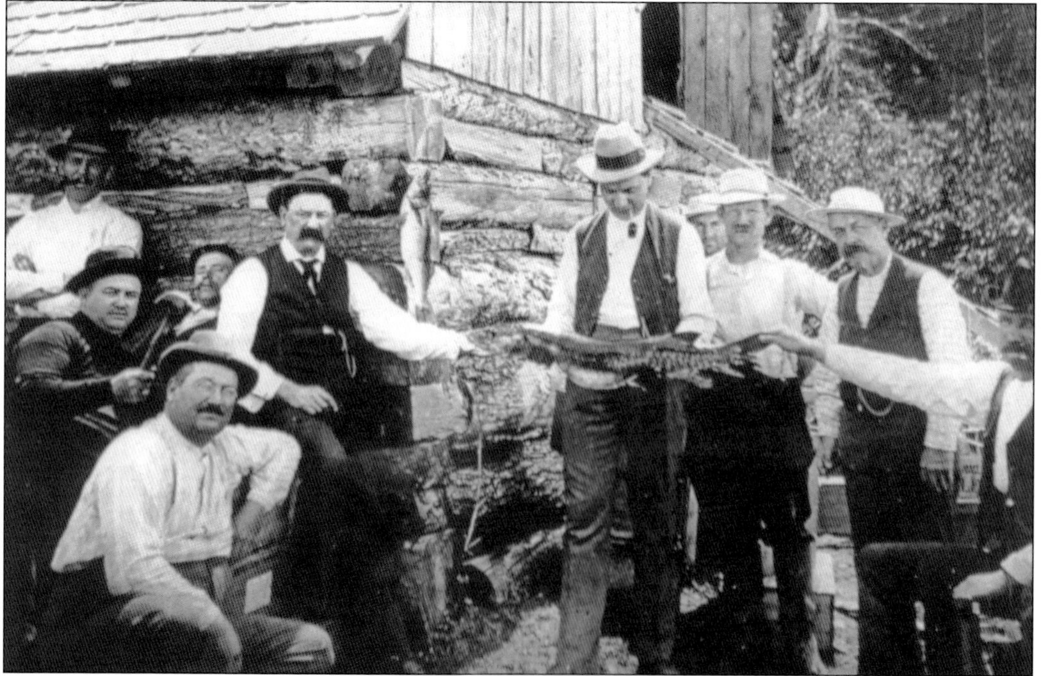

These members did not have a good day fishing. Only a small muskie and a walleye hang on the end of a log. Note the bark on the logs of this shed had not been peeled. (Courtesy of the Big Sand Lake Club.)

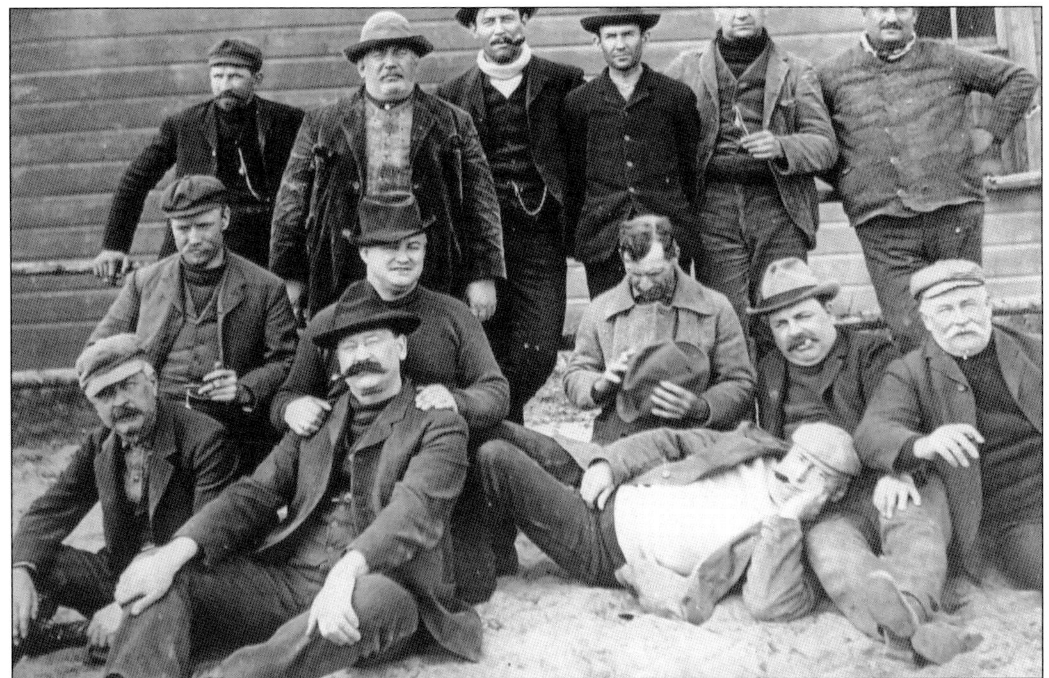

A few of the early members of the Eagle River Fishing and Shooting Club seem laid-back, enjoying the camaraderie. An outing in northern Wisconsin in those days must have been the equivalent of a trip to the wilderness of Canada or Alaska nowadays. Access to this region of northern Wisconsin was limited in transportation and was very remote. (Courtesy of Big Sand Lake Club.)

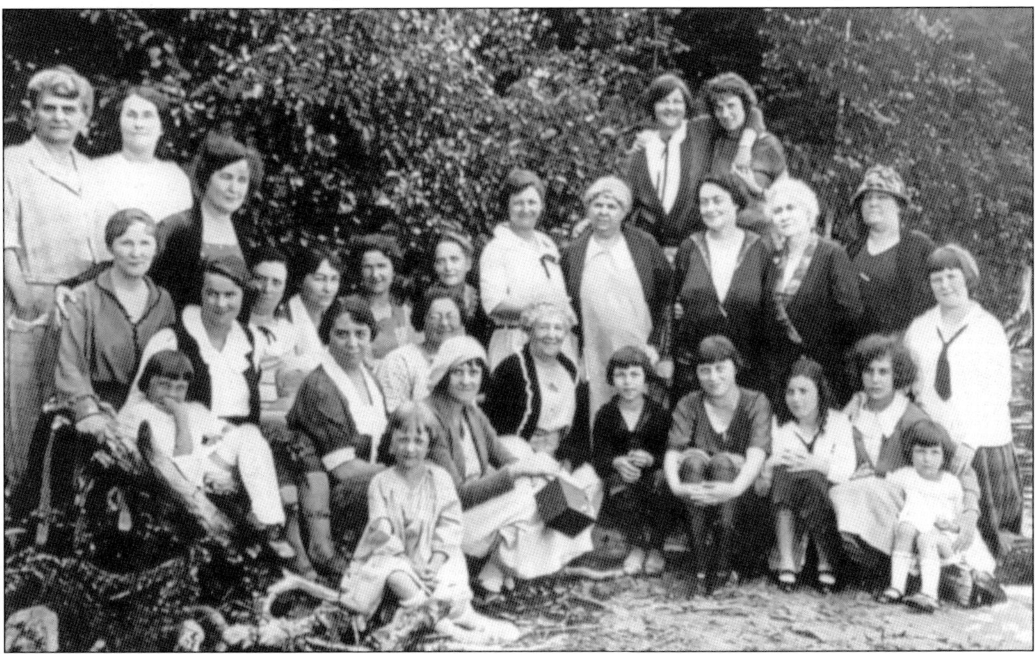

Gradually, beginning in the early 1920s, women and children were allowed to join the men at the Big Sand Lake Club. This photograph was taken in the 1930s and shows women and girls posing on the club grounds. (Courtesy of Big Sand Lake Club.)

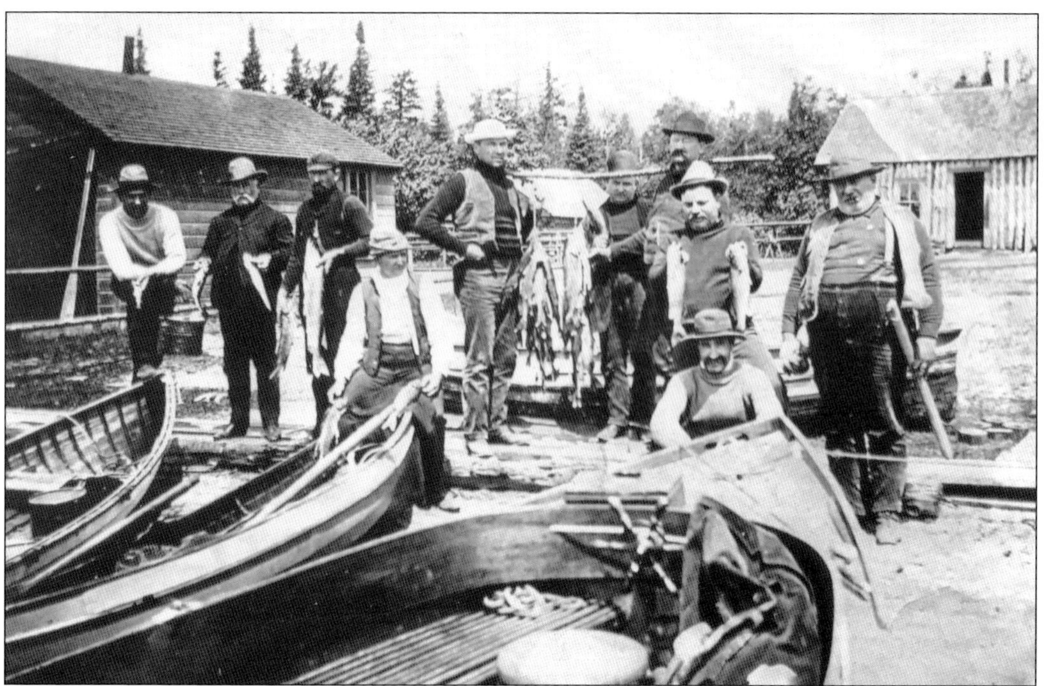

Fishermen display their catch of walleyes on Big Sand Lake. The driver of this inboard boat sits on a stool right up front in the boat, with a bench seat along the side. (Courtesy of the Big Sand Lake Club.)

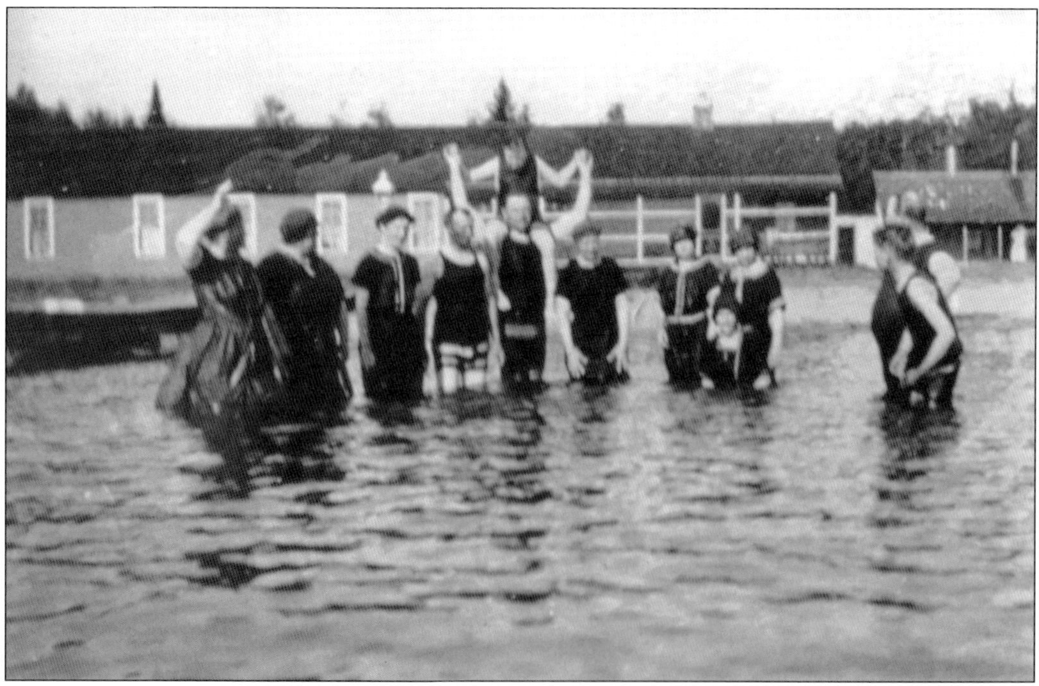

The summer heat finds these members, both men and women, in their full-dress bathing suits around the early 1900s. The clubhouse can be seen in the background at the far left. The bathers stand right about where the club pier is now. (Courtesy of Big Sand Lake Club.)

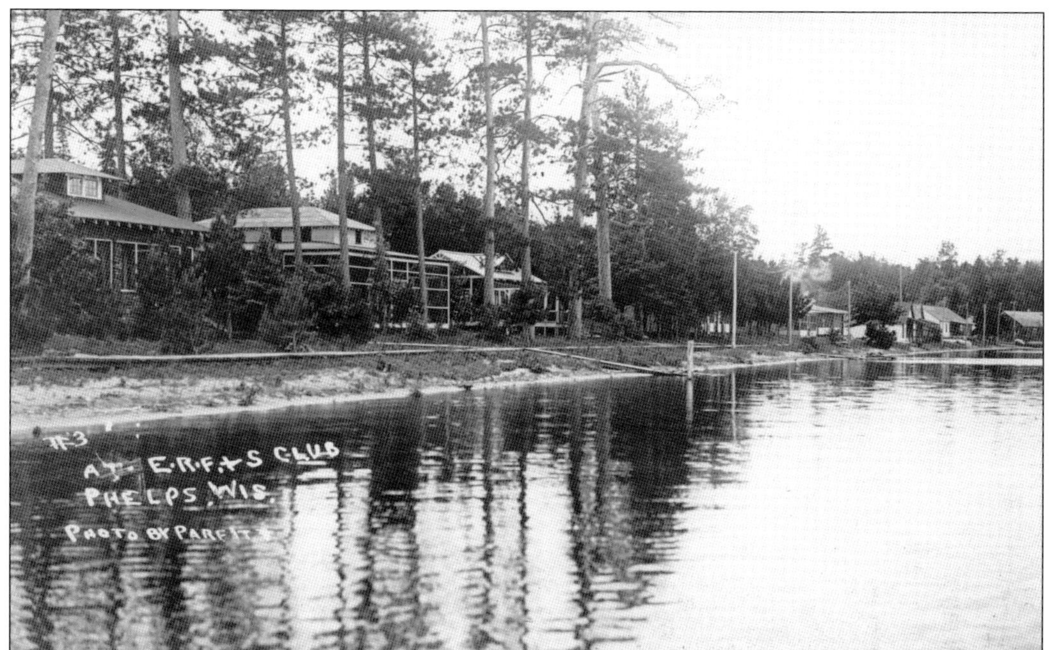

As more land was acquired, membership grew. The original rustic cabins gave way to larger cottages and homes. The homes seen here on the left in this photograph are located north of the clubhouse. A wooden boardwalk connects the homes on both ends for easy access to the clubhouse.

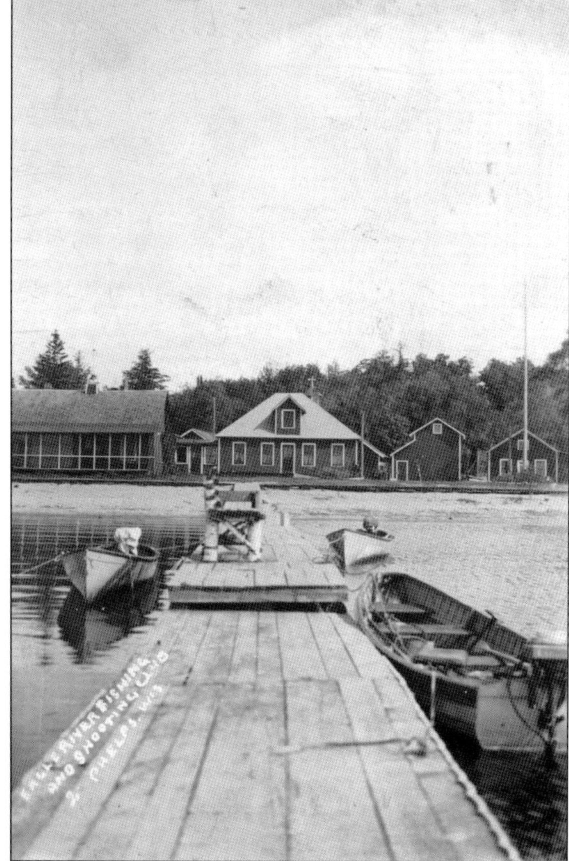

Boats with outboard motors attached are tied to the main pier in this stamped postcard dated 1927. The card was probably sent later, since the old clubhouse seen here already burned down. The caption reads, "Eagle River Fishing & Shooting Club 2 – Phelps, Wis."

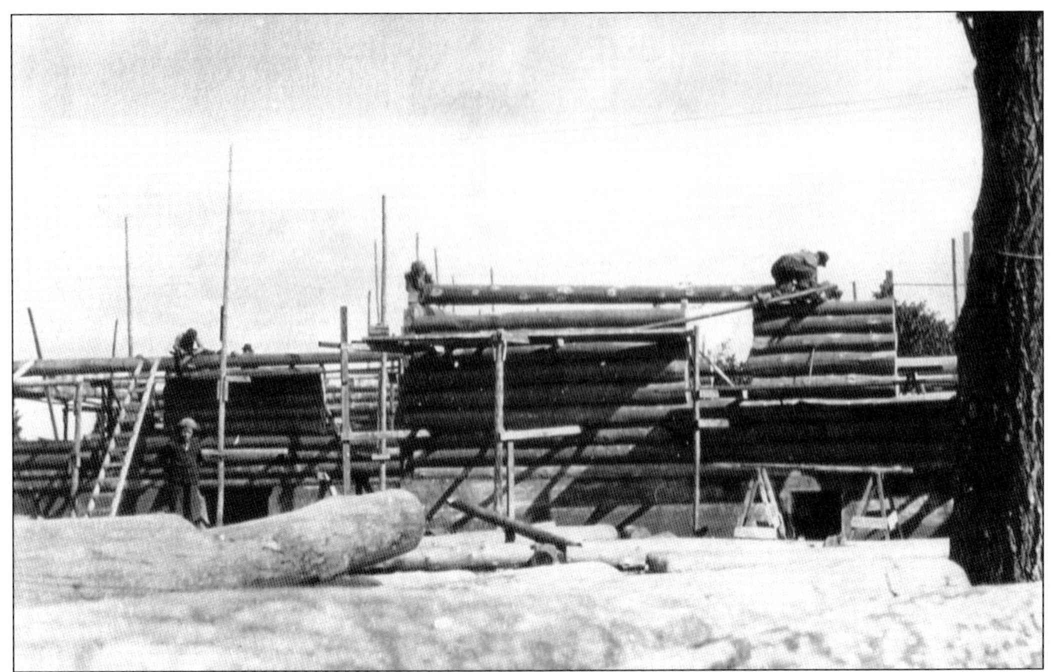

Shortly after the old clubhouse burned down in late 1924, construction of the new building began and was completed in 1926 by the Northern Log Cabin Company. The assembly of the hemlock logs with snow already on the ground can be seen. This clubhouse still remains today, with a few upgrades or repairs over the years. (Courtesy of Anne Grogan.)

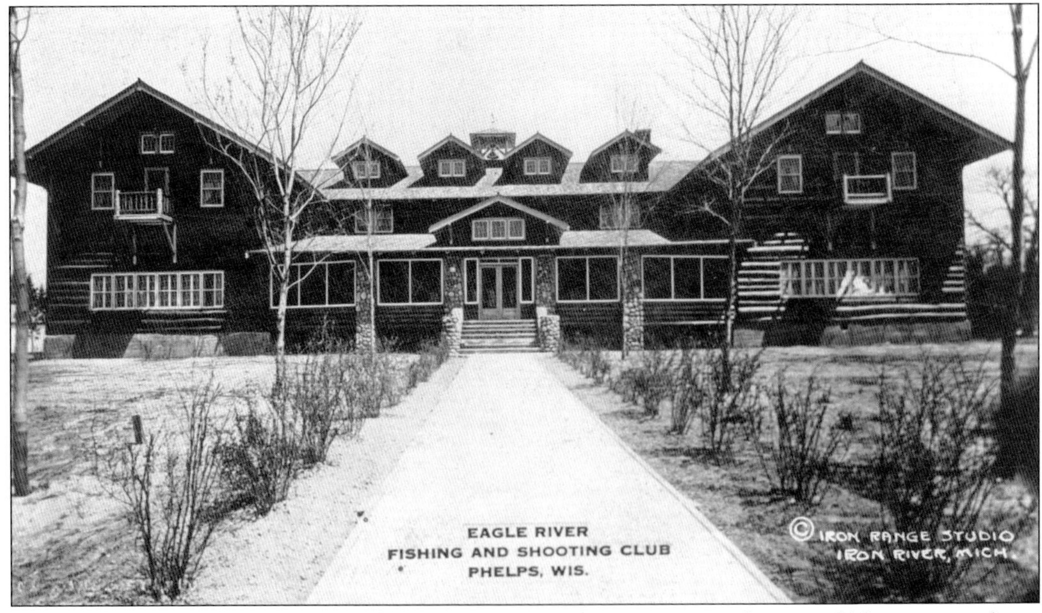

This view from the lake depicts the 15,000-square-foot structure that would have cost about $125 when completed in 1926. In 1927, the name of the club was changed from the Eagle River Fishing & Shooting Club to the Big Sand Lake Club. There was a desire to make the name less specific to just Eagle River.

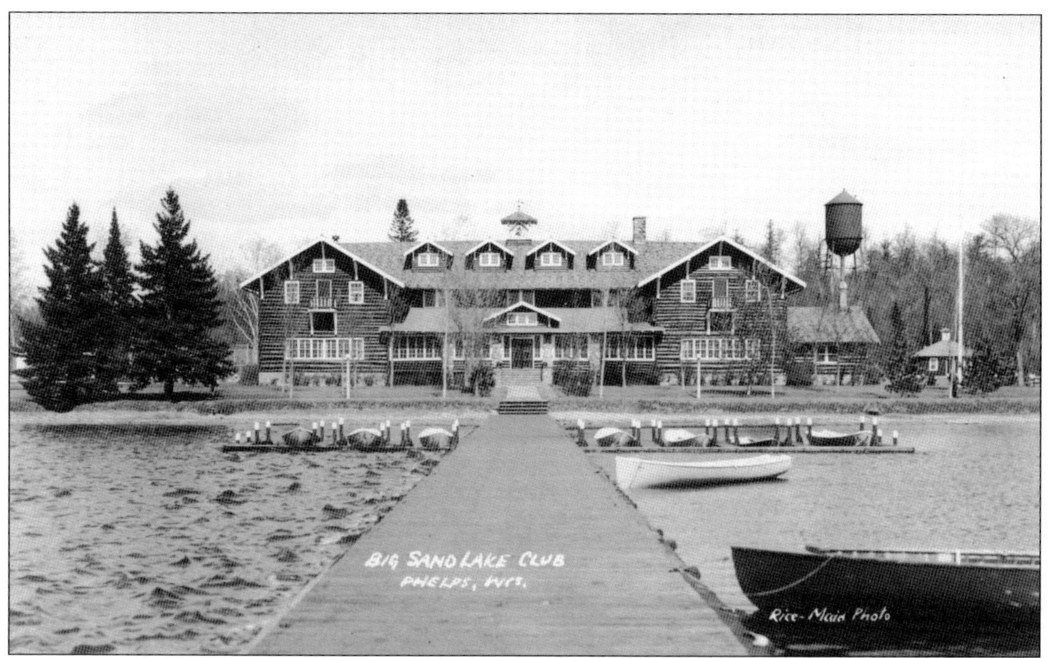

The new clubhouse became the largest log building in Wisconsin of its time and one of the biggest in the country. The water tower on the right was erected in approximately 1910, long before the new clubhouse was built. Its main use was for fire protection.

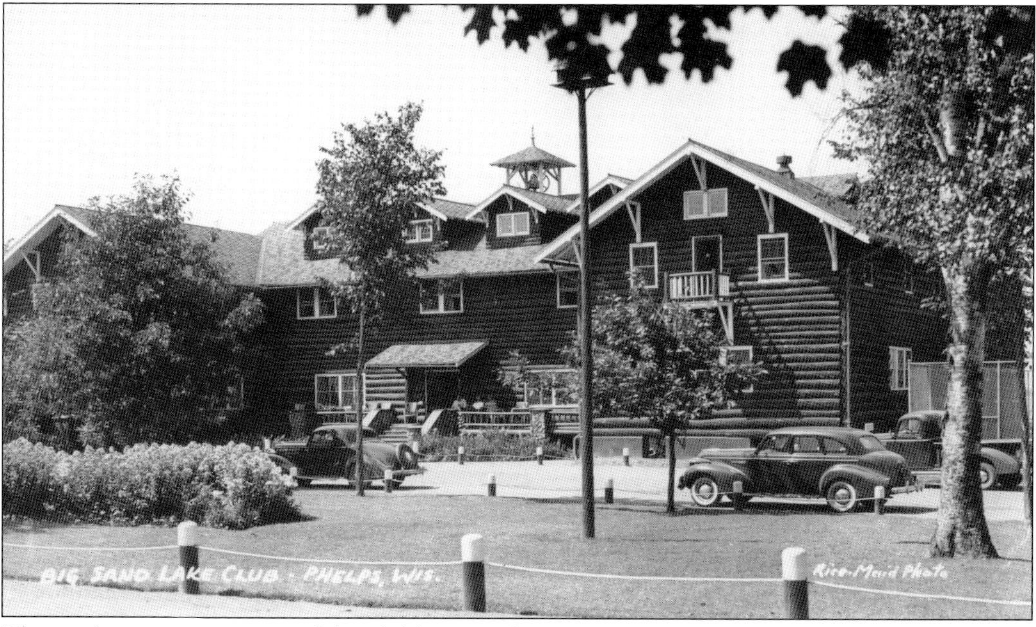

This is the main entrance of the clubhouse. The four gabled dormers are also incorporated on the lakeside of the building. A bell tower on top of the roof called the members to meals three times a day. Most memberships were facilitated by current members of the club who were friends or co-workers. This mailed postcard is dated 1941.

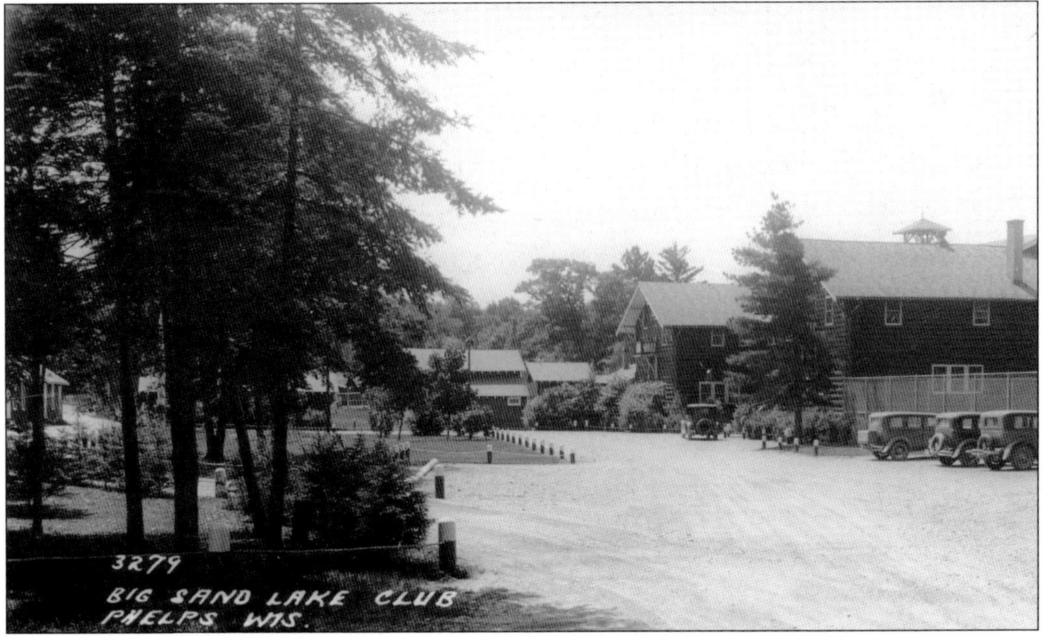

Although most family members came via the Chicago & North Western Railway to Eagle River, Conover, and then the spur to Phelps, some drove their automobiles, as shown here, in the late 1920s on ever-improving roads.

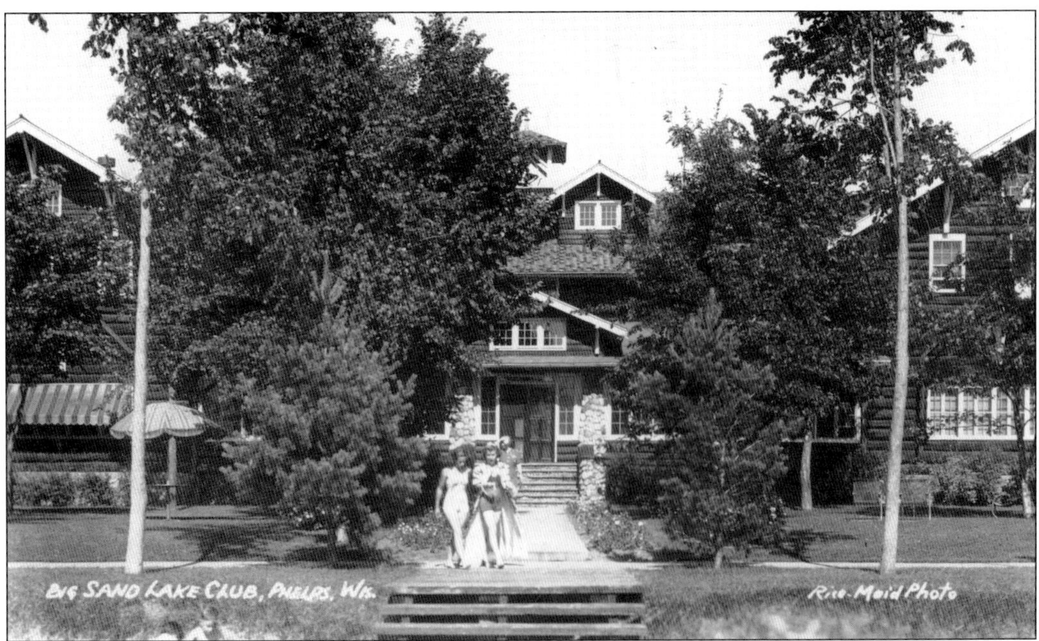

Perhaps a mother and daughter are heading to the club's private beach in this postcard dated 1940, while a boy (lower left) is already playing in the sand.

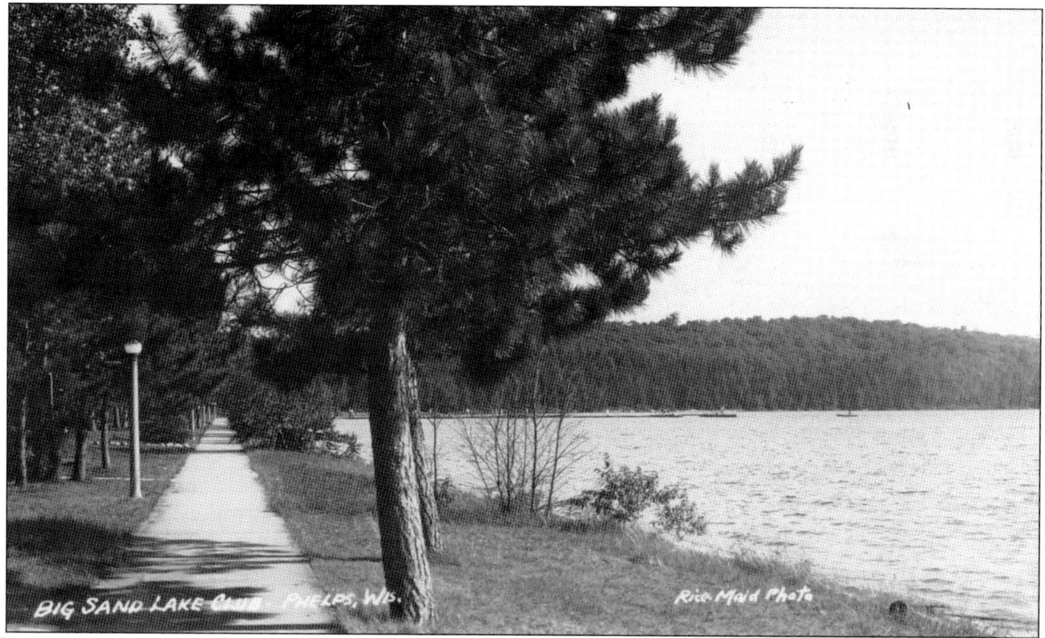

The old wooden boardwalk was replaced with a concrete sidewalk and pole lamps. It served as a path to the clubhouse and the main pier. It could also be used as a bike path for children or just for a stroll along the shore.

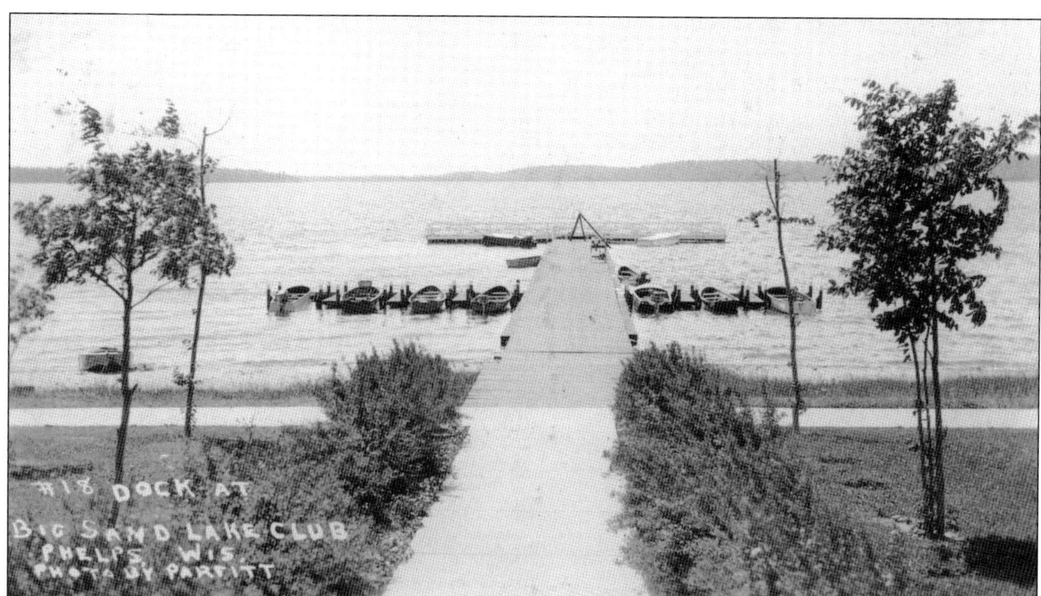

This view looking west shows most of Big Sand Lake. The dock terminates into a T-shaped section. The pier was also positioned to line up with the lake entrance of the clubhouse. Midway down the pier, members parked their boats in designated spots.

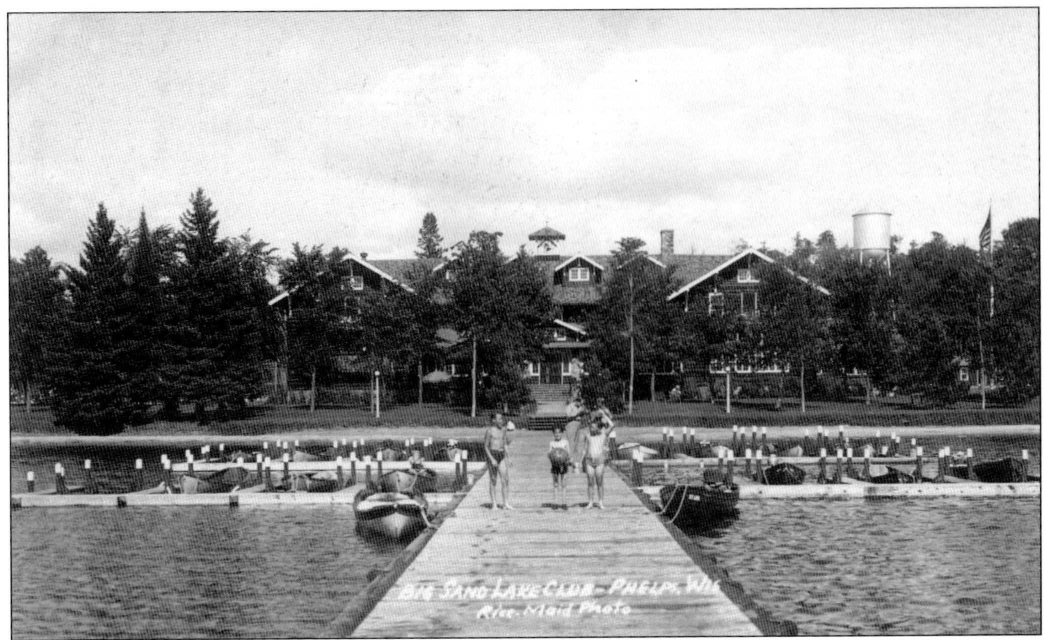

The large wooden dock is a popular spot, not only for fishing, swimming, and boating but also as a gathering place for club members. It looks like these children are ready to jump in the lake or sit at the end of the dock with their feet dangling in the water.

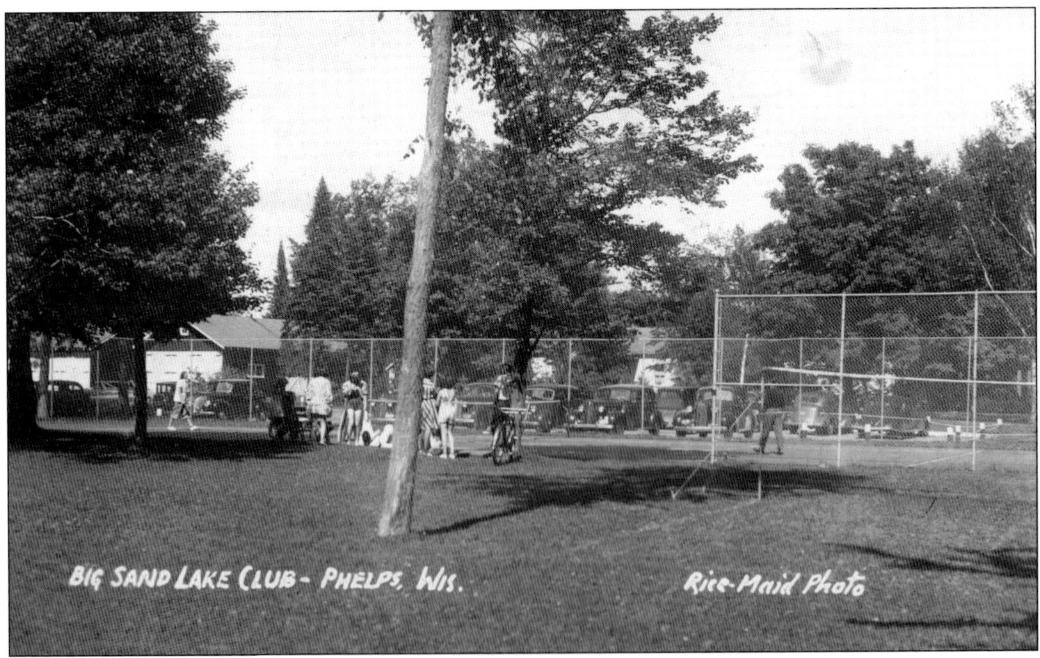

"The Club is full and there are a lot of children here," reads this 1947-dated postcard. These two tennis courts, side by side, are located next to the clubhouse and were constructed about the same time. The club also provided beach access, boat use, and meals during the day.

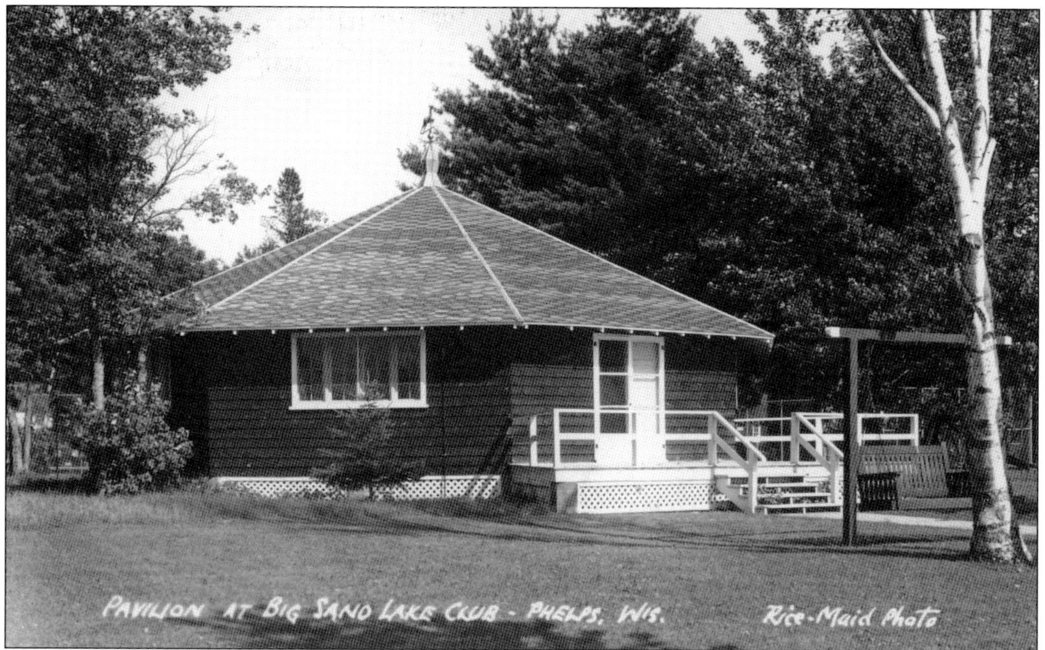

The pavilion was another favorite place to meet with friends and gather for dances, card games, and storytelling. It was a great place to hang out on rainy days. The pavilion was removed in the 1970s to make room for the second tennis court.

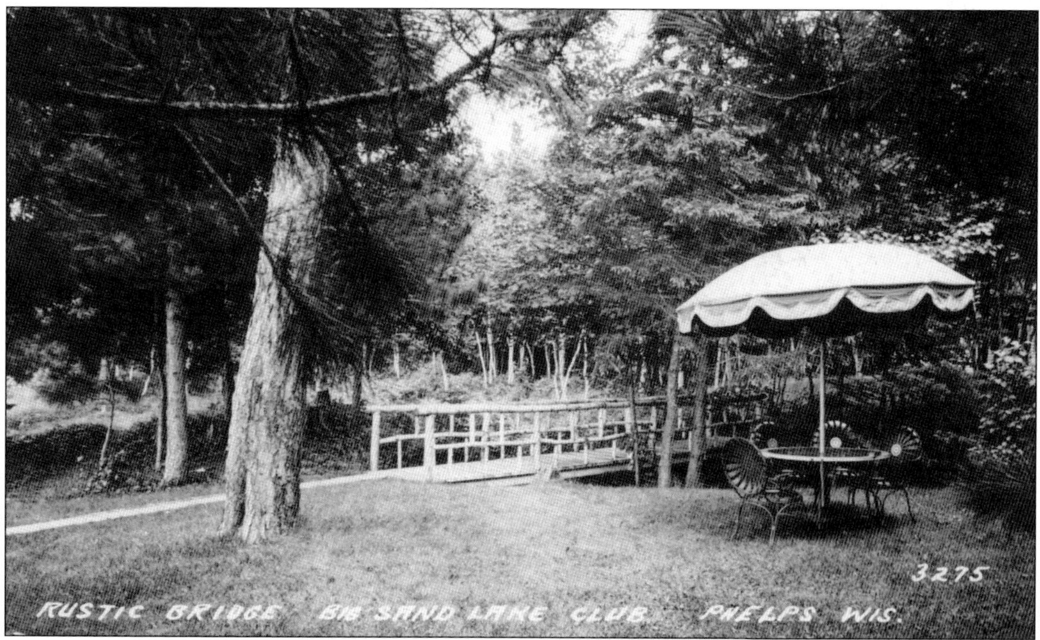

A rustic bridge constructed of hewn and peeled logs spans a creek bed south of the clubhouse. A new bridge with fieldstone guardrails has since replaced the one shown here. It is affectionately known as "the Bridge of Hope over the River of Doubt."

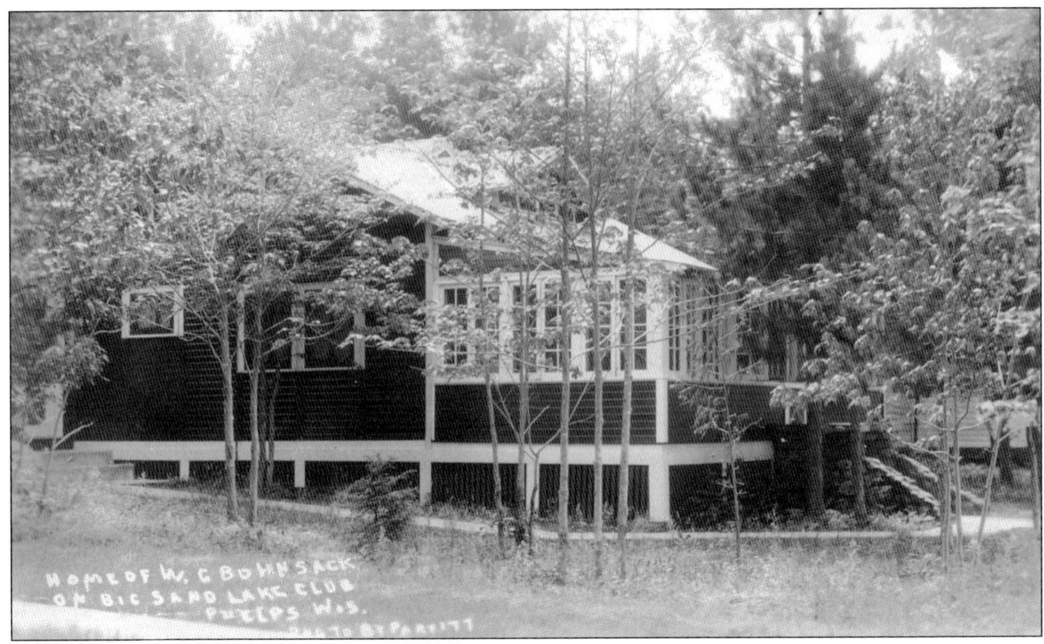

Pictured here is the home of W.G. Bohnsack, a member of the club. He was the grandfather of Lois Milburn, who still resides at this house during the summer season. A cousin of Lois, Helen Adams, also has a summer home at the Big Sand Lake Club. These two ladies have spent the summers here since they were little girls.

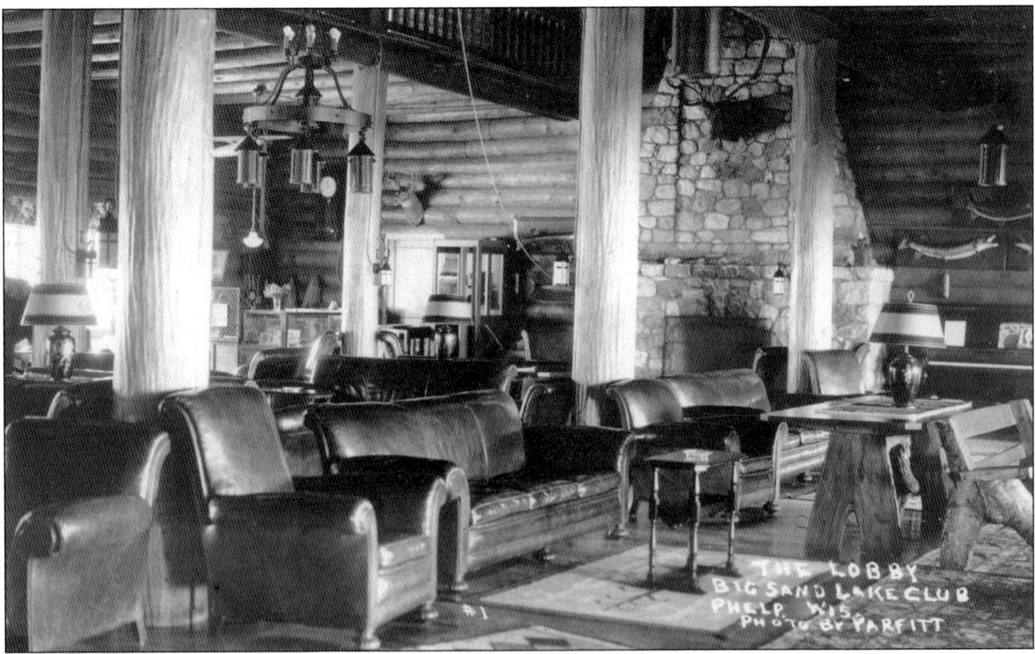

The main lobby of this clubhouse is an impressive three-story-high room with a large fieldstone fireplace that extends to the ceiling. Young and old congregate around the fireplace and lounge in the comfort of the club's leather couches and chairs.

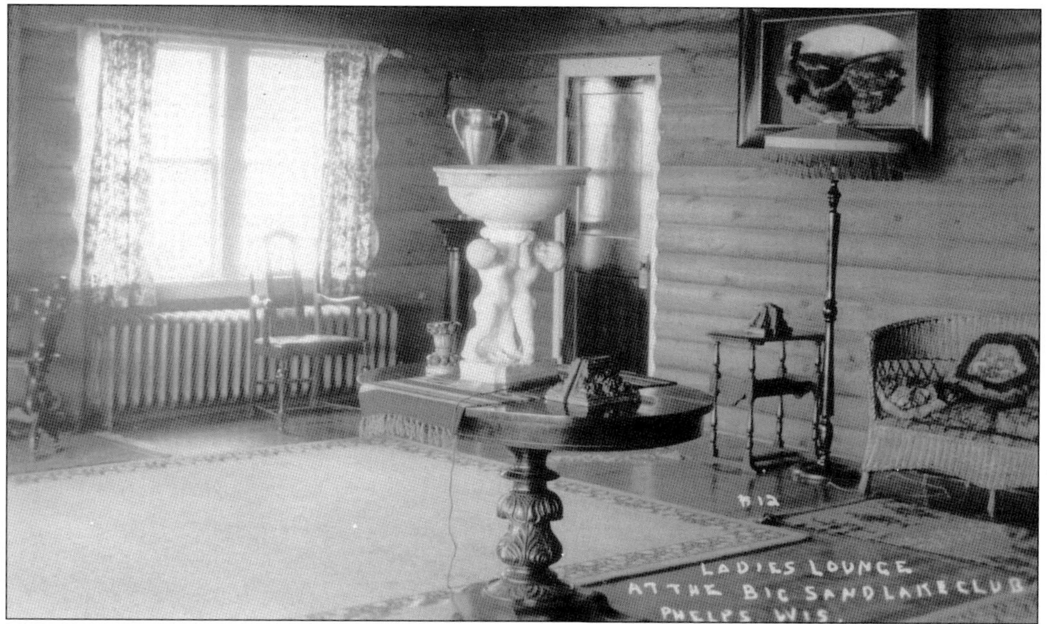

The ladies' lounge was also called the women's card room. Note the white ceramic pedestal bowl on top of the table and the hot water radiator below the window.

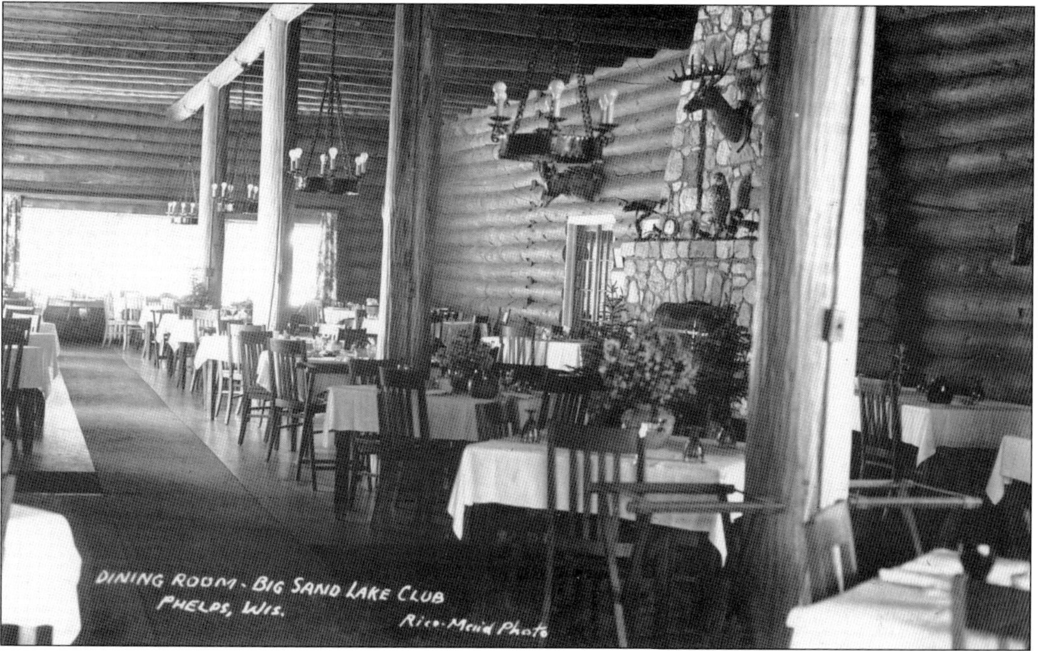

In readiness for the next meal are white tablecloths covering the tables with water glasses turned over. The dining-room fireplace on the right in this photograph is back to back with the one in the lobby.

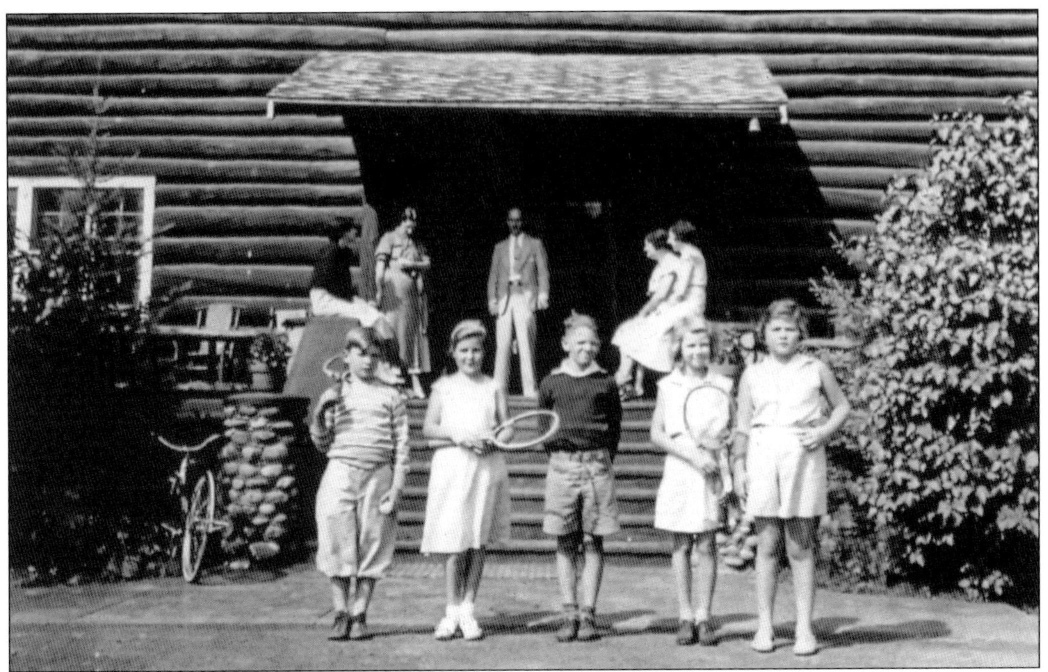

This photograph at the west, or lake, entrance shows the staff on the porch. There were approximately 12 staff members employed. They tended mostly to the cleaning and landscape maintenance of the club. The gentleman among them is the "keeper," a term used for manager. The children, members, and guests are ready to play tennis. (Courtesy of the Big Sand Lake Club.)

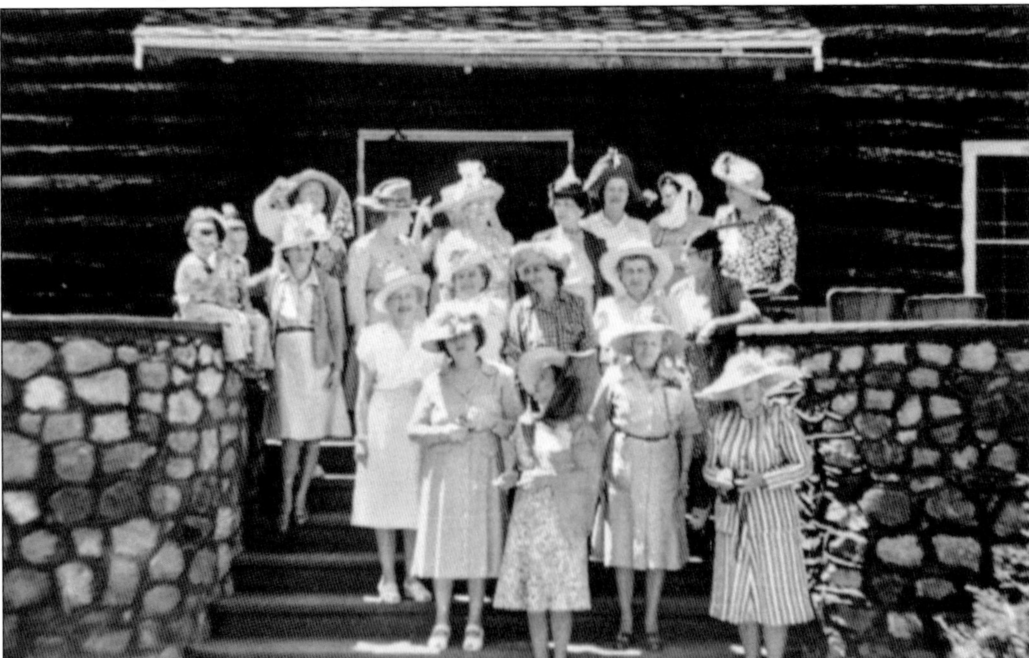

Ladies of the club and two youngsters, sitting on the retainer wall, pose on the steps to the rear, or east, entrance of the club building. Formal attire was typical on vacation in those days. (Courtesy of Big Sand Lake Club.)

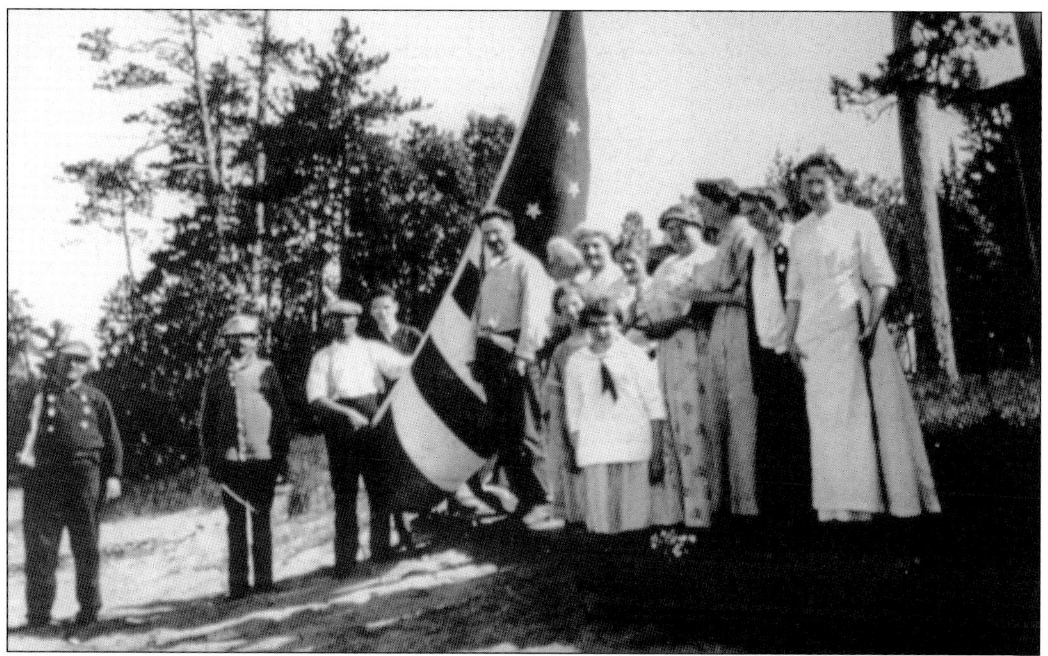

This is perhaps a Memorial Day gathering at the Big Sand Lake Club. Pictured are a large American flag, as well as a man, most likely a veteran, holding a rifle over his shoulder. Holiday weekends were and still are busy times at resorts in the Northwoods with parades and other activities. (Courtesy of the Big Sand Lake Club.)

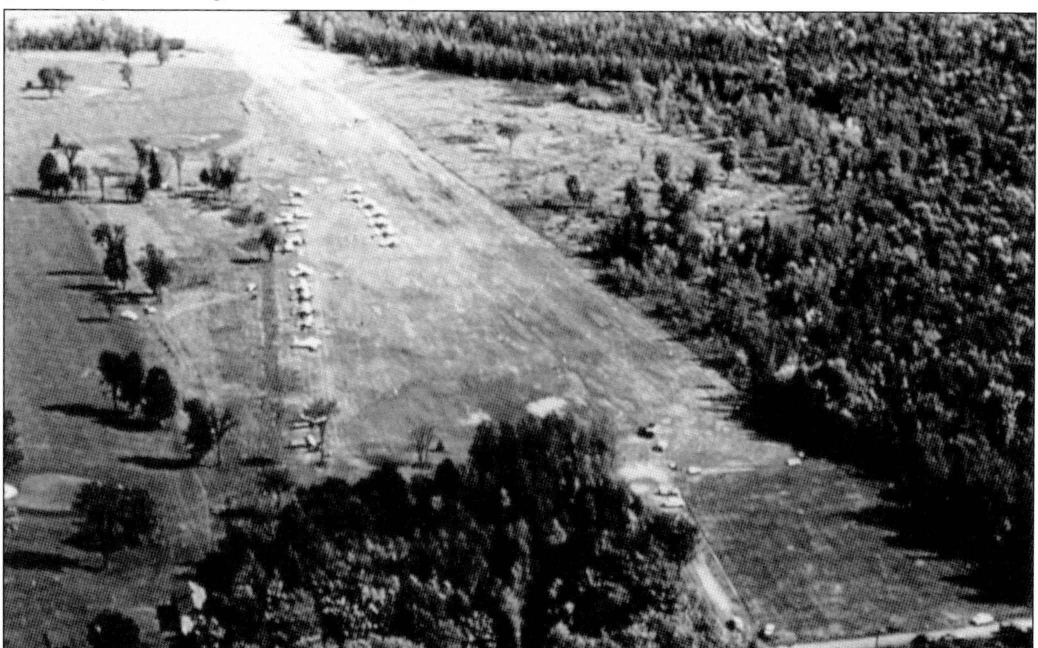

This aerial view shows the airstrip and part of the golf course of the club. It signifies a special occasion, as noted by the many airplanes parked on both sides of the runway. The airstrip was originally part of the club's property, but it was turned over to Phelps in 1957. In 1985, it was deeded back to the club and closed as an airstrip in 1991. (Courtesy of Anne Grogan.)

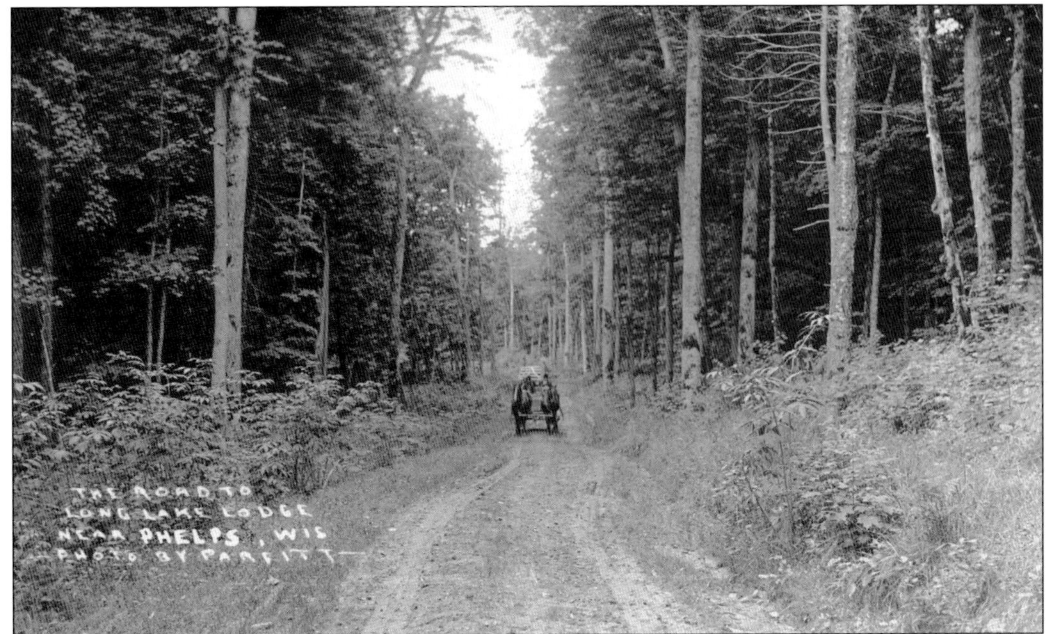

A horse-drawn wagon is being pulled along the road leading to Hazen's Long Lake Lodge. It was the same road the early members of the Big Sand Lake Club traveled to Long Lake. From there, they traveled by boat to Big Sand Lake through the thoroughfare channel. The early members of the Big Sand Lake Club, formally called the Eagle River Fishing and Shooting Club, were residents of Chicago that had a desire to have adventures in the Northwoods. Many were also business associates of Homer Galpin.

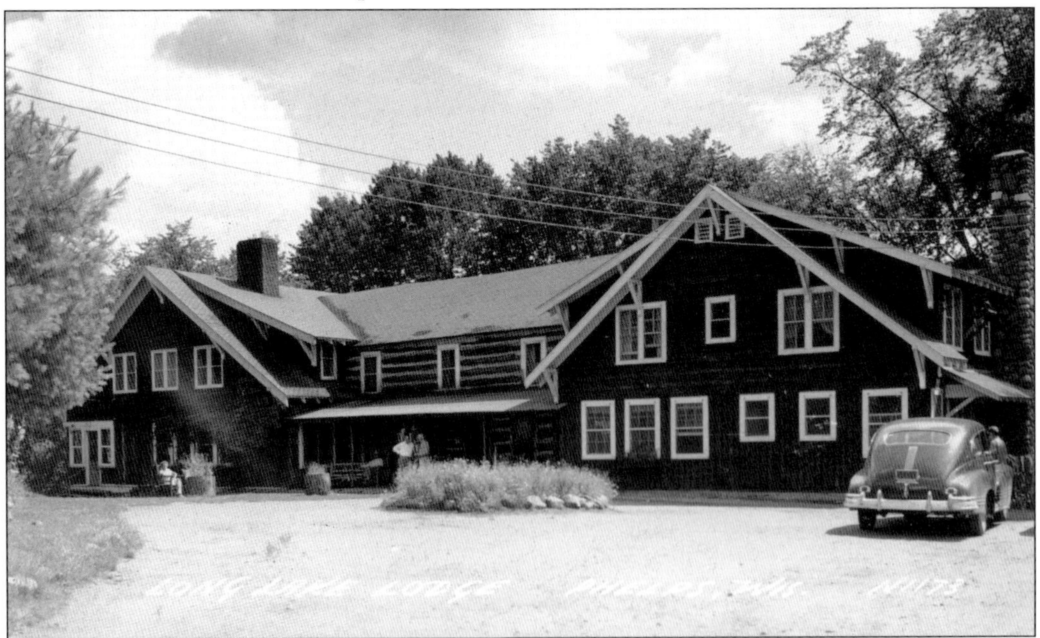

With the growing tourism to the Northwoods, entrepreneurs like Charles Hazen purchased 53 acres and started building a resort in 1901 on the banks of Long Lake. Early vacationers are seen here in front of the Long Lake Lodge in this 1948-dated postcard.

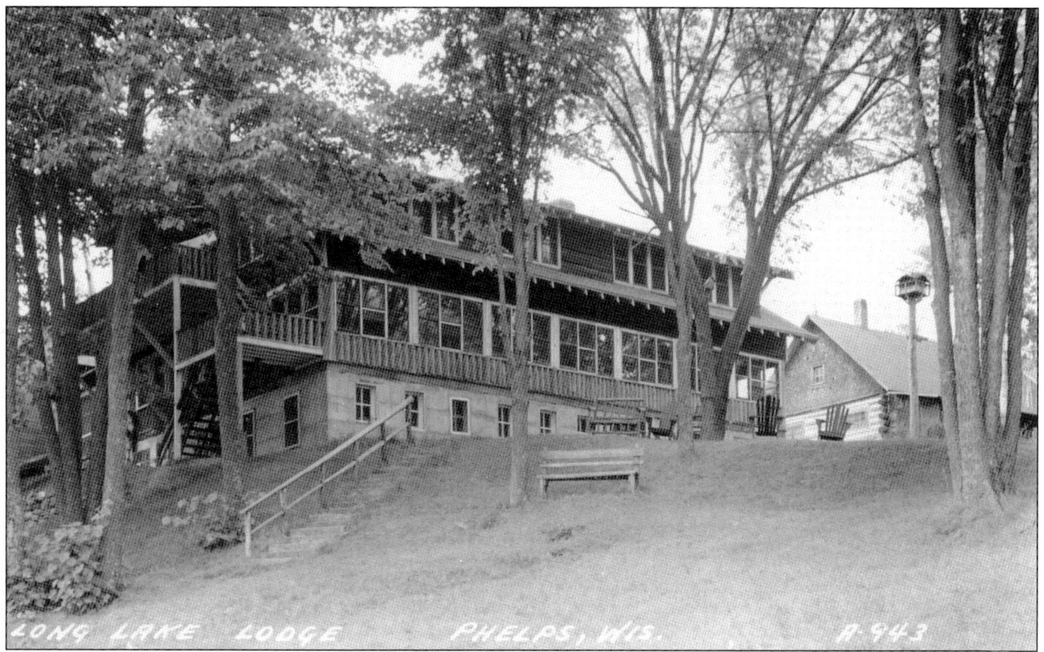

One of the earliest resorts in this area, the Long Lake Lodge continued to prosper for 75 years. Harvey Hazen eventually took over the operation from his father and later passed it down to his daughter Sunny Fondris. On the second floor, the enclosed veranda can be seen overlooking the lake. Hazen's Inn is now a private residence.

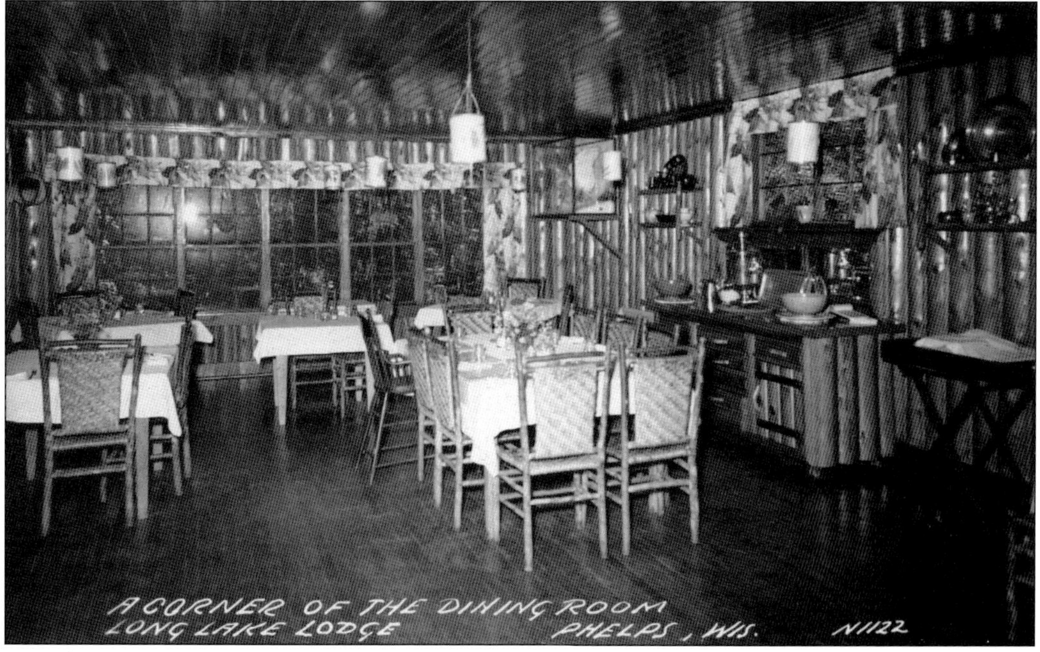

Seen here is a corner of the large dining room at the Long Lake Lodge. The Long Lake Lodge was completed in 1901 and even began producing much of its own food, including vegetables and even maple syrup. Harriet Hazen, the wife of Charles, ran the kitchen at the resort.

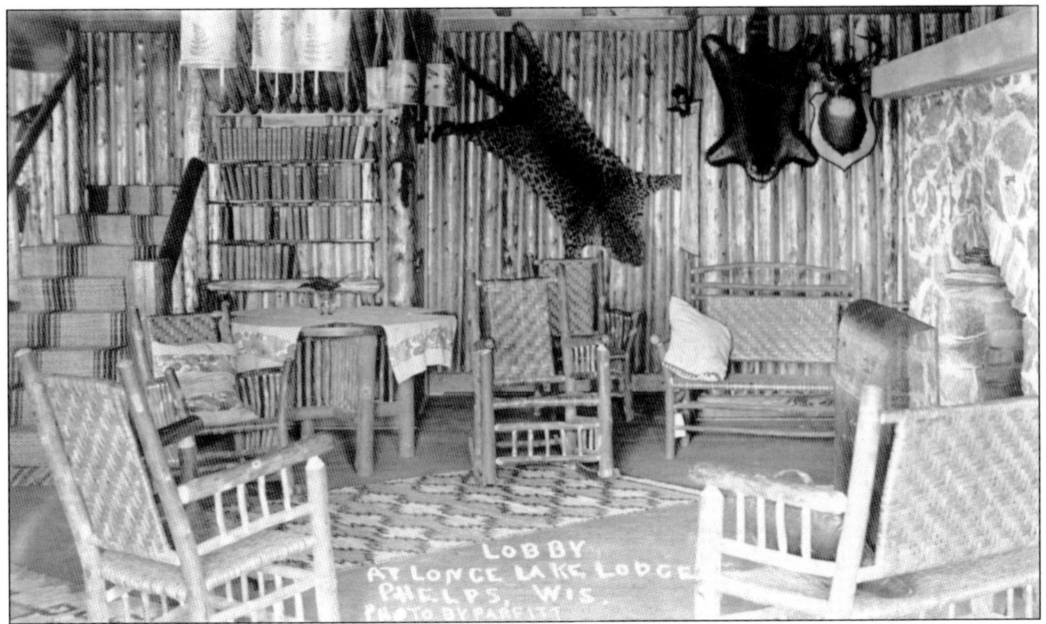

Rustic furniture, wall mounts, and a bookshelf adorn the lobby at the Hazen's Inn. The outside was constructed of tamarack logs. By 1920, the lodge grew to 10,000 square feet, providing all the modern amenities. There was a complete kitchen and 12 bedrooms.

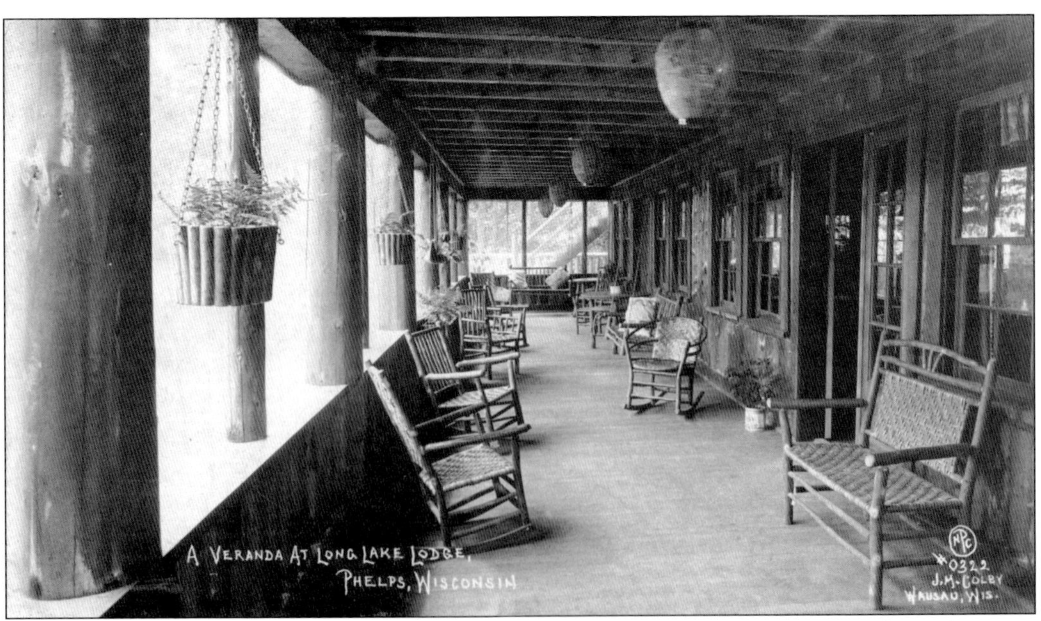

Sitting here would provide a beautiful view of Long Lake in 1925 from the veranda at the Long Lake Lodge. The resort was one of the first in the area to have electricity, which was from a 15-horsepower-engine generator.

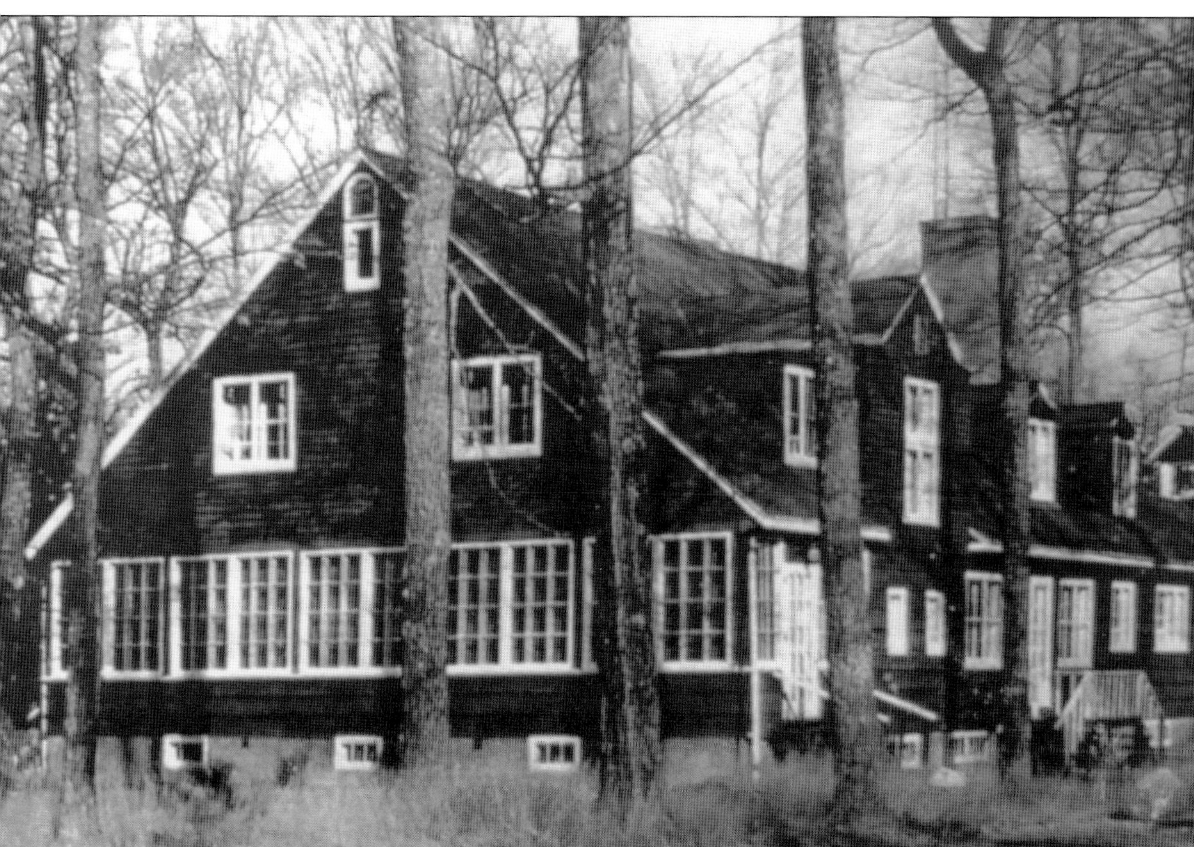

The main house, also referred to as the "Big House," at the old Frankenthal Estate in Phelps was built by Chicagoan Dr. Lester E. Frankenthal Sr. in 1920. Frankenthal was born in 1864 and lived to the age of 80. He named the estate, which, at one time, was about 950 acres, Poh-Wah-Gom, which means "Place Dreamed Of" in the Canadian Cree Indian language. His estate spanned over Long Lake and part of Big Sand. The estate's original boathouse was on Long Lake until it burned down in 1955. Generations still have some smaller holdings leftover from the original estate, and they continue to enjoy the area of the Northwoods. (Courtesy of Steve McMillan.)

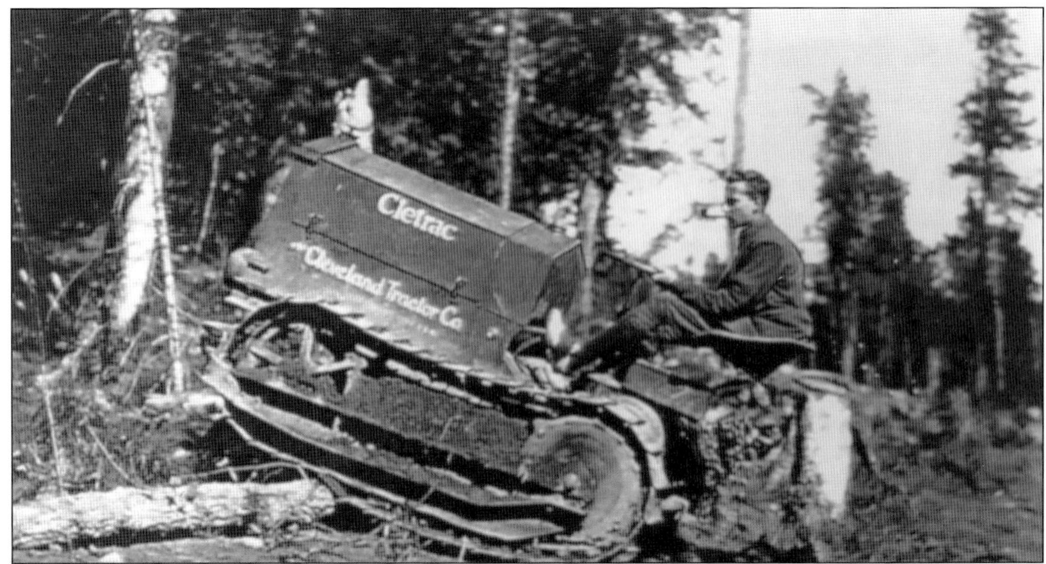

Lester E. Frankenthal Jr. (pictured here) met and would eventually marry Katherine Anderson. Katherine Anderson's parents, Bishop Charles Palmerston Anderson and his wife, Janet, had a cabin near Haven's Resort on Long Lake. He had purchased the land for $50 an acre and built a cabin in 1902 under the condition that his family takes their dinner at the lodge on the resort. Even though both are from Chicago, Lester and Katherine met on Long Lake in Phelps. They were married to each other for their entire lives. (Courtesy of Steve McMillan.)

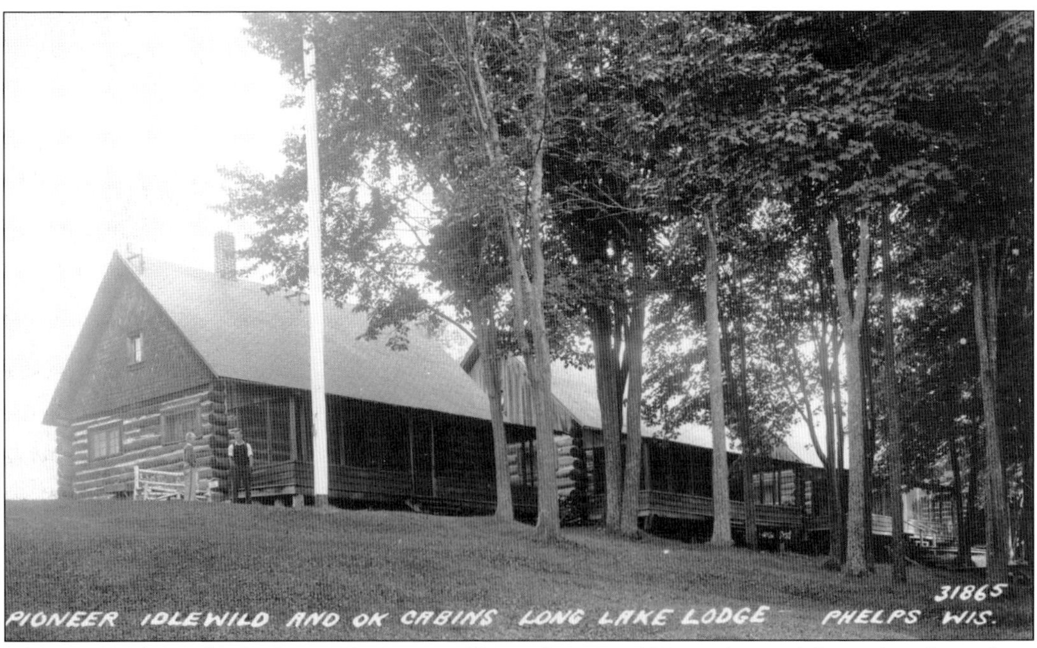

The Long Lake Lodge had several cottages. Shown here in 1937 are three of the earliest log cabins with fireplaces. They were named the Pioneer, Idlewild, and OK cabins.

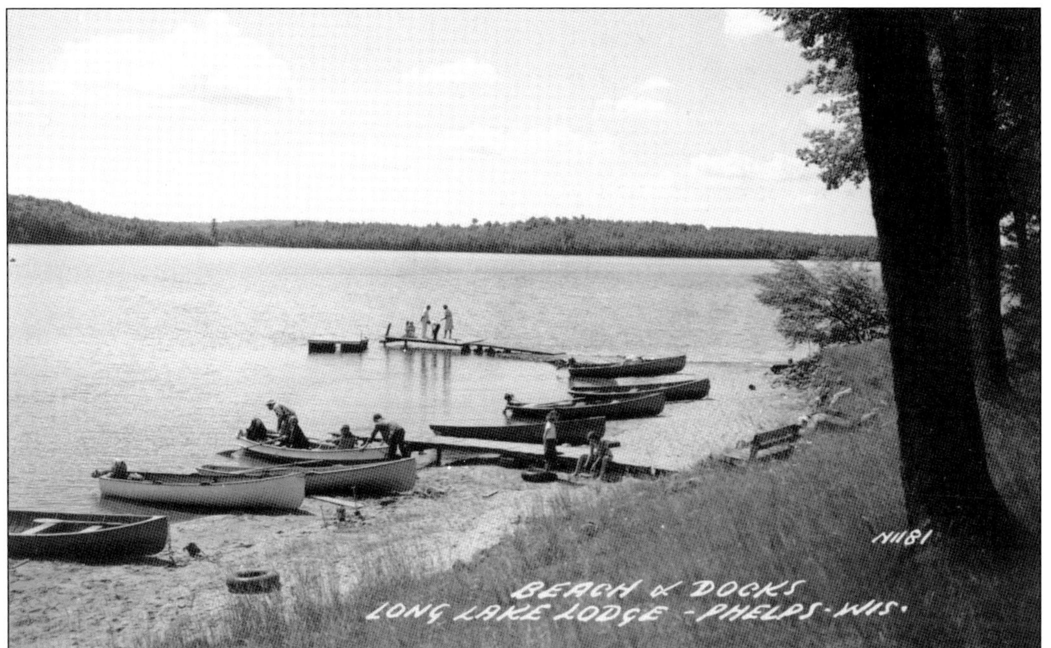

Pushing a boat off the shore, a party is seen heading out on the lake to enjoy a little fishing. To the right of the tall pine on the left in the background is the entrance of the thoroughfare creek connecting Long Lake with Big Sand Lake. This photograph was taken in 1951.

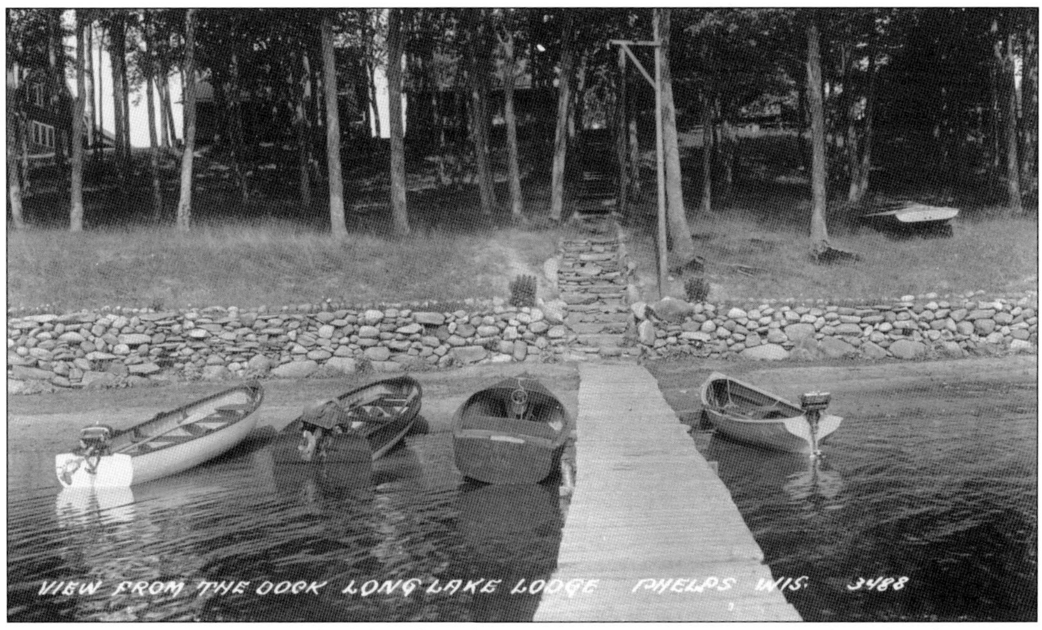

Waiting to be taken out on the lake, these boats, some with motors attached, are lined up along the shore. Note the fieldstone seawall and staircase going down to the lake. Three cabins and a small portion of the lodge can be seen in the background.

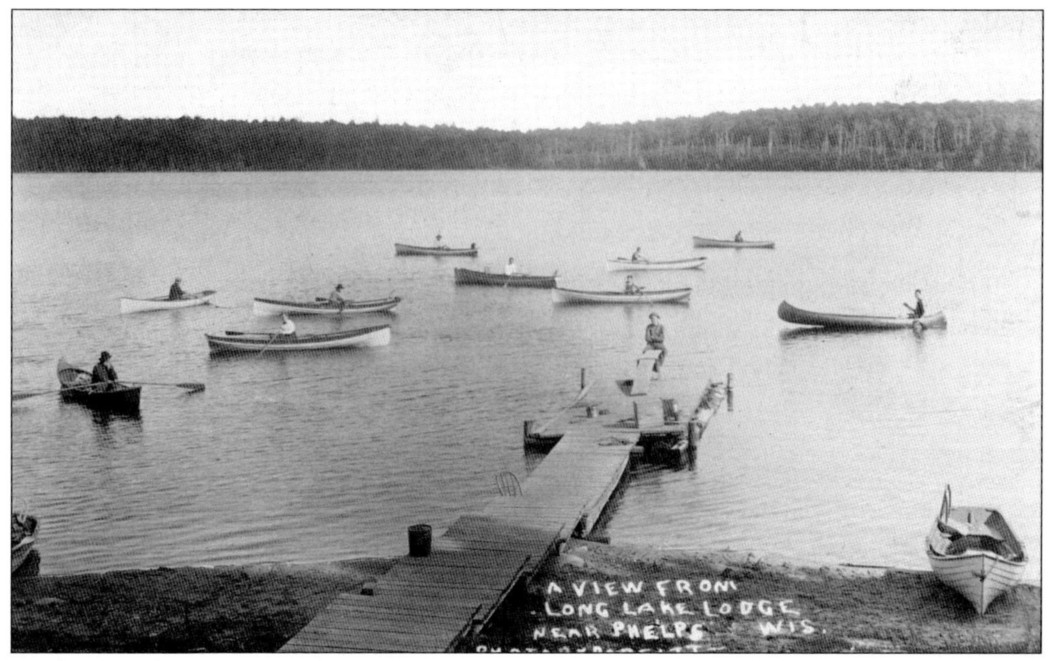

Rowboats and one canoe gather past Hazen's pier. The date of this postcard is marked 1917.

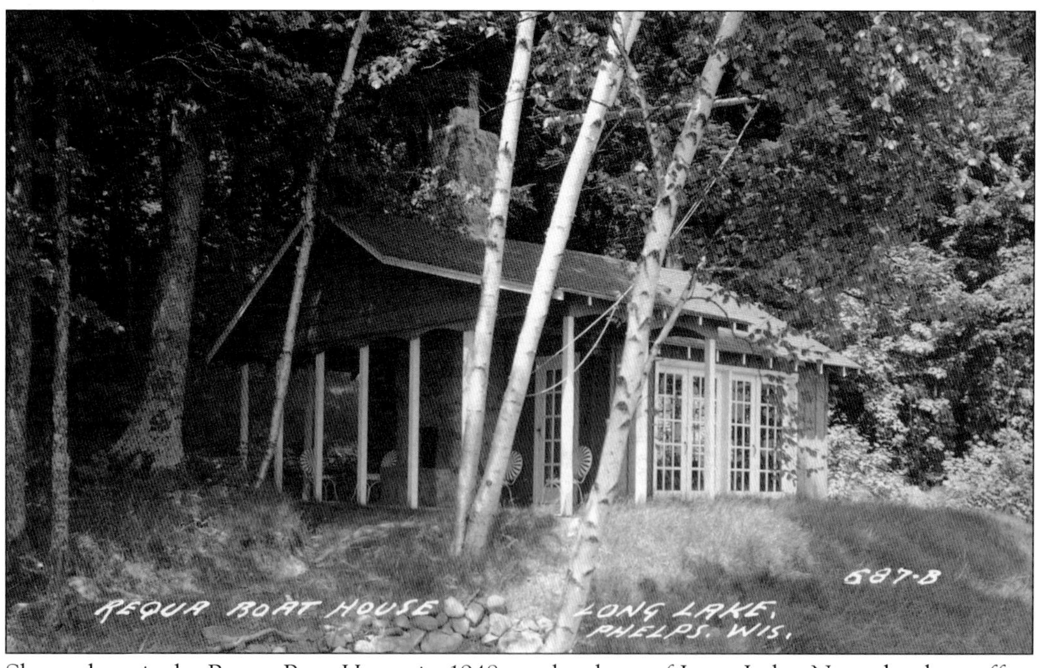

Shown here is the Requa Boat House in 1948 on the shore of Long Lake. Note the drop-off to the lake.

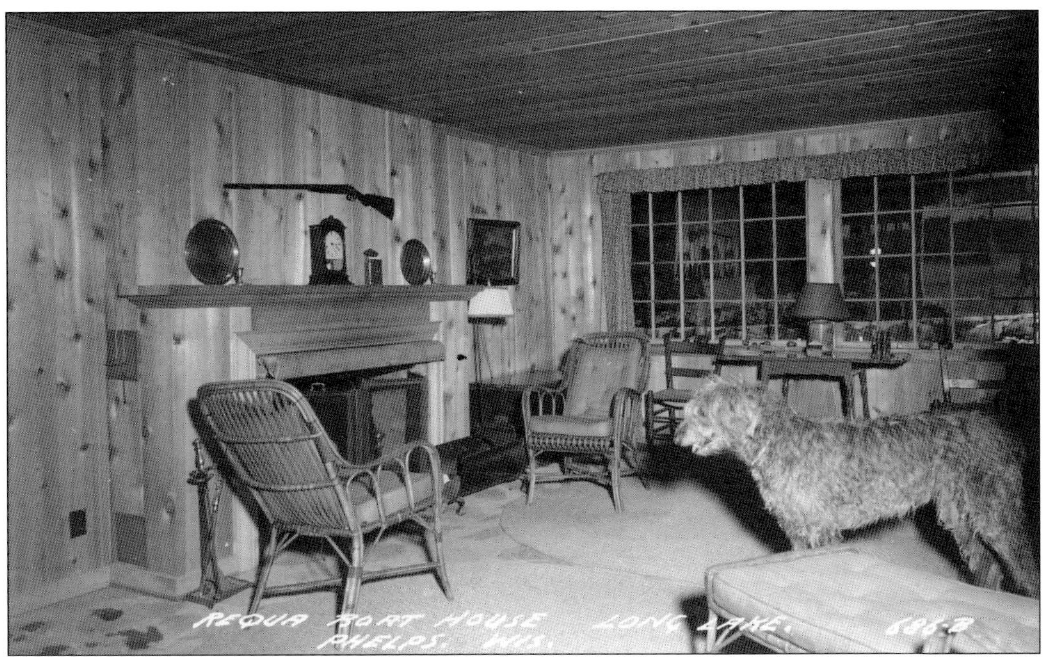

This view of the interior of the Requa Boat House was taken about 1948. Knotty pine, for the rustic look, was typically used to cover interior walls and ceilings in cabins.

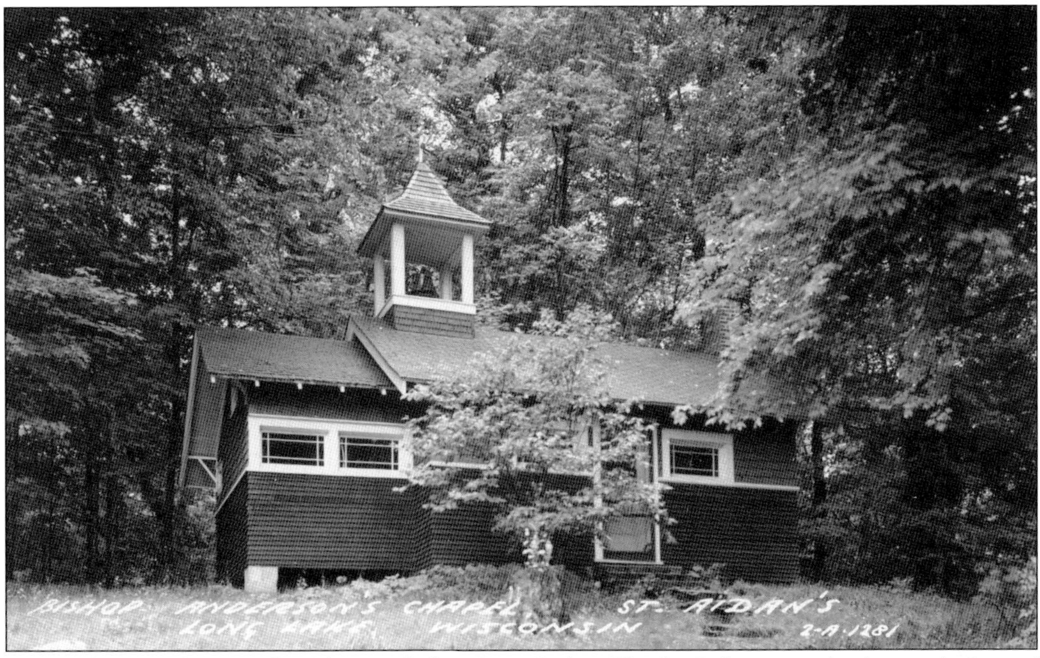

The Bishop Anderson Chapel is nestled on Long Lake. Charles Palmerston Anderson, bishop of Chicago, became the presiding bishop of the Episcopal Church of America in 1929. He used this cabin for his studies. The bell tower shown here was added in later years.

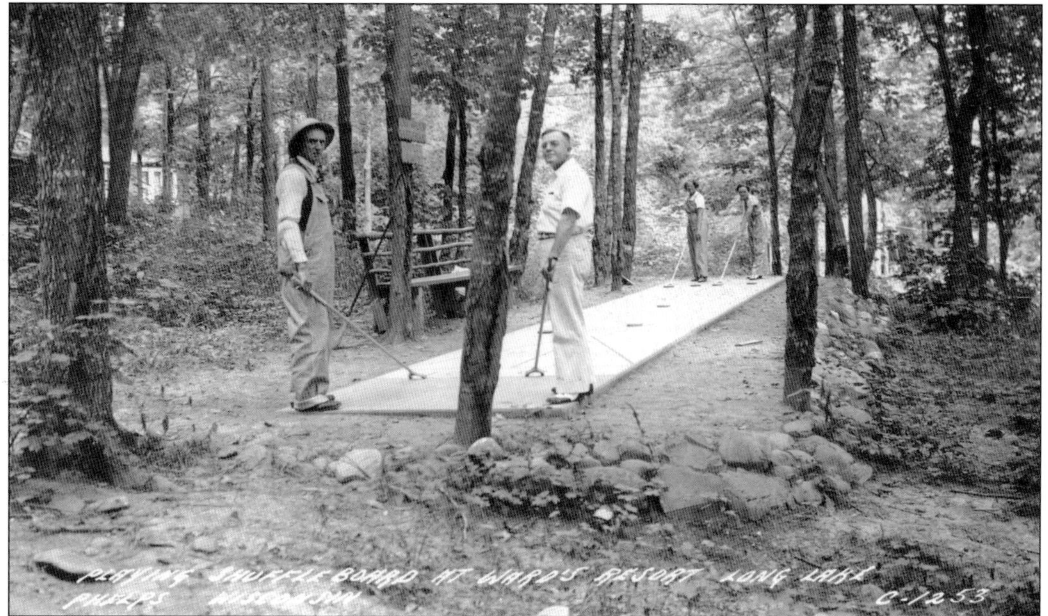

Four men are seen at Ward's Resort on Long Lake playing shuffleboard. Leveling the board over the irregular train would have been some serious manual labor. Note that the board is raised and leveled with sand and fieldstones.

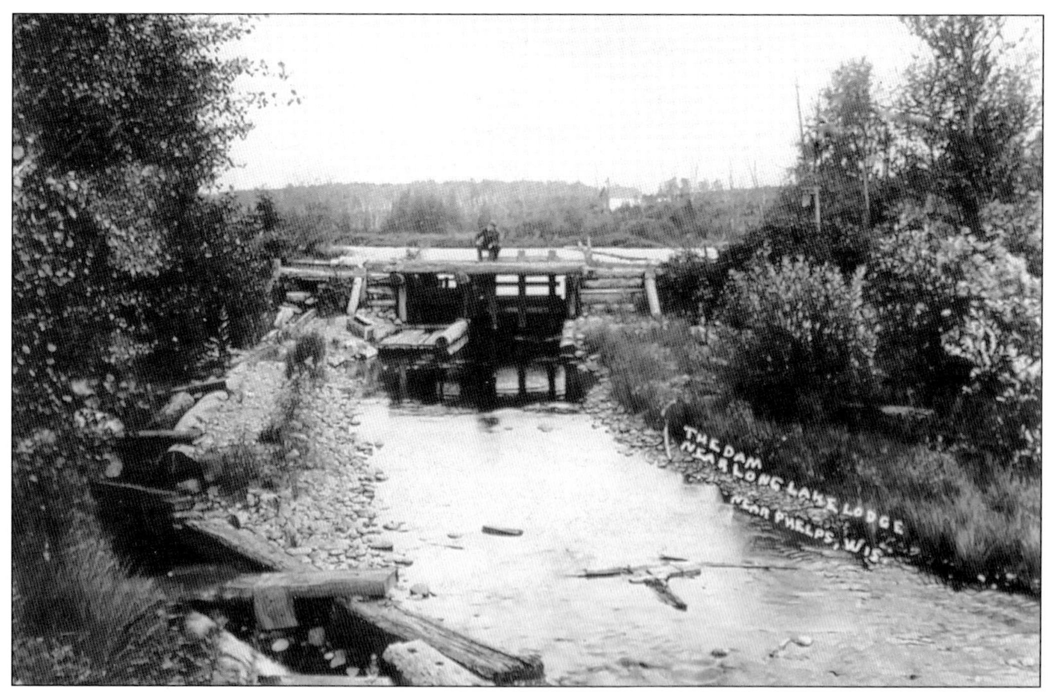

A man is sitting on an early log dam located on the south end of Long Lake, which regulates the water flow of the Deerskin River. The Deerskin River, as well as the headwaters of the Wisconsin River, start in Phelps.

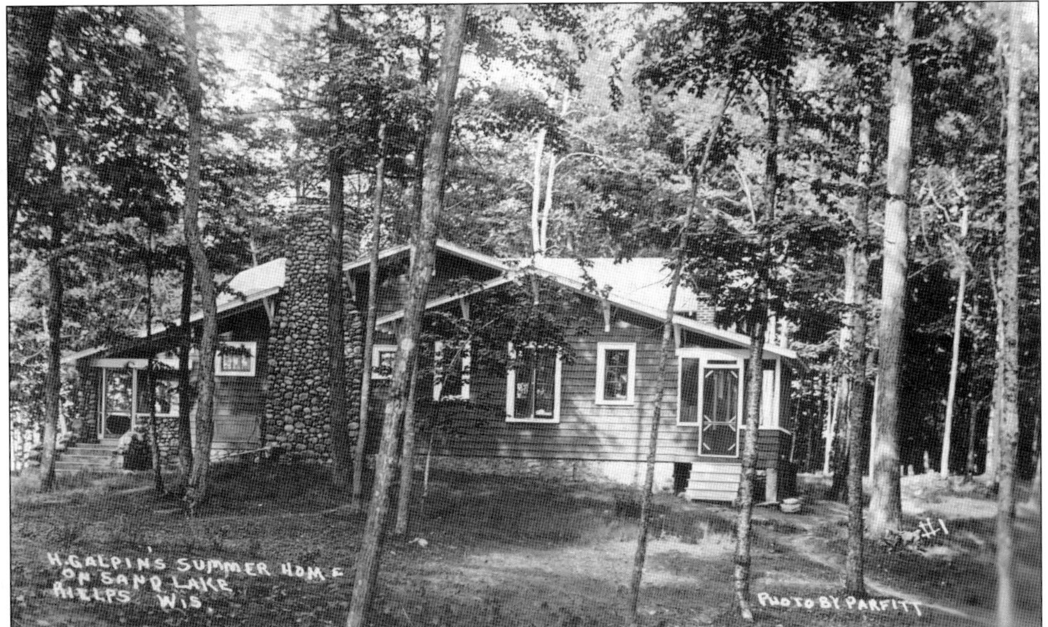

Homer and Hilda Galpin purchased 700 acres on the south shore of Big Sand Lake in 1917 and named it Fort Eagle. The house shown here was built in 1919 and transformed in a dramatic 1927 remodeling to the colonial mansion that is seen today.

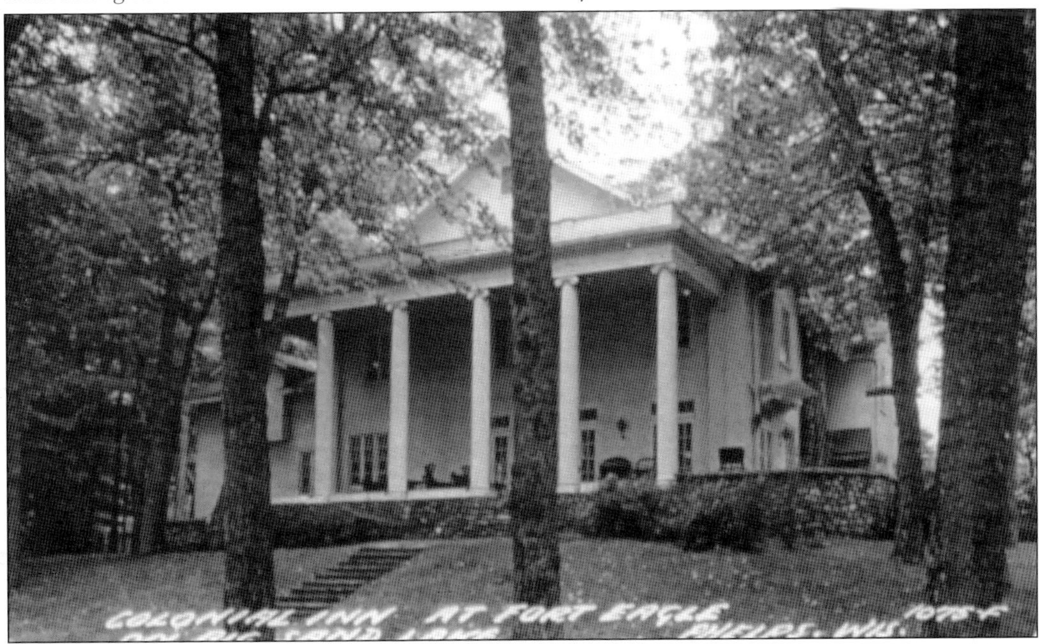

Fort Eagle was the residence of Homer Galpin, chairman of the Cook County Republican Committee under Republican mayor "Big Bill" Thompson. Homer Galpin built this three-story Victorian mansion in 1927–1928 with 17 rooms, including three fireplaces. The property included a three-stall boathouse, a six-car garage, a caretaker's house, two log cabins, and several other small buildings. Fort Eagle is a private residence and is listed under the National Register of Historical Places.

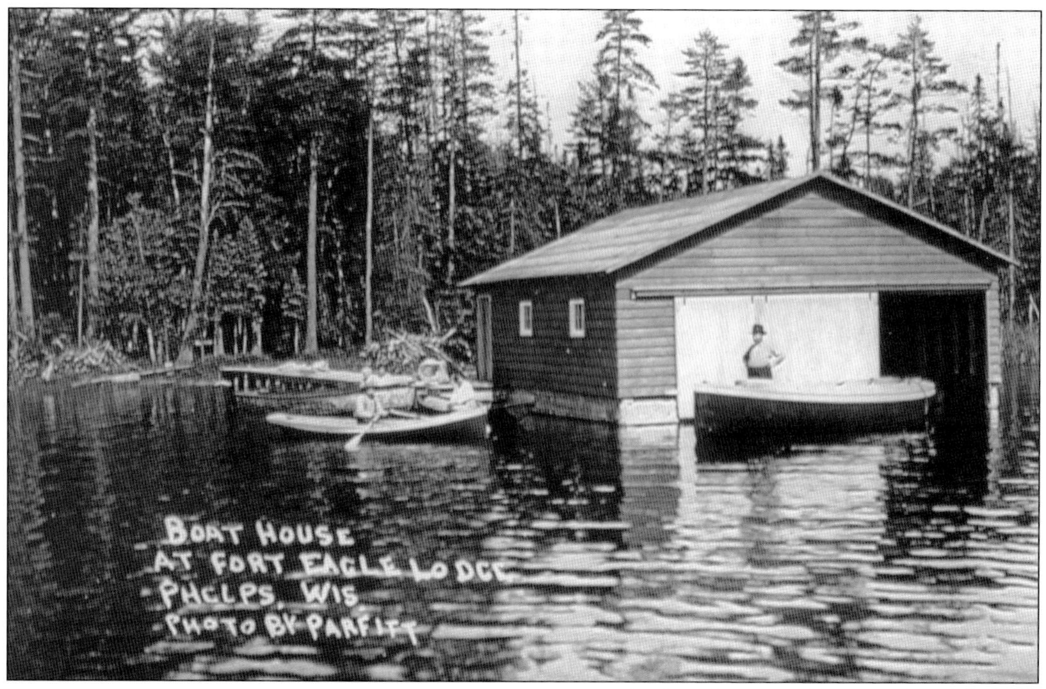

The boathouse at Fort Eagle was constructed about the time the first house was erected. Located in the bay, this boathouse was replaced with an even larger three-stall boathouse when the mansion was built. Hilda Galpin, in the white dress, can be seen in the boat behind the man in the rowboat. Standing in front of the boathouse is Homer Galpin. He was an avid boater, frequently arriving via the water in his Hacker Craft to the Big Sand Lake Club. (Courtesy of Anne Grogan.)

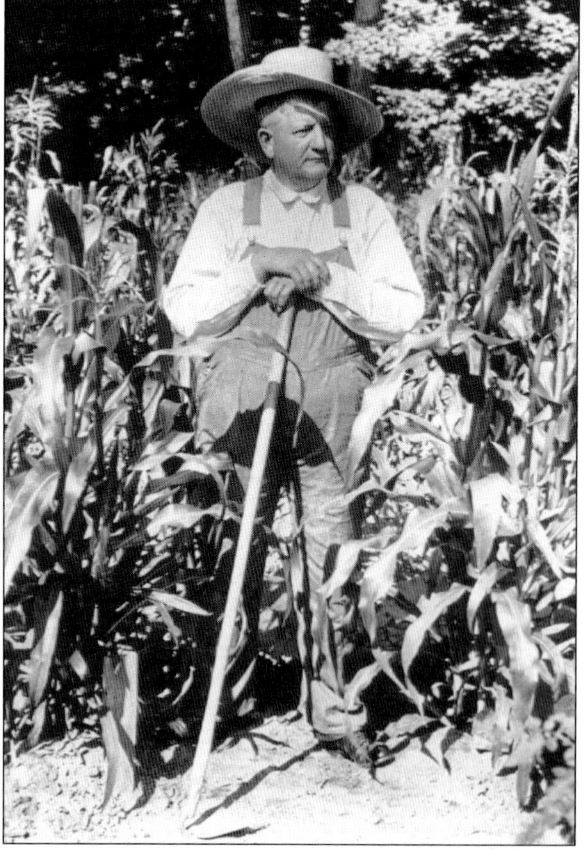

Gardening was one of Homer Galpin's hobbies. Attached to the caretaker's house was a greenhouse with stepping-stones leading south to the garden. He is seen here in a maze of corn.

Four

Conover's Station and Beyond

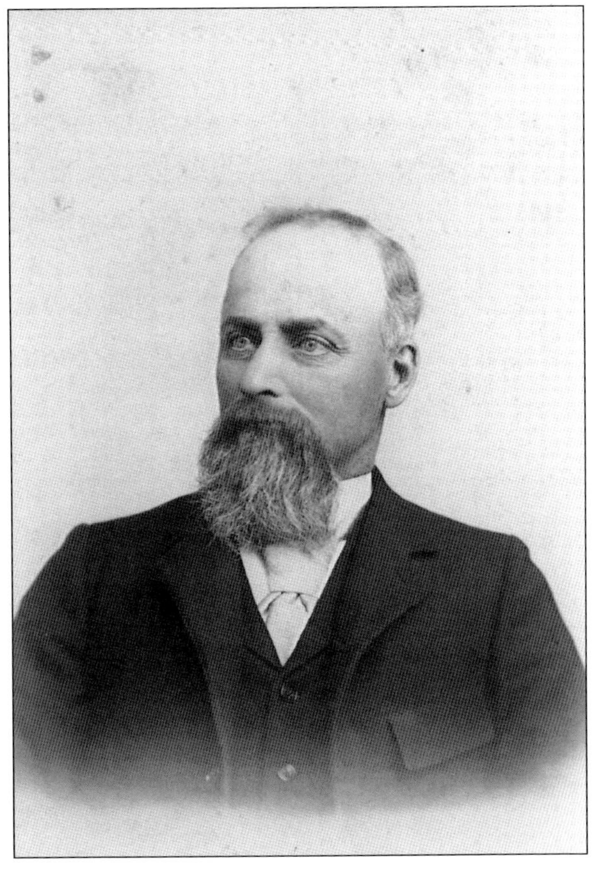

The man for whom this town is named is Seth H. Conover, who originated from Plymouth, Wisconsin. A prominent cheese buyer, he worked in his younger days as a cheese maker in his father's cheese factory. His father, Hiram Conover, was born in 1821 in New York. Seth was born in 1852 and had four children. Fishing and hunting brought Seth to the wilds of northern Wisconsin. He died in 1932. (Courtesy of Jim Hedberg.)

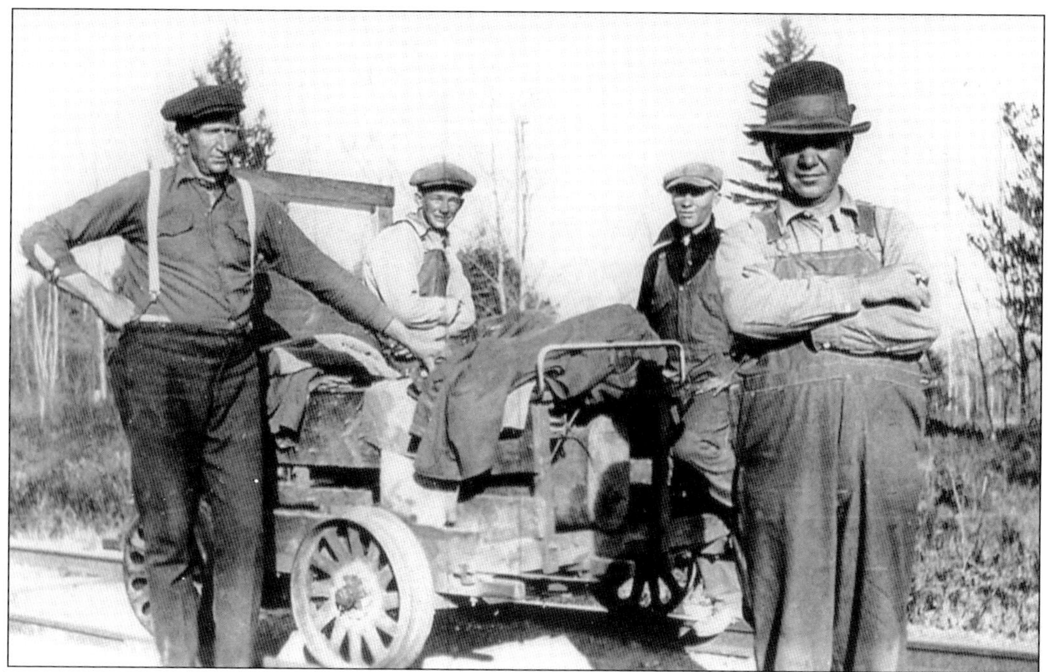

Many of the early settlers to the area worked for the railroad. Seth Conover's fishing hobby is what drew him to ride the logging train to the same spot over several trips. The railroad men began referring to it as "Conover's station" and eventually erected a station in that location. The person on this tracked vehicle is Martin Pearson, who worked for the Chicago & North Western Railway all of his life. (Courtesy of Jim Hedberg.)

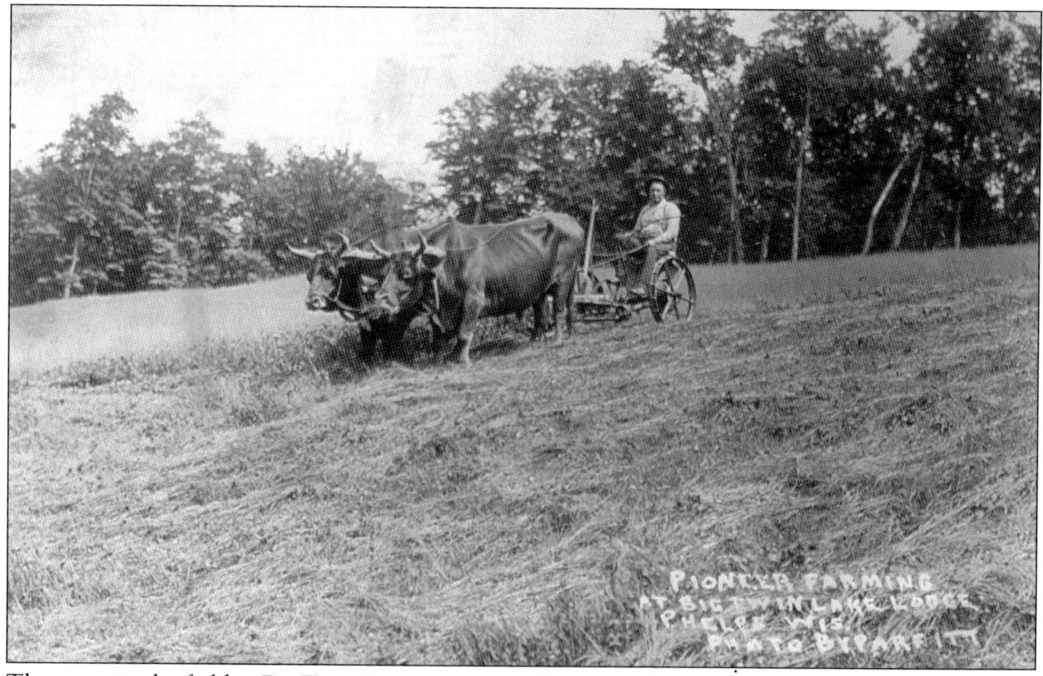

The team in the field at Big Twin Resort is pictured cutting the crop for animal feed. Many of the area resorts raised much of the meat and poultry served to the guests. (Courtesy of Jim Hedberg.)

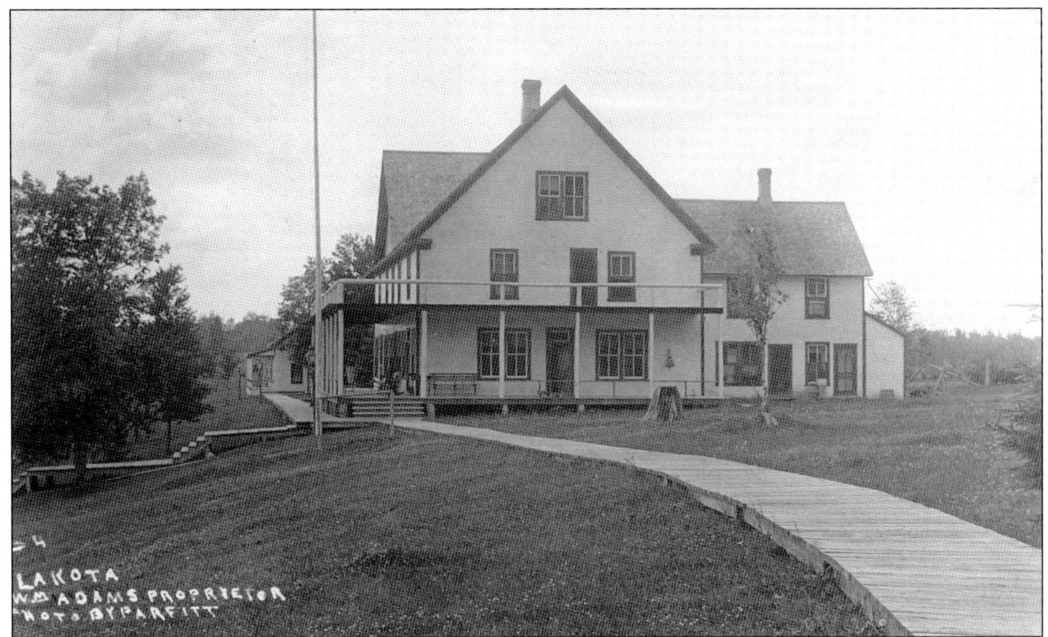

Records from the Office of Register of Deeds show that 73 acres of land were deeded to Seth Conover on April 24, 1891. This was the region on Big Twin Lake he had frequently fished. He then started the Twin Lakes Fishing Club there. Seth owned it for less than a year before it was sold to Harvey L. Goodall. It was renamed Lakota Resort, as shown in this 1918 postcard.

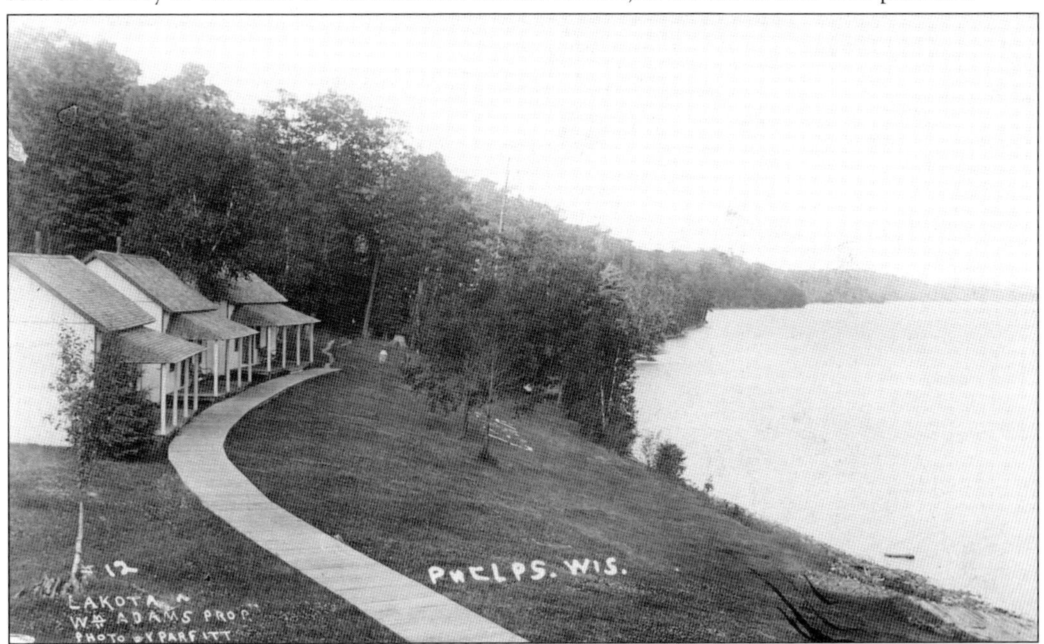

The original Lakota Lodge was made of logs, as were the cabins. Finished in August 1893, the lodge burned down in September of the same year. As a result, Harvey Goodall, the owner at the time, sold the property in 1895 to Dan Sargeant. Sargeant rebuilt and had a prosperous business. The cabins shown here sat on the bluff contoured from the lake with a spectacular view of Big Twin Lake.

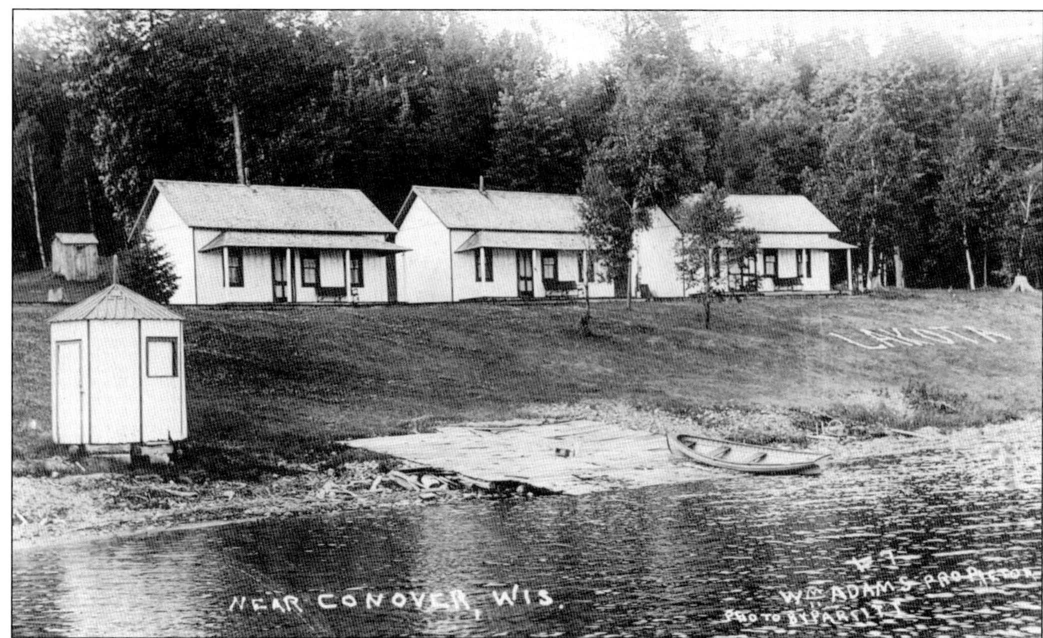

The boat slip on the lake got a lot of use as the business flourished after William Adams purchased the Lakota Resort in 1903. Adams already owned the adjacent Adams Resort and purchased the adjacent Sanborn Resort as well. The Lakota resort is shown here in 1920. Combined with the other two resorts, there was a lodge and 15 cabins. Note the storage building and the outhouse in the background.

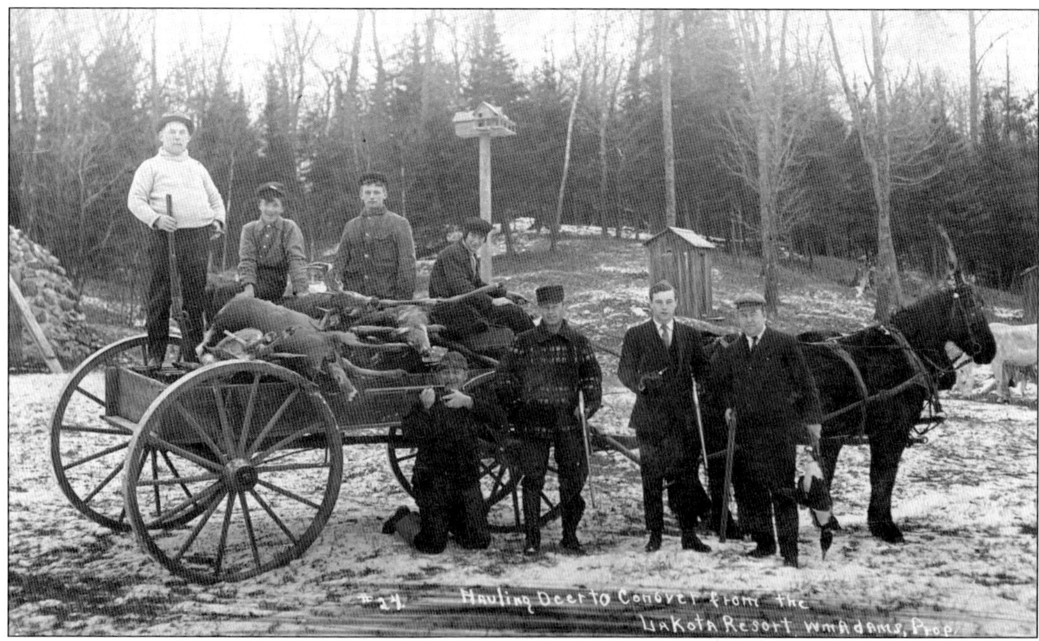

Hunters are shown here with a wagon loaded with the day's kill of whitetail deer as they are getting ready to transport them to Conover. Donkeys were packed with grub and supplies for extended hunting trips to Pioneer, Long, and Big Sand Lake by Dan Sargeant, owner of the Lakota Resort.

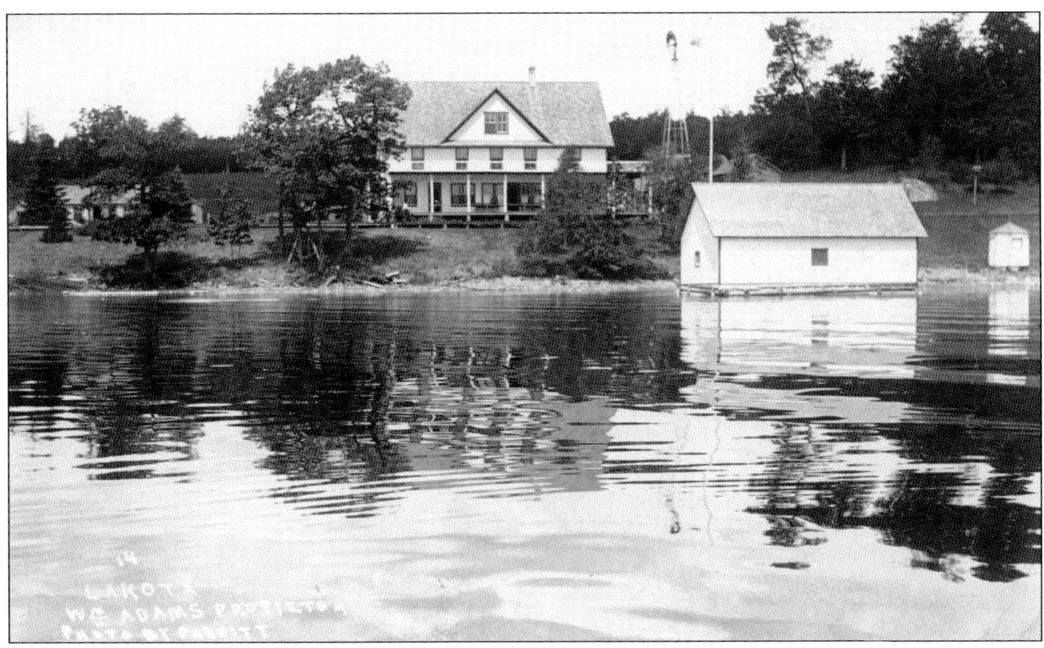

In the 1920s, William Adams constructed a boathouse on the lake. The structure was moved to downtown Conover in later years and sits today on private property once owned by the Adams family near the motel on Adams Road. This photograph shows the Lakota Resort in 1922 with William Adams.

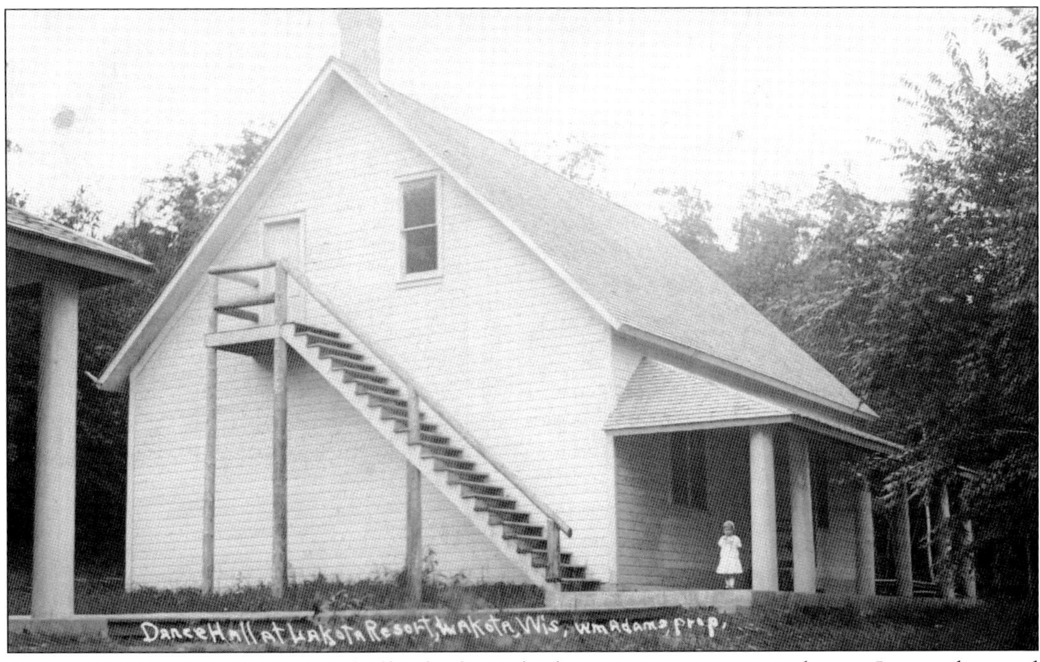

The Lakota Resort had a dance hall, which made the vacationers more at home. It was also used for other entertainment, such as card playing and just hanging out on rainy days.

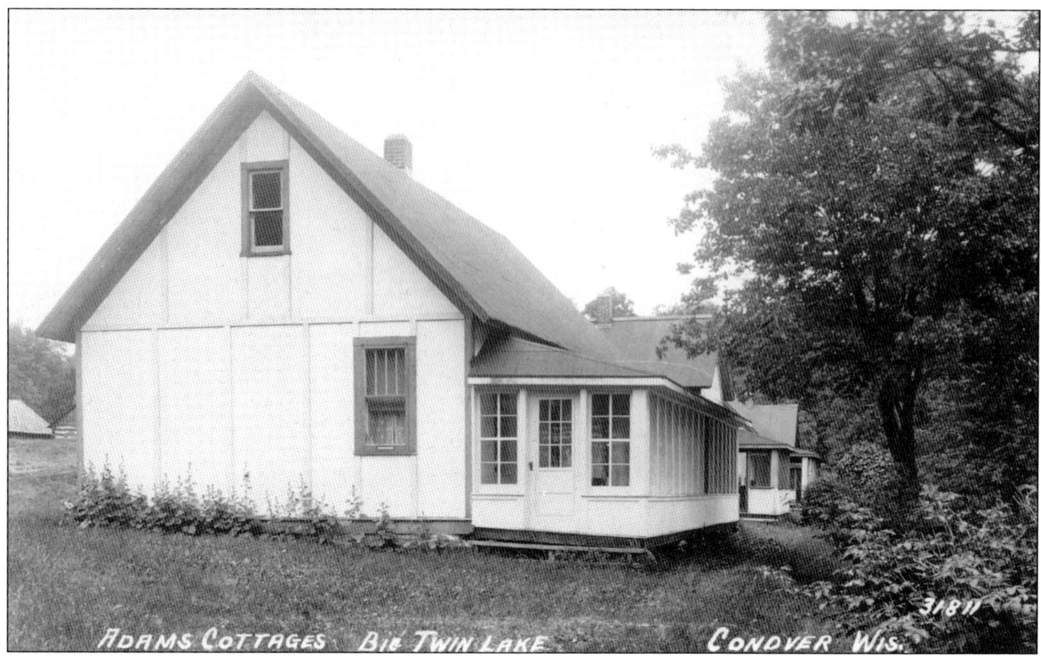

The log cottages were later improved as more vacationers came via the railroad and some by automobiles from Chicago and beyond. The Lakota Resort covered 248 acres, including a half-mile of lake privileges.

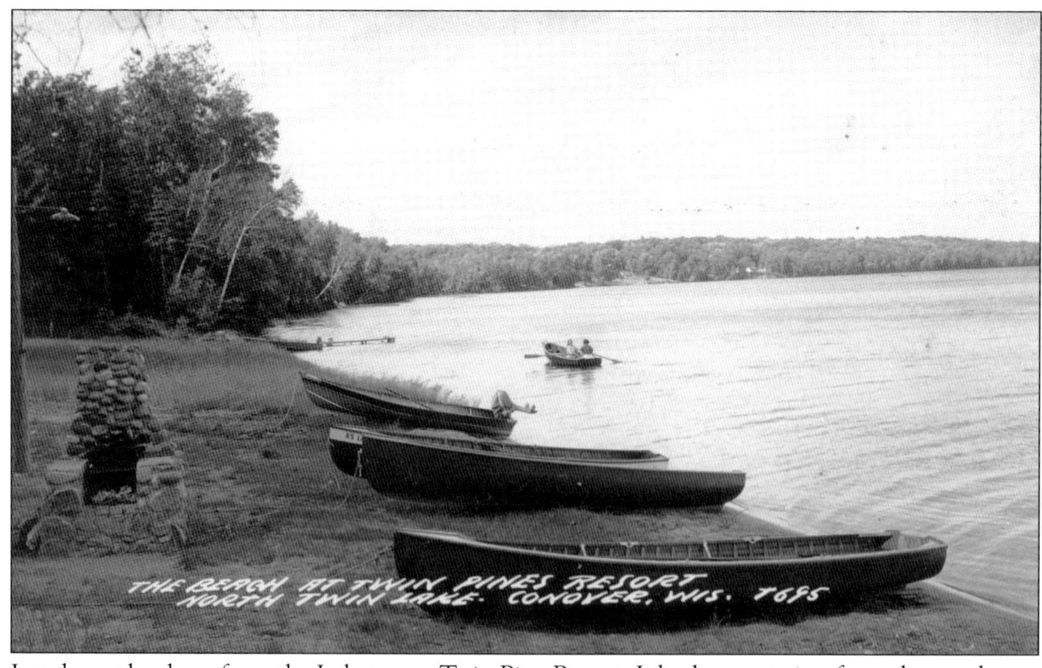

Just down the shore from the Lakota was Twin Pine Resort. It had a great view from the northwest end of the Big Twin Lake to the mill in Hackley (now Phelps).

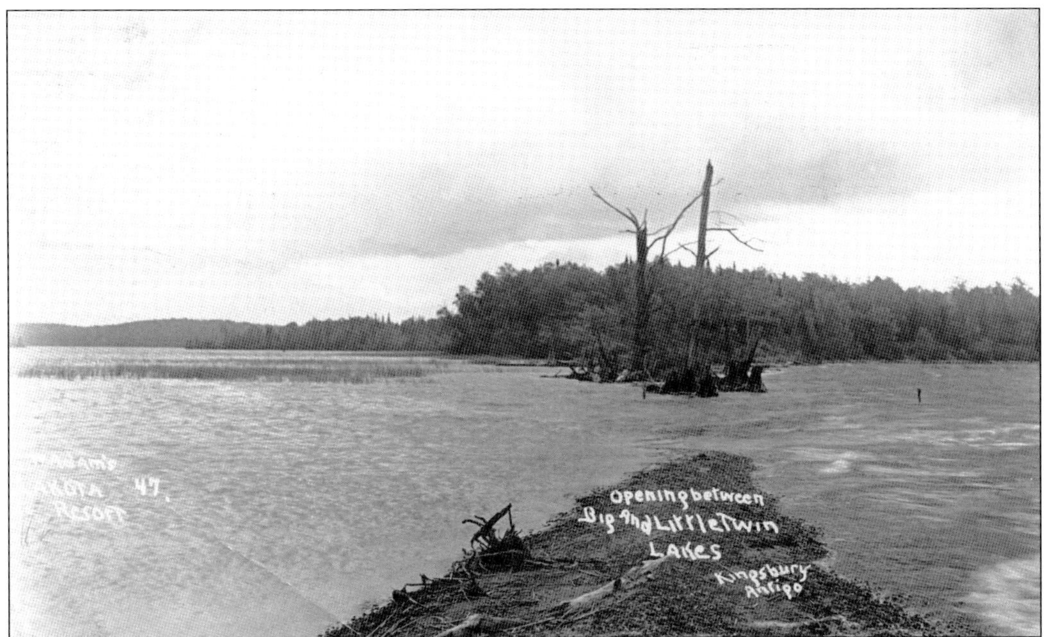

The narrow and shallow connection is seen here in 1920. This narrow channel connects Big and Little Twin Lake. At a low level, care must be taken to cross here with an outboard or an electric motor, and rowing is advised.

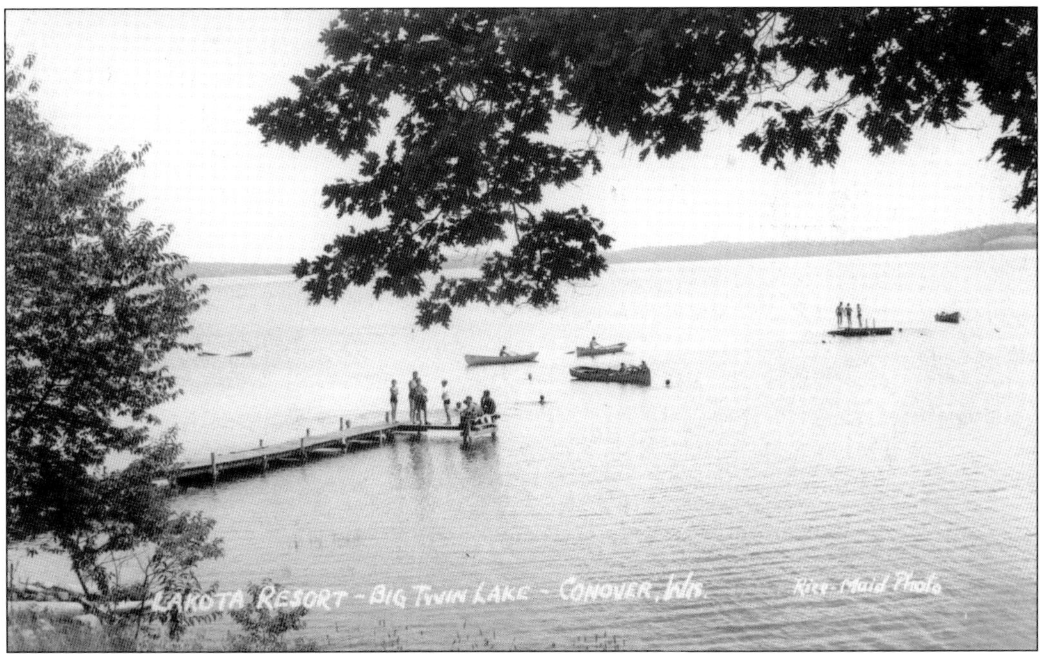

The Lakota Resort became a family destination where everyone enjoyed being in or on the water. The largest muskellunge, or "muskie," landed with Al Adams as a guide was a 50-pounder. The bait was a leaf of red cabbage on a silver spoon. The guiding fee was $1.25.

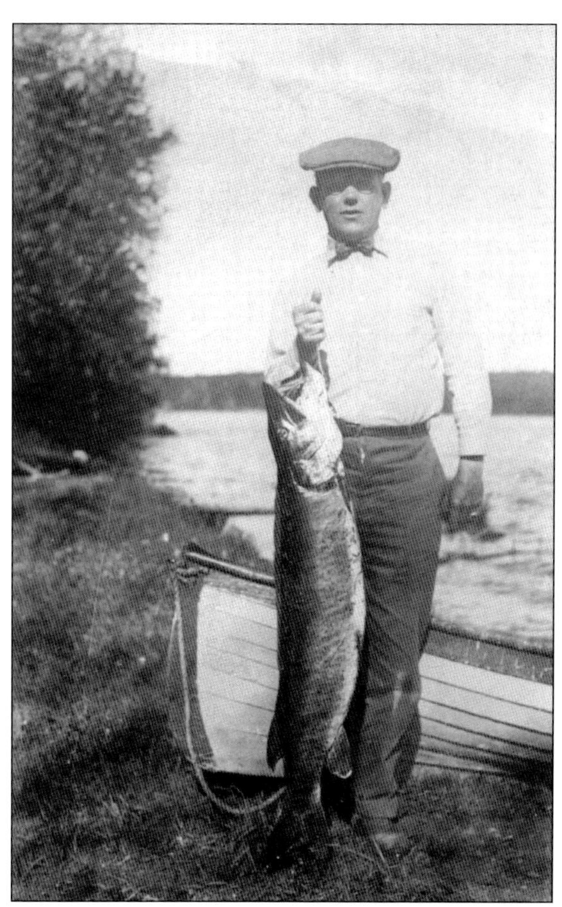

The great fishing is what drew Seth Conover and others to this area with a bountiful amount of lakes. This postcard, written by John A. in 1924, relayed the details of his 80-minute struggle with this muskie out of Lake Buckatabon in Conover. He eventually landed it, weighing in at 35.5 pounds and measuring 42 inches. The muskellunge is the largest member of the pike family, Esocidae. The origin of the name derives from the Ojibwa words *maashkinoozhe*, meaning "ugly pike."

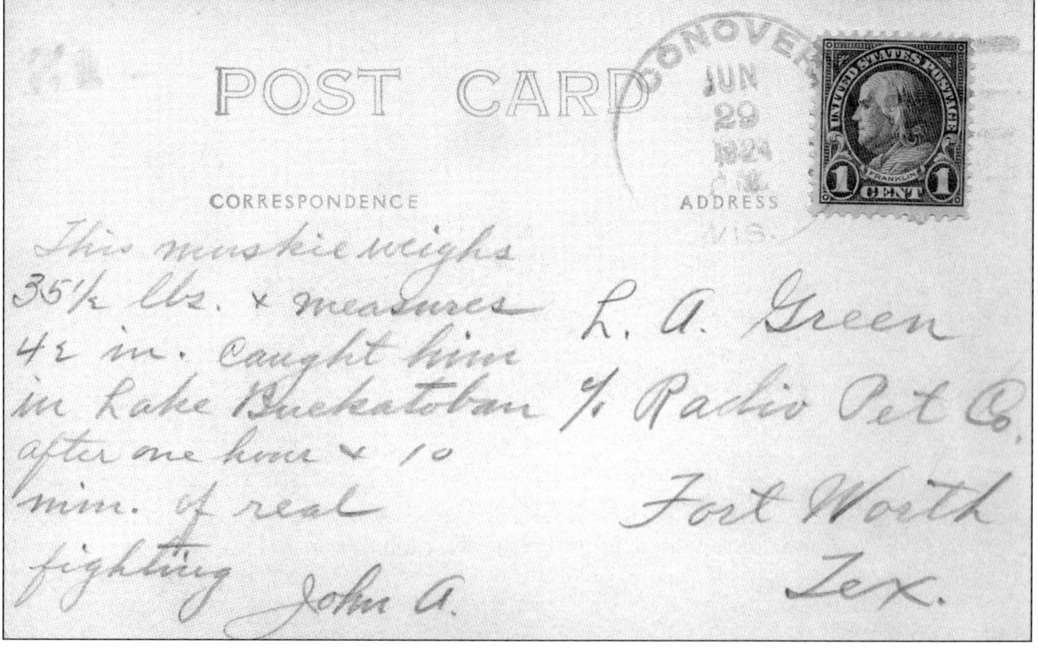

POST CARD

CONOVER JUN 29 1924 WIS.

UNITED STATES POSTAGE FRANKLIN 1 CENT 1

CORRESPONDENCE

This muskie weighs 35½ lbs. x measures 42 in. Caught him in Lake Buckatoban after one hour x 10 min. of real fighting John A.

ADDRESS

L. A. Green
% Radio Pet Co.
Fort Worth
Tex.

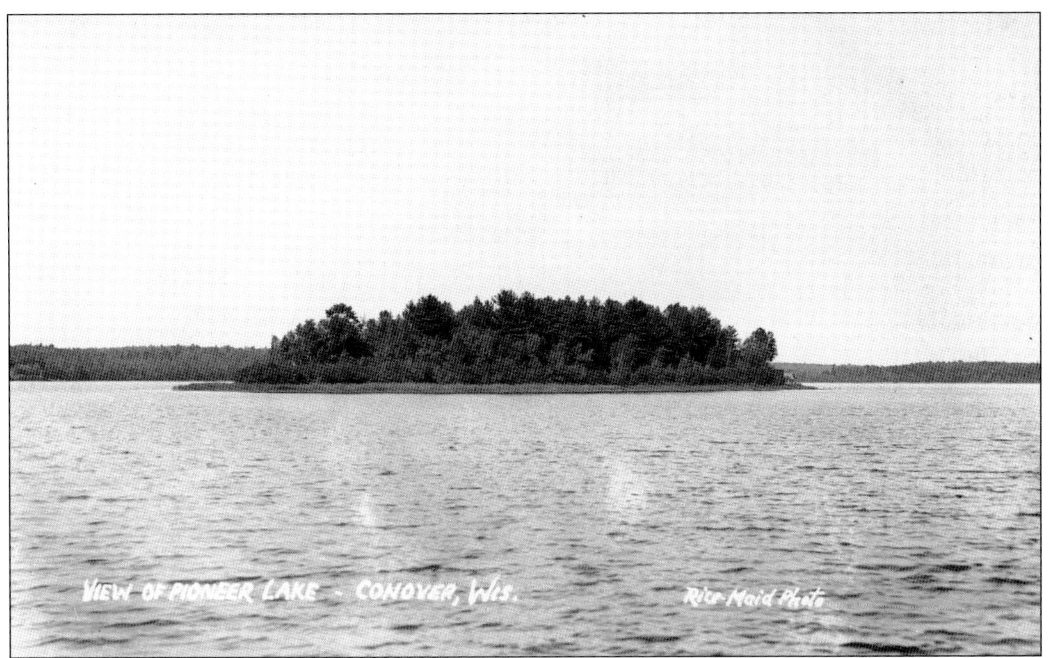

Pioneer Lake was another body of water that the Twin River flows into. It too became a popular lake for fishing and other recreation. William Adams lived on the island on Pioneer Lake when Teddy Roosevelt was president. The island is now privately owned, but no one occupies it any longer.

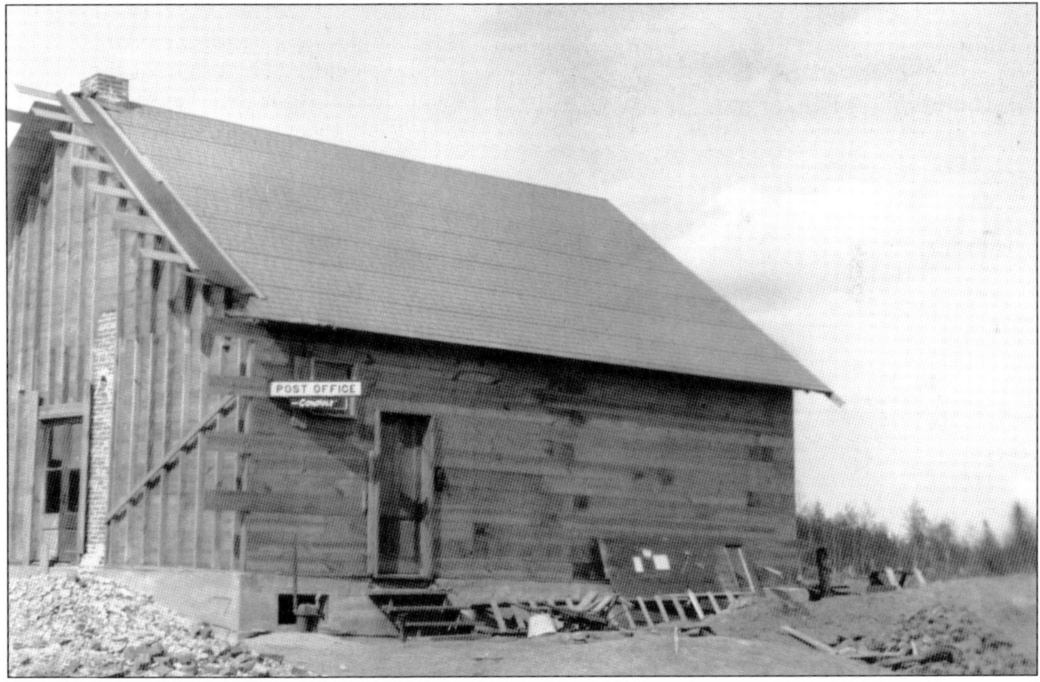

The first post office was in the home of postmaster C. Blohm from 1904 to 1906. After several other locations over the years, George Dobbs built a new post office, shown here, next to his general store. Shortly thereafter, in 1921, Dobbs was appointed postmaster and remained in that position until 1932.

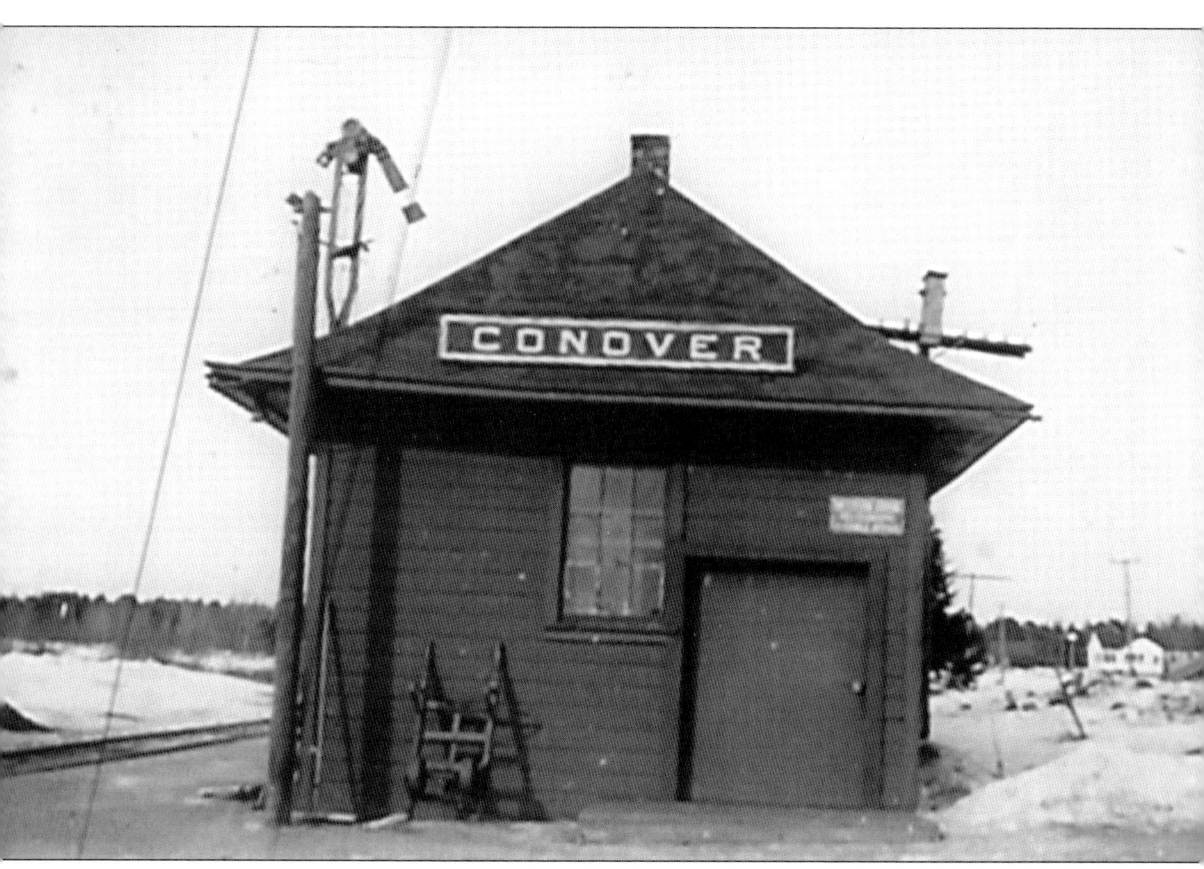

The depot of the Chicago & North Western Railway depot in Conover is pictured here in a view looking north. The old depot was the only building on the west side of Highway 45 from Rummels Road to County K. In 1960, the children from the Conover School left their classes to witness the last steam engine pull out of town. The depot remained standing for several years before it was torn down. (Courtesy of Jim Hedberg.)

Five

Finding a Retreat

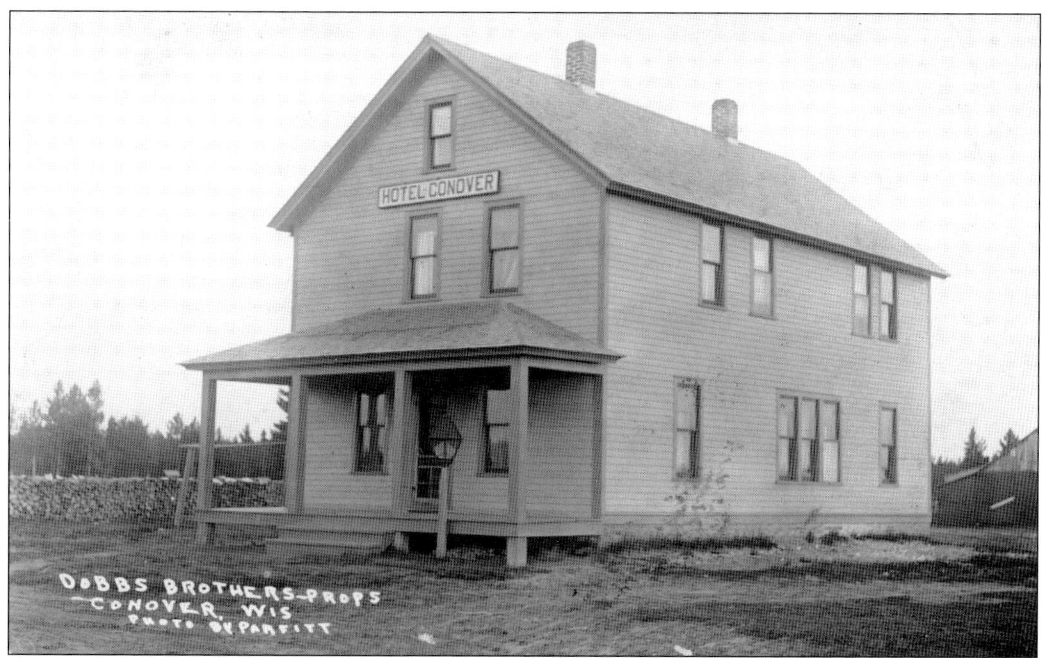

Hotel Conover was a property owned by the Dobbs Brothers. The building was relocated when the highway was improved many years ago. Today, the hotel is a group of rental units.

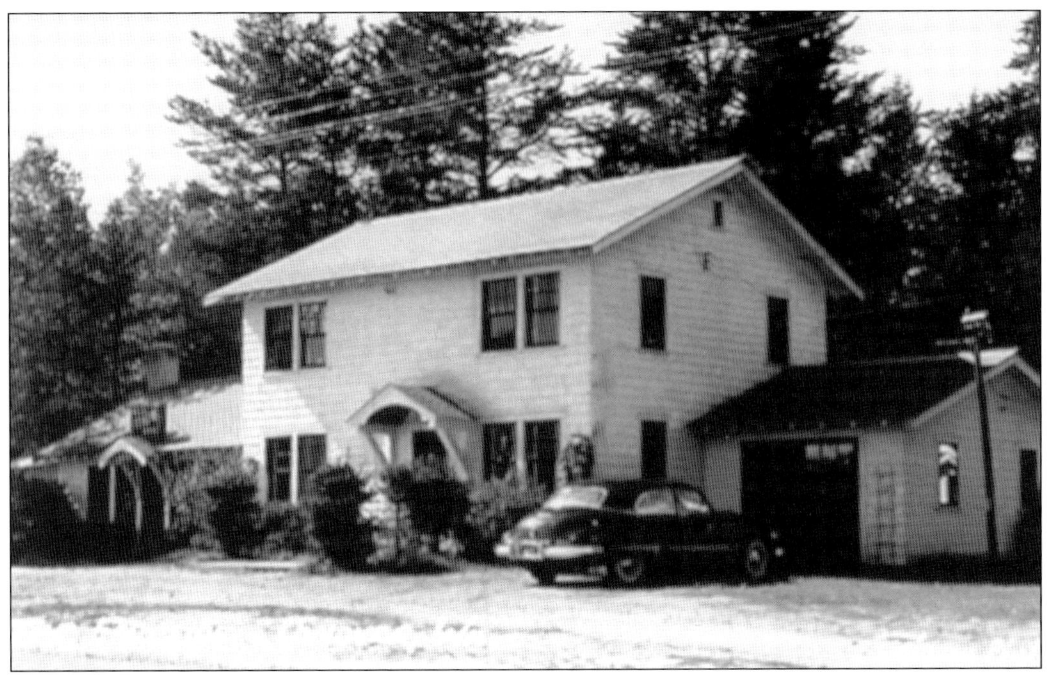

One Conover landmark, which is still in the same location, was the Fireside. To many locals today, memories of Tony and Mary Bosich will be associated with their turtle soup. Large snapping turtles taken from the area lakes were prepared by these Bohemian owners and was a great attraction. Fireside remains open today as a supper club and has been known as Lanny's Fireside since 2005. (Courtesy of Jim Hedberg.)

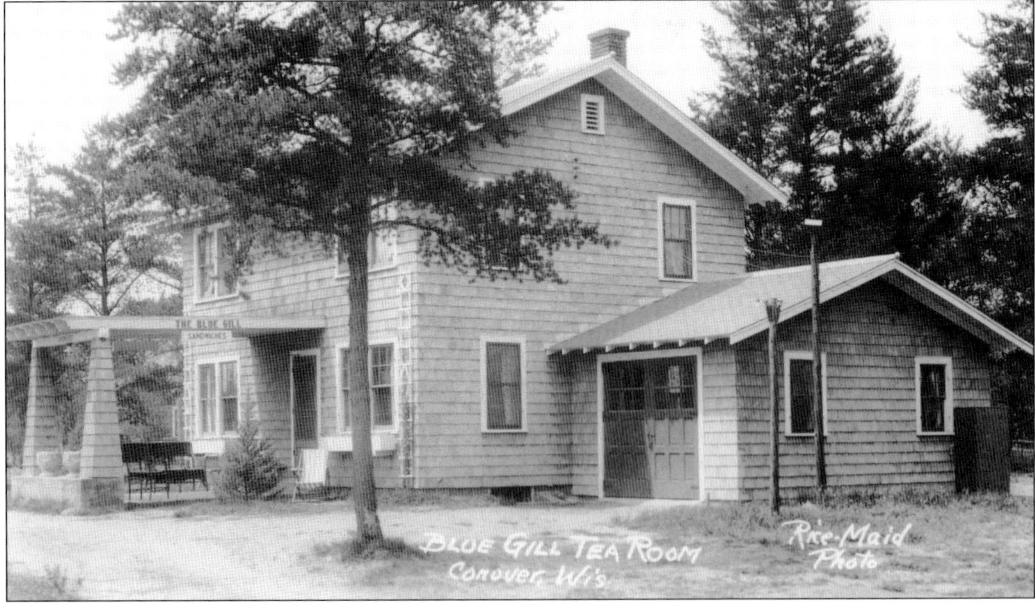

Along with the Bluegill Tea Room, as it was called, were several cabins to make up the Bluegill Campground on Pleasant Lake. Hamburgers served on white bread with fried onions were their specialty, and old bread was given to patrons to feed the bluegills on the shoreline. Pleasant Lake is now used by the Chain Skimmers, a water-ski show out of Eagle River. (Courtesy of Jim Hedberg.)

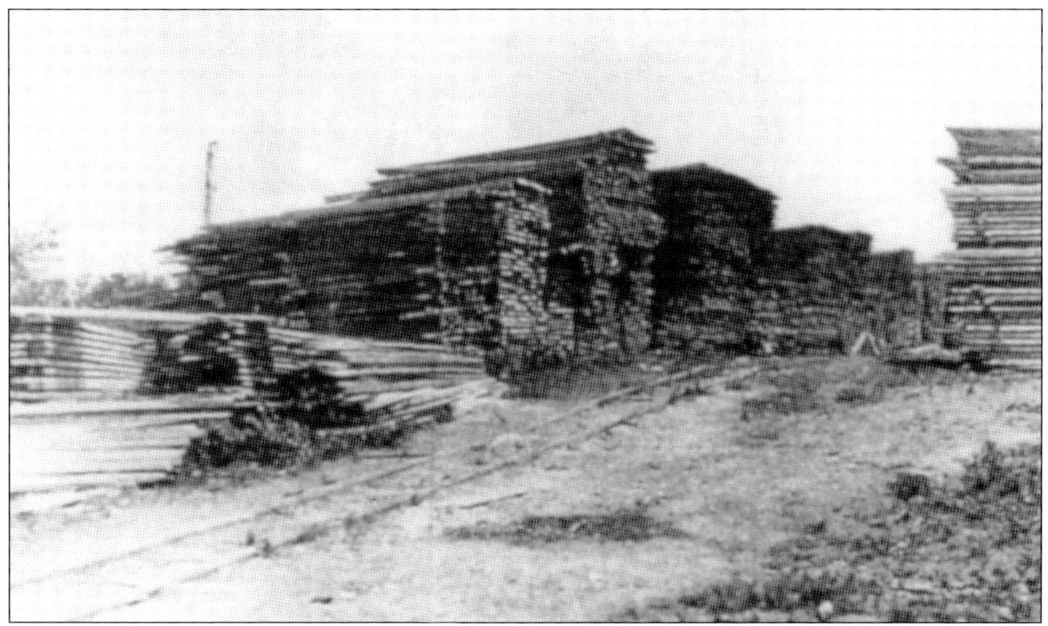

Engelbrecht Saw Mill on County Road S near Joyce Lake and Rummels Road is pictured here. The lumber from this mill was processed from local tree cutting and used to build many local homes and resorts that were continuing to expand. The interior of the old Conover town hall got all of its lumber from the mill. The mill was a large facility for its time. Note the narrow-gauge railroad tracks running between the lumber stacks on what is now Rummels Road. (Courtesy of Jim Hedberg.)

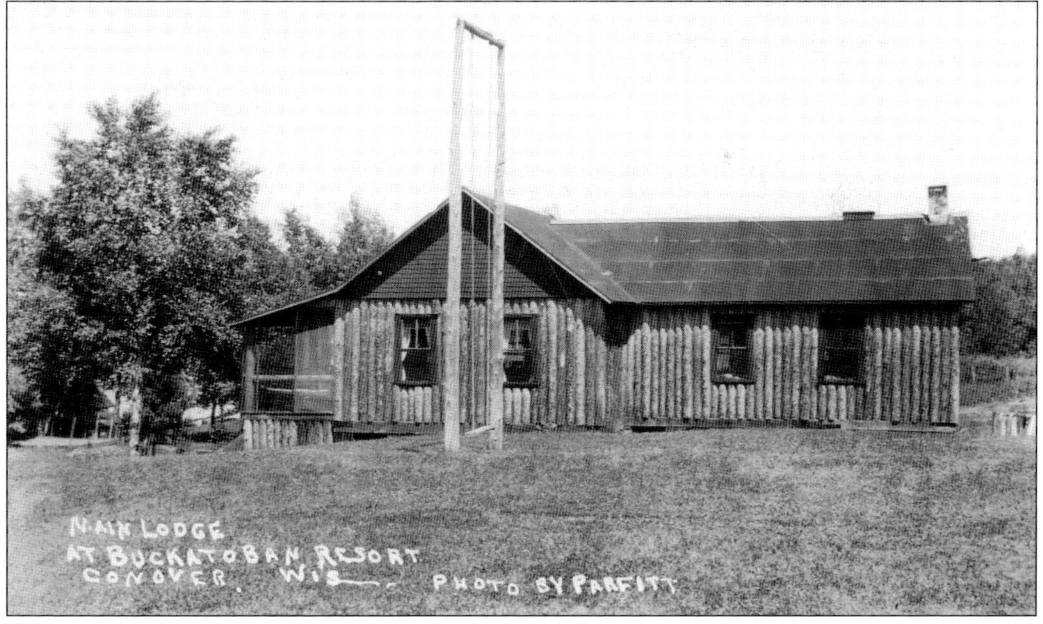

"Main Lodge" was written on this 1923 postcard. The Buckatabon Lodge with vertical log construction was located on Buckatabon Lake in Conover. The resort was located on Lower Buckatabon Lake. There is a channel that allows access to Upper Buckatabon Lake. The Buckatabon Resort still is in operation today.

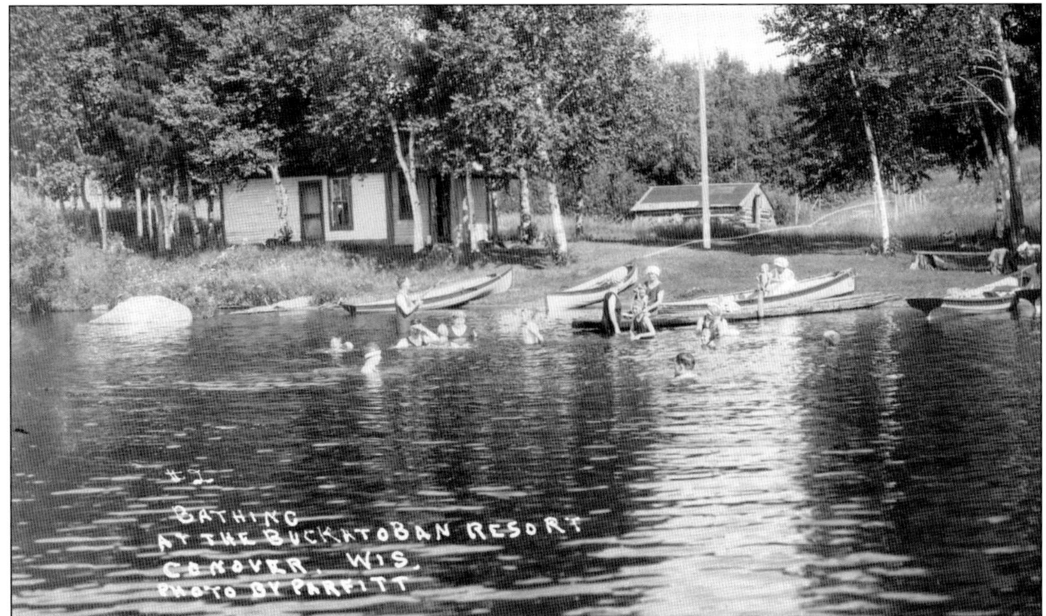

Escaping the summer heat and enjoying the refreshing water of the Lower Buckatabon Lake at the Buckatabon Resort in Conover. The lower lake, which houses the location of the resort, is nearly 378 acres and has a maximum depth of 16 feet. The other part, Upper Buckatabon Lake, is another 493 acres and has a maximum depth of 47 feet. Today, the lakes still provide fishing and resort life to many.

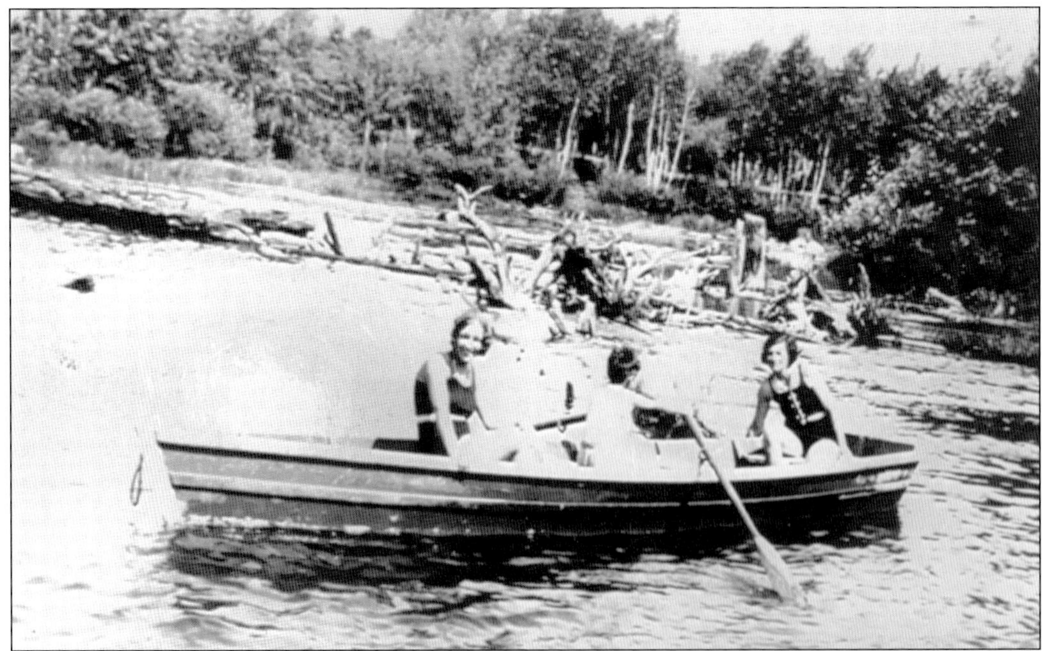

In 1934, in front of the dam on Buckatabon, Eugene Conti (pictured center) is rowing Hattie Bemke (left) and Mary Conti around the lake. The name Buckatabon was derived from the Ojibwa language. In 1946, this area would later become the location of Bauer's Dam Resort. (Courtesy of Donna Miller.)

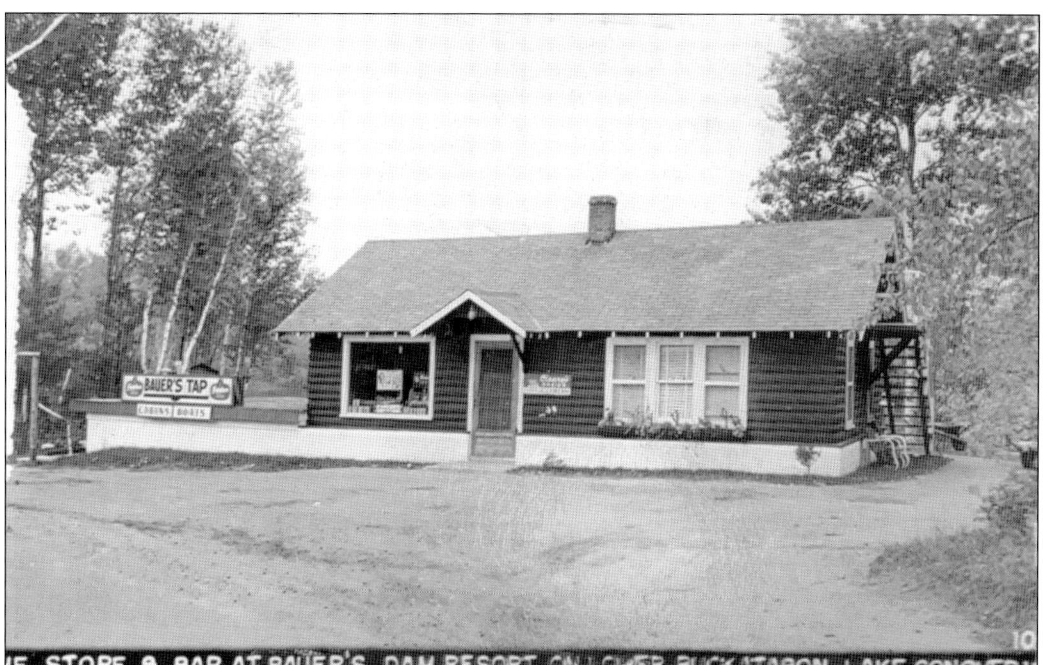

Situated on a peninsula of Lower Buckatabon Lake, Bauer's Dam Resort has been in business since it was established by Syl and Al Bauer in 1946. In 1973, it transferred ownership to Bob and Jeanne Bauer. Since 1992, Bauer's Dam has been successfully running as a three-cabin, five-room house resort under Glen and Donna Miller. There also remains the restaurant and bar, pictured here years ago. (Courtesy of Donna Miller.)

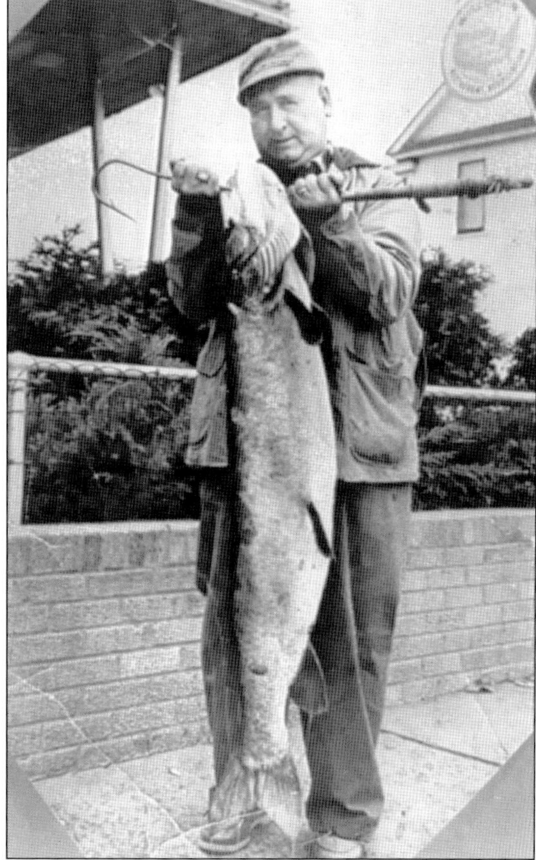

Bill Hoeft from Wausau is seen here in 1961 with his muskie catch out of the Lower Buckatabon Lake behind Bauer's Dam Resort. The muskie weighed in at 44 pounds and was 54.5 inches in length. (Courtesy of Donna Miller.)

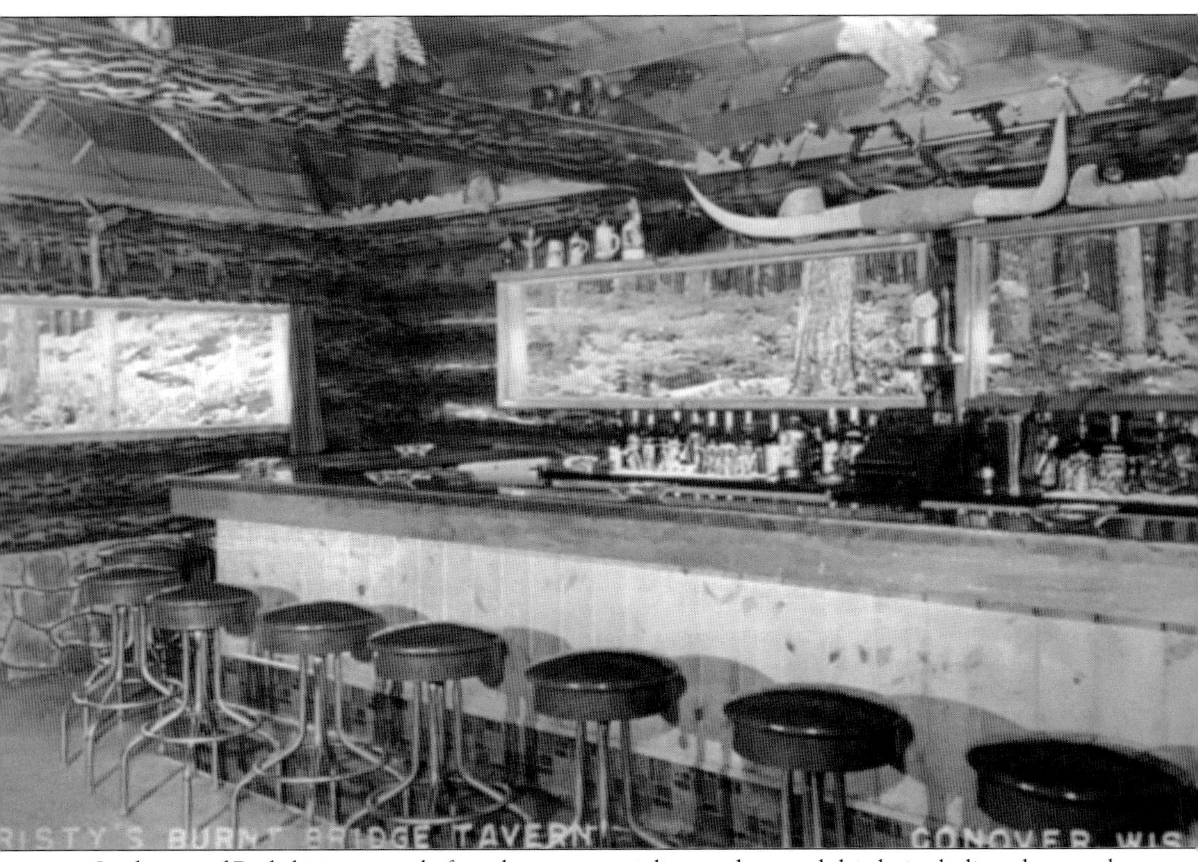

In the era of Prohibition, people found ways to socialize, gather, and drink, including the people of Conover. The town folk used the phrase "meet at the burnt bridge," referring to the logging road bridge that burned in an early 1900s fire. They would drink their moonshine here. After Prohibition was repealed, Fred LaMason built a log cabin for people to now gather and drink legally just west of the old gathering spot and on County Highway K. This is now the current dining room of the Burnt Bridge Tavern & Restaurant. This is an older view of the interior when the name was Christy's Burnt Bridge Tavern. Burnt Bridge has been operated by the Singer family since 2015. (Courtesy of Andrew Singer.)

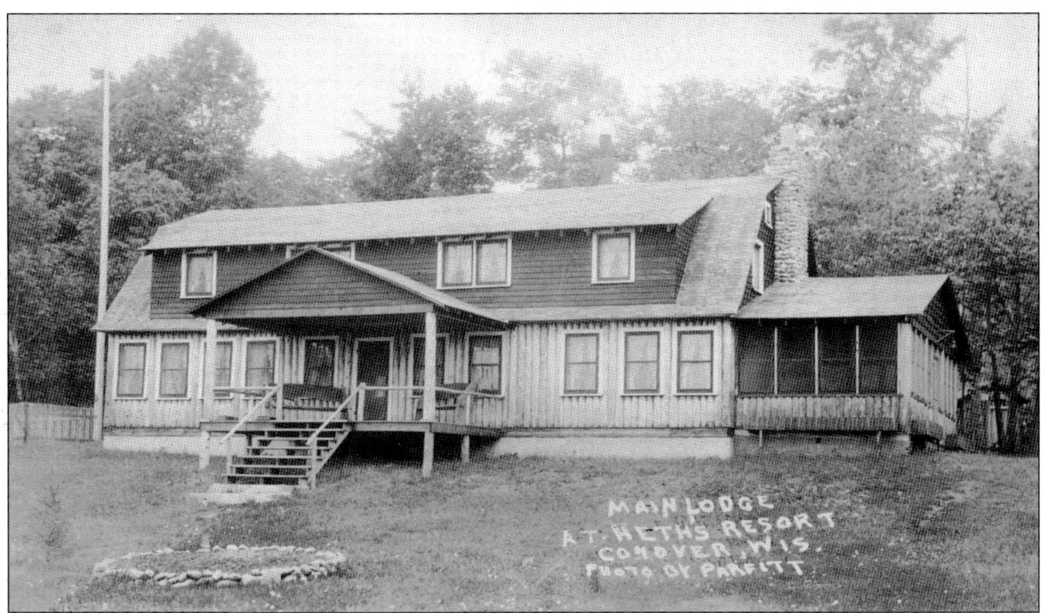

Ernest Heth and his wife, Vera, established Heth's Resort on the west shore of Little Twin Lake in Conover in 1916. At that time, the Chicago & North Western Railway was the only means to travel to the resort, and conveniently, it was on the railway. In later years, it became the Silver Birch Resort and then a Jewish boy's camp. Now remodeled, it is a private residence.

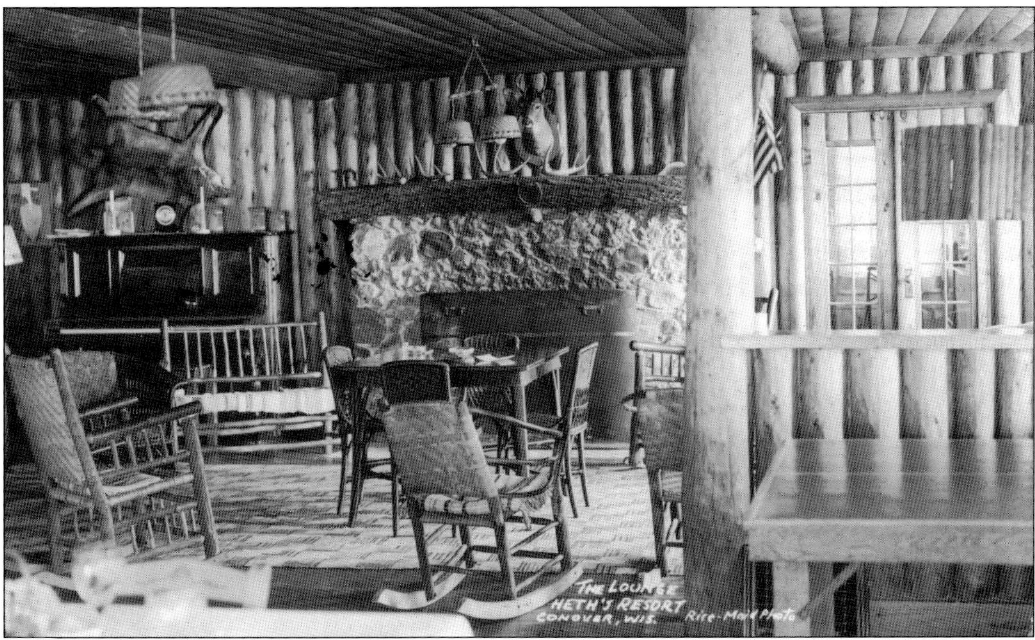

Sitting rooms and dining rooms were a common place for Northwoods resorts. The lounge at Heth's Resort in 1939 is surrounded by a fireplace and the typical wicker chairs and benches. Vera Heth ran the dining room at the resort. The staff raised their own vegetables and poultry and also operated their own dairy.

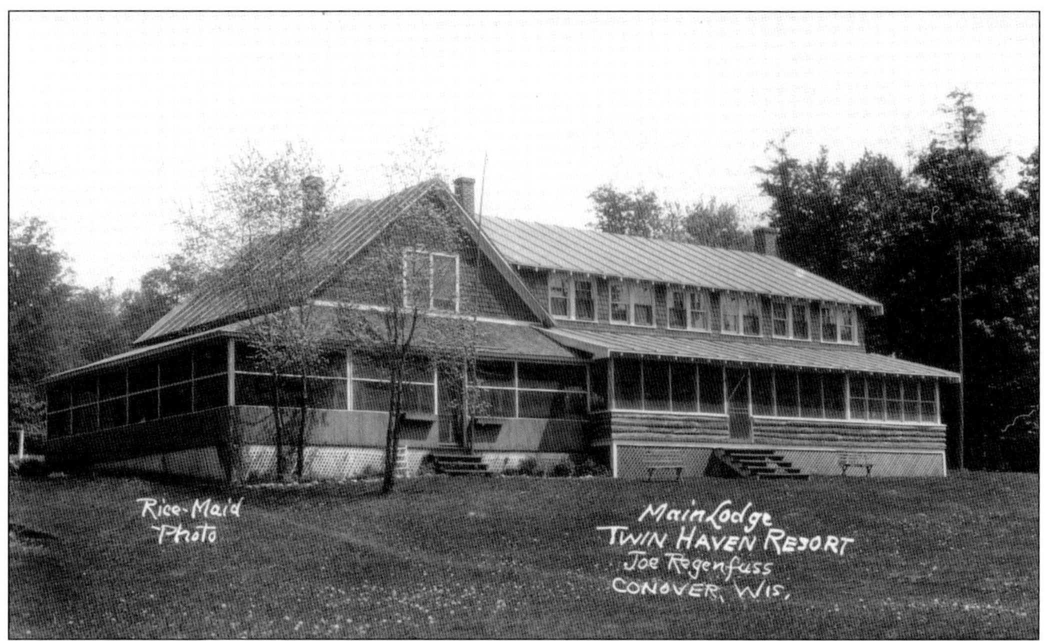

Joe Regenfuss built Twin Haven Resort, originally named Regenfuss' Resort, on the north shore of Big Twin Lake. In the 1920s, it was a lovely two-story log structure with an enclosed veranda and several log cabins. It was owned and operated by several other families over the years.

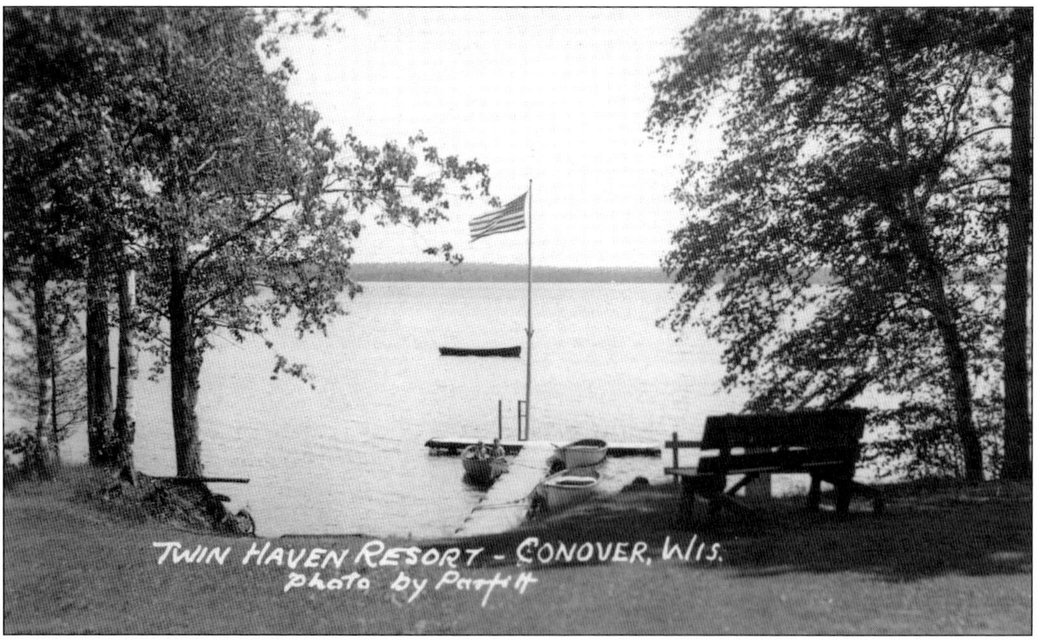

This is a typical view of the shoreline with a bench, a pier, boats, and the lake. The scene is at Twin Haven Resort on Big Twin Lake. In the 1980s, a chimney fire burned the original Twin Haven lodge to the ground, and a smaller lodge was erected shortly after. This lodge subsequently burned down again in 2017. As of today, nothing has been rebuilt in its place.

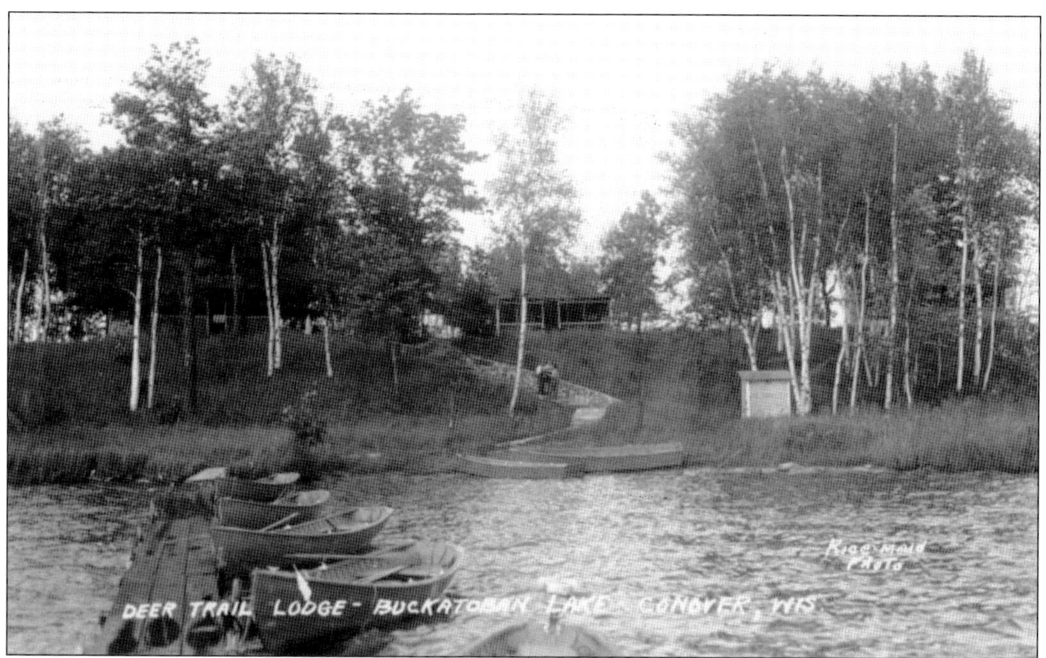

Boats are lined up at the pier-beckoning fishermen to try their luck on the lake. This scene is at the Deer Trail lodge on Buckatabon Lodge in Conover.

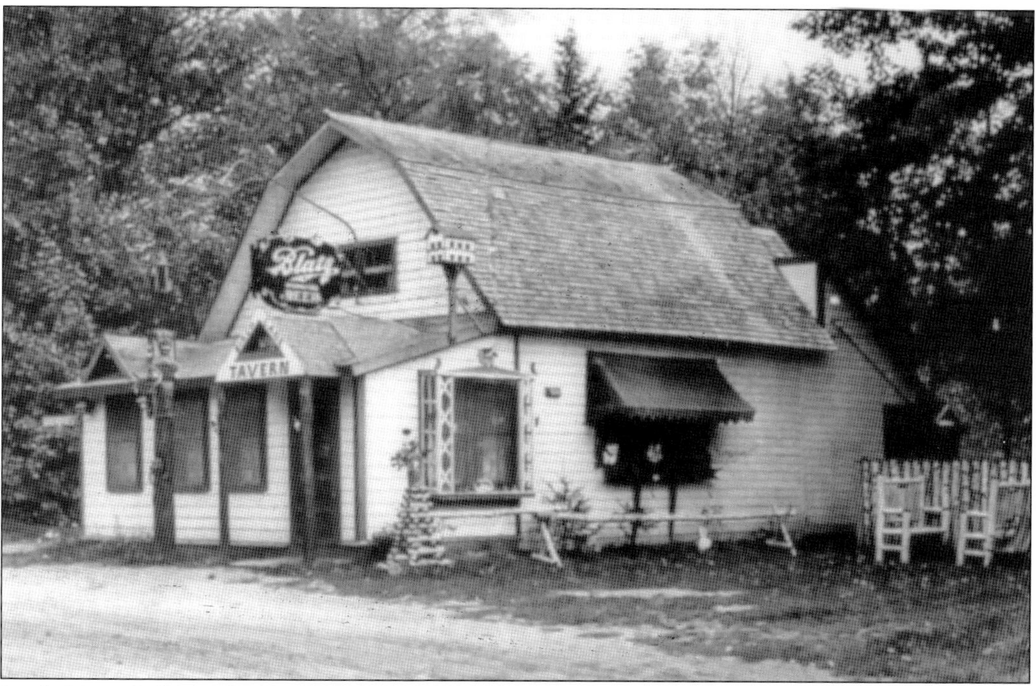

Little Twin Lake had several resorts on the lake, but this tavern was not on the water. It was located on Twin Lake Road. In its history, it had several names, but the most remembered one is the Sundown Tavern. This early photograph is hardly recognized from its appearance today. Sundown was owned and operated by Betty Sue Lynn (singer Loretta Lynn's daughter) in the 1980s. It is still currently open and is known as Twin Lake Pub.

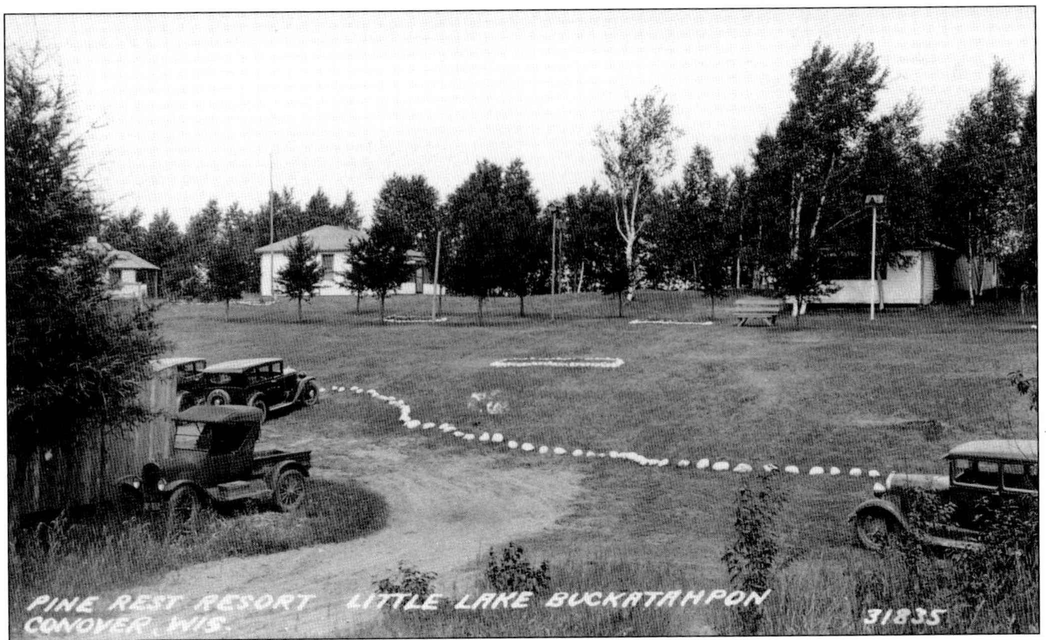

Although most vacationers came by train, only a few drove automobiles, as shown here in 1928 at the Pine Rest Resort on Lower Buckatabon Lake just past the dam. Painted field stones line the parking area, which gave children ample room to play.

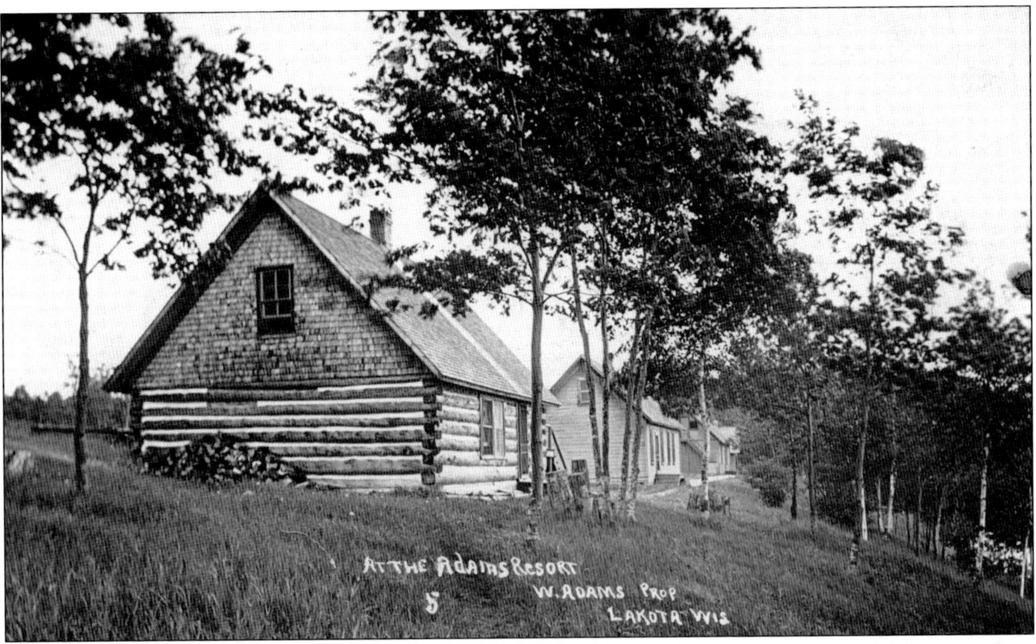

William Adams established his resort, Adams Resort, on Big Twin Lake around 1903. He also purchased the Lakota and the Sanborn Resorts, which adjoined it. In later years, the Adams Resort became the Huettenbar resort. The Sanborn Resort had a dance hall, which later became the bar area of the Huettenbar Resort. The bar is now the current location of Dublin's Bar & Grill, purchased by Jon Racine in 2012.

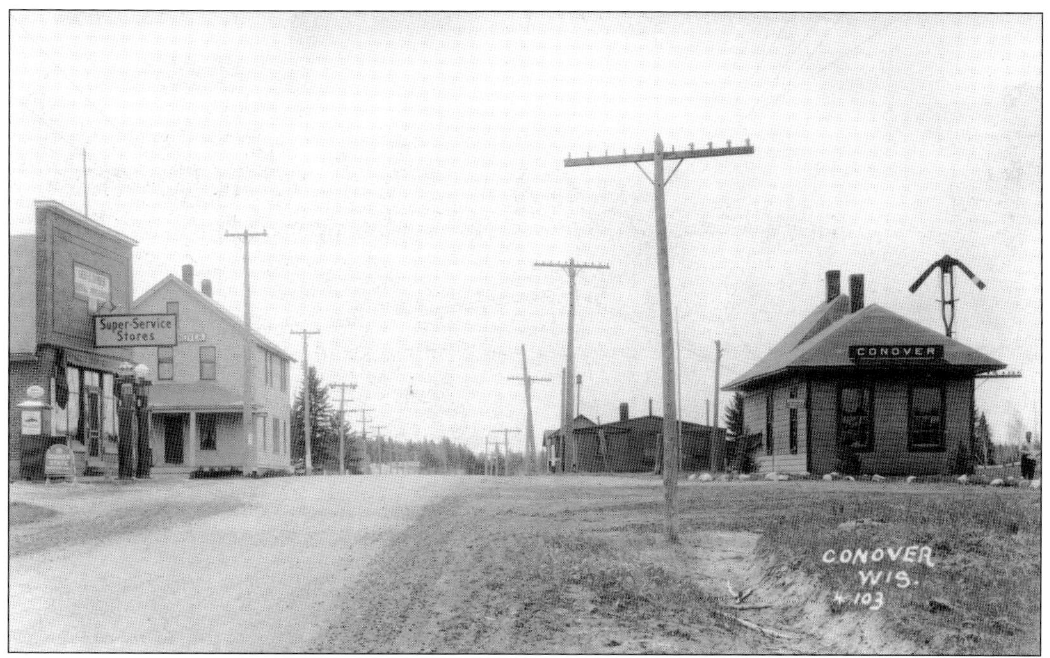

This 1936 postcard shows the Dobbs Brothers General Store with gas pumps (left). Beyond the store is the Hotel Conover. The Chicago & North Western depot sits in the right foreground. South of the station were the buildings of the brickyard and Schlack's Tavern.

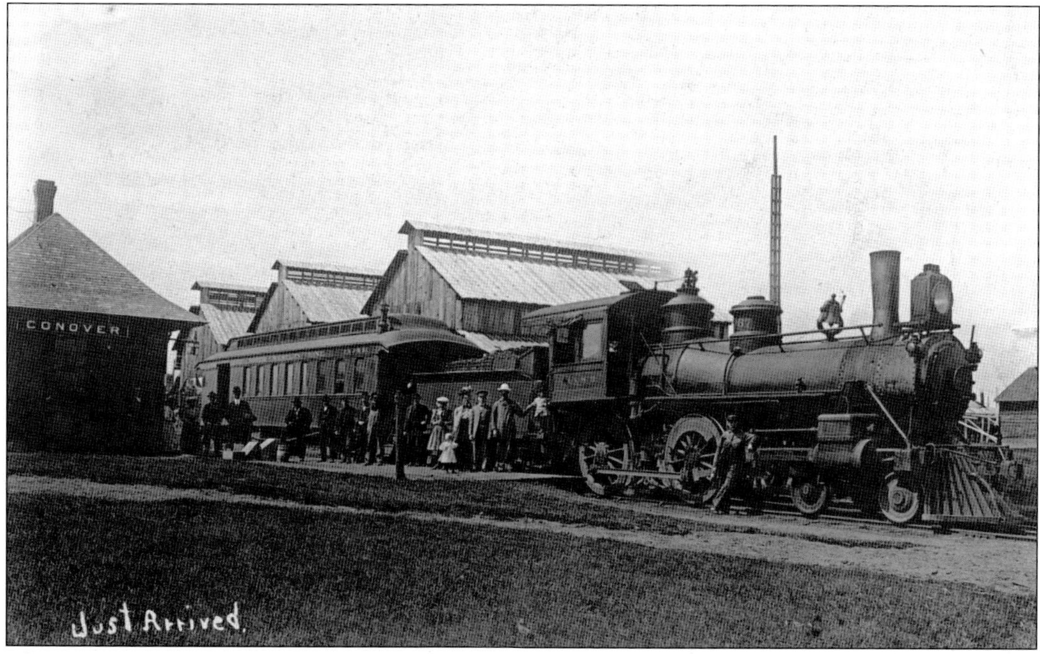

This one passenger car steam locomotive is heading north and stopping long enough to drop passengers off while having their photograph taken. The buildings across the tracks were probably storage buildings for grain and other goods.

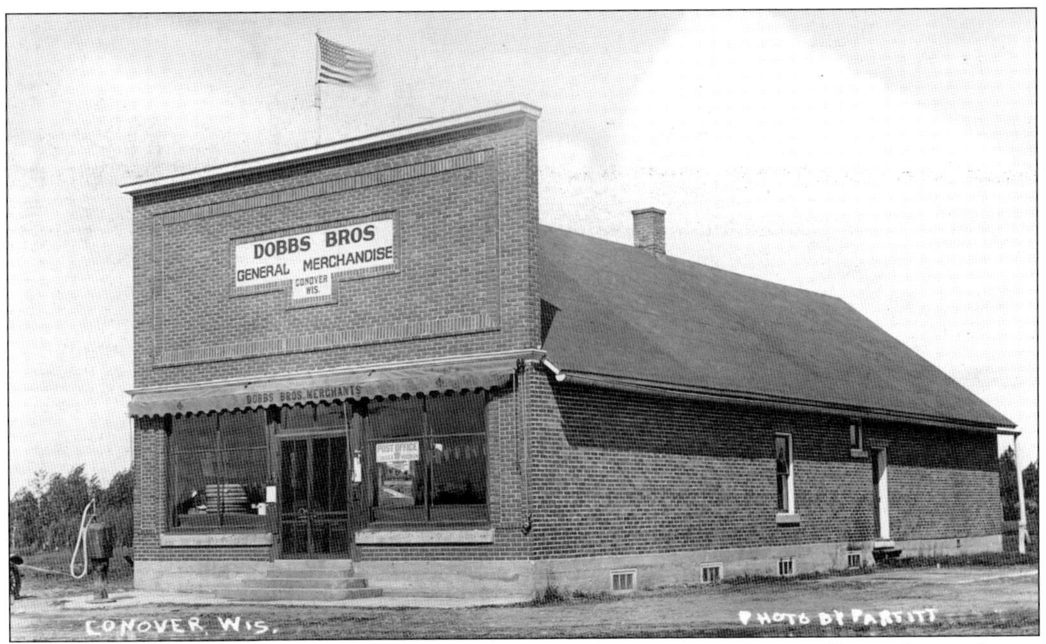

The Dobbs Brothers General Store is one of the few remaining buildings still standing today in Conover. The brothers built the store in 1918. Note the gas pump at the corner of the building. In 1921, the brothers went their separate ways. George purchased his brother Fred's interest, and Fred moved to Three Lakes, Wisconsin, and opened his own successful business there.

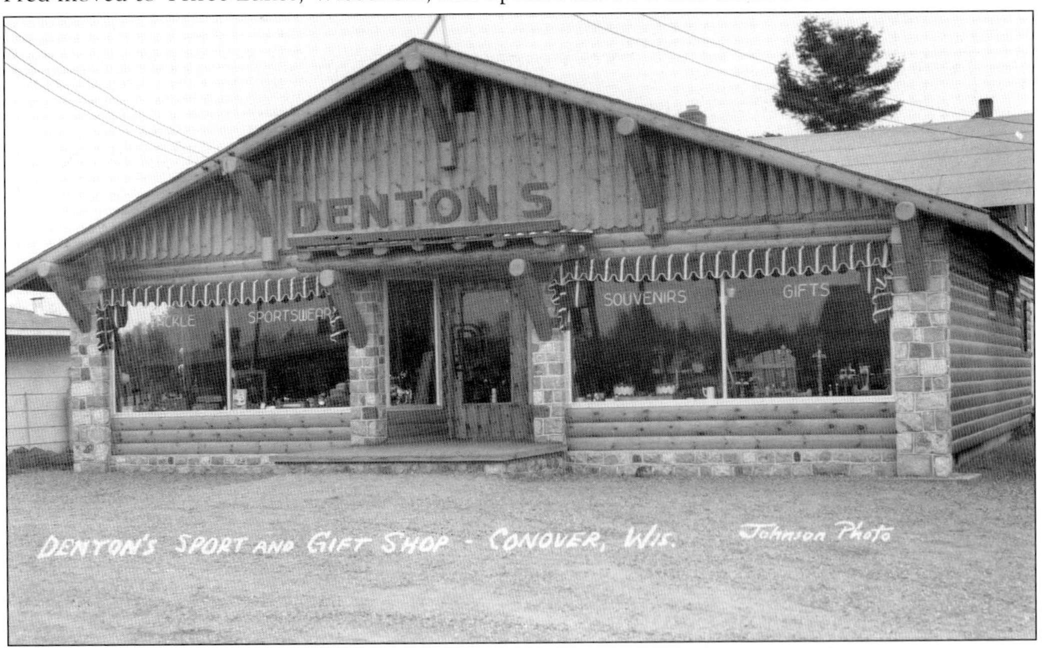

Denton's Sport and Gift shop was just south of the Dobbs Brothers General Store. It was built in roughly the 1950s by Glen Denton. Many of the gifts in the store were wooden knickknacks that his brother Milo had made. Milo created these gifts in his woodworking shop at his residence, which was located at the corner of Highways K and 45 on the west side. Denton's is still in operation today as a gift shop.

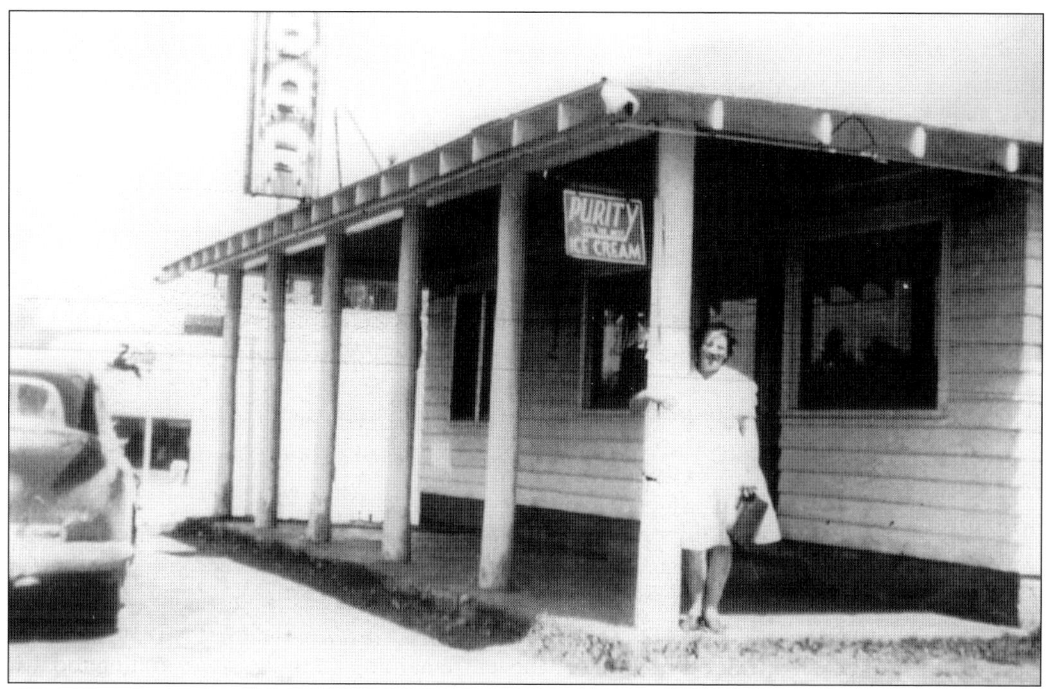

Chet Dussault had a bar on the north corner of Highways K and 45. He later built a Mobil gas station adjacent to the bar. (Courtesy of Jim Hedberg.)

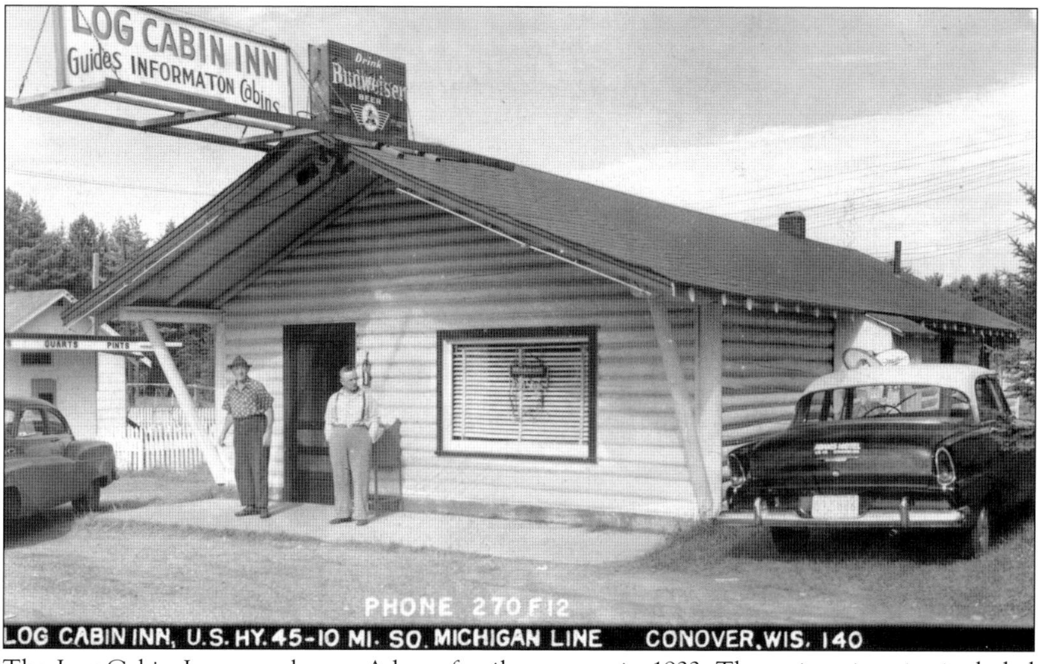

The Log Cabin Inn was also an Adams family venture in 1933. The unique interior included miniature light fixtures with log cabin designs, bar stools made from tree trunks, large beams, and chinked logs. The Log Cabin Inn is still in operation today.

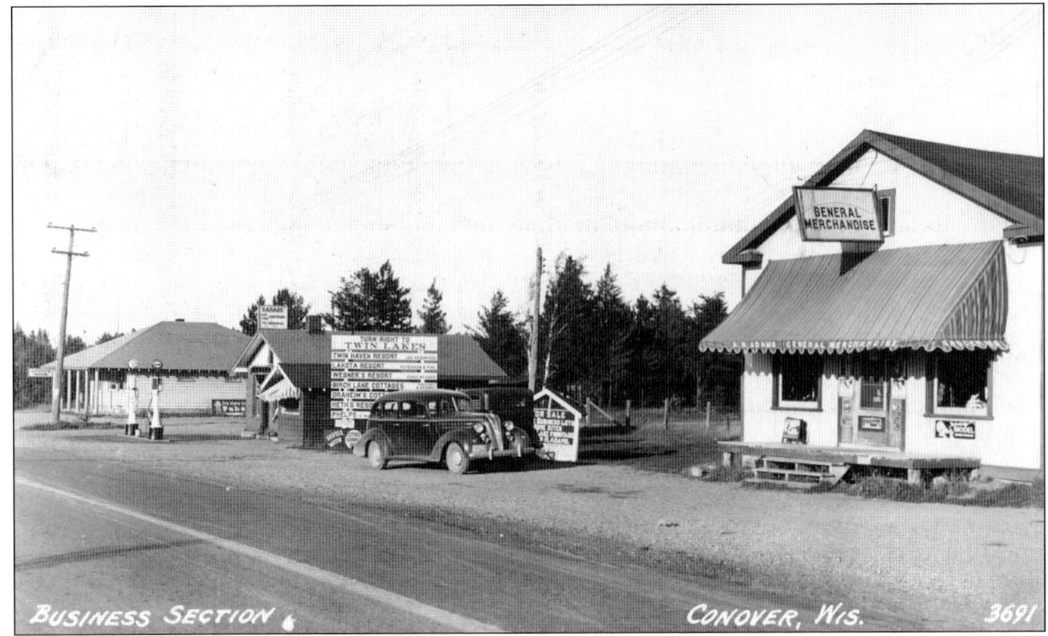

This business section in Conover on Highway 45 shows, from right to left, the A.H. Adams General Merchandise store, the gas station, and Dussault's Bar. The gas station and store no longer remain in operation. Dussault's Bar is still open today under the name Wild Turkey. (Courtesy of Jim Hedberg.)

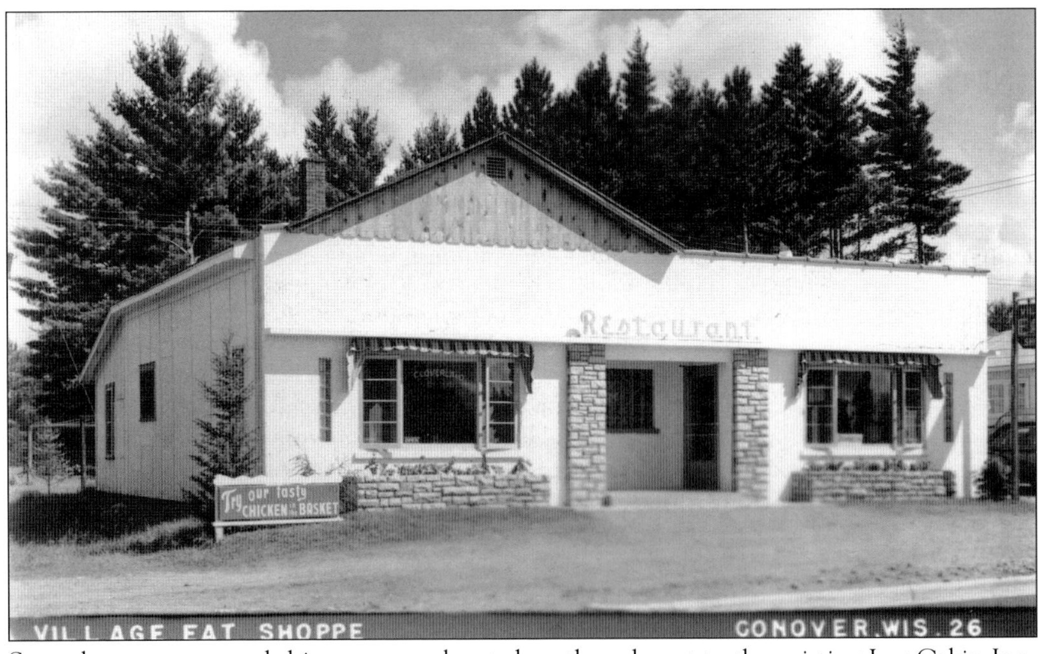

Several owners operated this restaurant located south and next to the existing Log Cabin Inn. In this picture, it is operating as the Village Eat Shoppe. This building is still erected but vacant. (Courtesy of Jim Hedberg.)

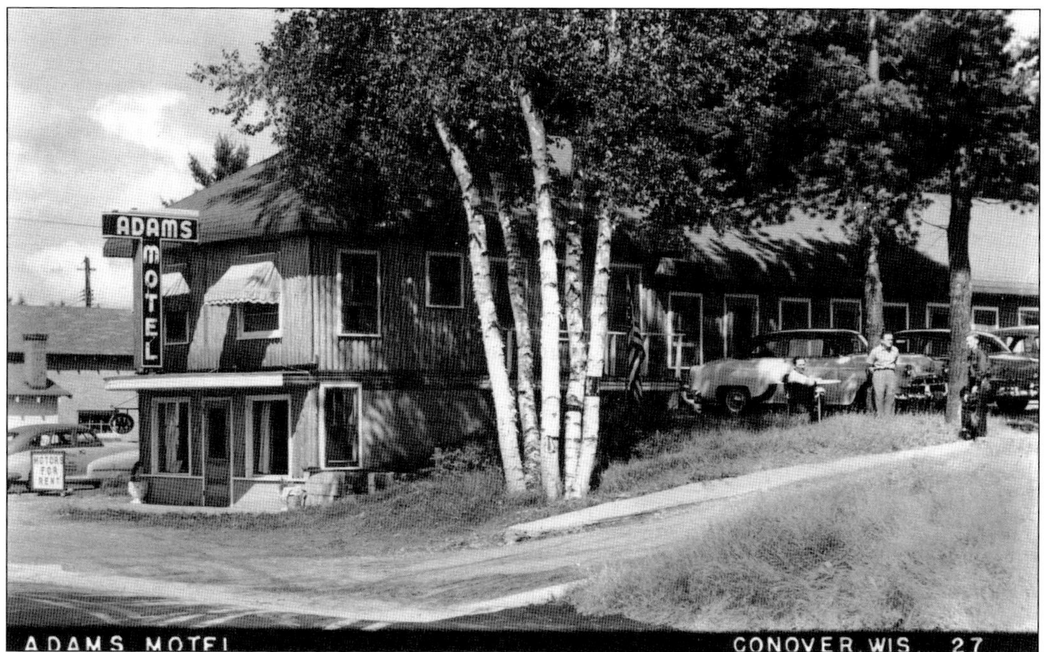

Adams Motel had a number of rooms lining its narrow-length building along the access road, fittingly named Adams Road. The year 1954 finds a few men relaxing after a long drive.

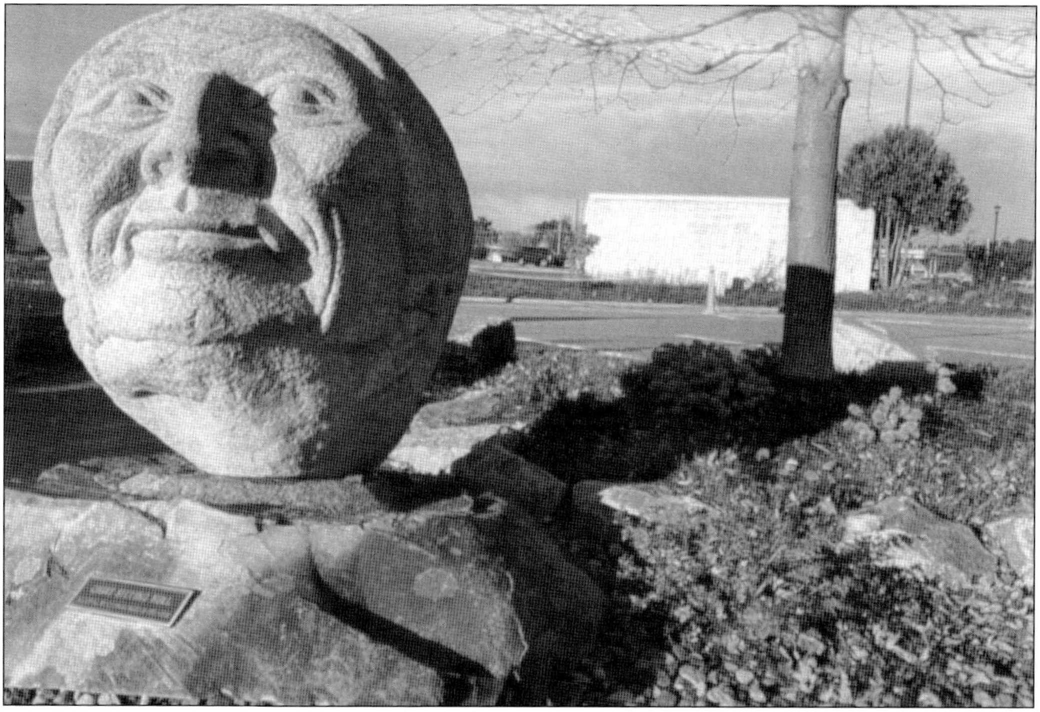

Charles Reed was a carver who created works of art from wood and stone. The most significant was a stone carving of Sitting Bull facing west on his property. Long after his death, the family donated the bust to the Vilas County Historical Society, where it can be viewed today.